POETS'

POETS' PERSPECTIVES
Reading, Writing, and Teaching Poetry

Edited by
Charles R. Duke
Sally A. Jacobsen

BOYNTON/COOK PUBLISHERS
Heinemann
Portsmouth, NH

Boynton/Cook Publishers, Inc.
A Subsidiary of
Heinemann Educational Books, Inc.
361 Hanover Street, Portsmouth, NH 03801
Offices and agents throughout the world

Several chapters originally appeared in *Reading and Writing Poetry: Successful
Approaches for the Student and Teacher*, edited by Charles R. Duke and Sally A.
Jacobsen, © 1983, Phoenix, AZ: Oryx Press, which is no longer in print.
Every effort has been made to contact the copyright holders and students for permission
to reprint borrowed material. We regret any oversights that may have occurred and
would be happy to rectify them in future printing of this work.

Library of Congress Cataloging-in-Publication Data

Poets' perspectives: reading, writing, and teaching poetry/edited
  by Charles R. Duke, Sally A. Jacobsen.
      p.   cm.
    ISBN 0-86709-304-8
    1. Poetry—Study and teaching.   2. Poetry—Authorship.   3. Reader
  —response criticism.   4. Reading.   I. Duke, Charles R.
  II. Jacobsen, Sally A.
  PN1101.P58   1992
  808.1'07—dc20   92-8499
                                                                       CIP

Printed in the United States of America.
92 93 94 95 96   9 8 7 6 5 4 3 2 1

Contents

Preface

Once, in a time best forgotten, many people thought that poetry could be found only in the graveyard, in the diary, or in the classroom. Certainly no one would be seen on a subway reading a collection of poetry! Since students seldom went to graveyards—certainly not to read epitaphs—and since the majority would not admit to keeping diaries or reading on a subway, young people's main perceptions of poetry were shaped by experiences in the classroom. This could have been a good thing because, traditionally, English teachers probably read more poetry than any other form of literature in their training. Yet, aside from having poetry read to them in the early grades, and having an opportunity now and then to write some of their own rhymed verse, most students have spent little time considering with their teachers what poetry might be or could become.

For too long, far too many students have considered poetry as some kind of mysterious artifact, meant to be observed at a distance always, under the eye of a critical curator. But this distancing is contrary to all we now know about how readers develop a liking for various types of literature. Growth comes from direct engagement, not from distancing of reader and text. We believe, therefore, that the teaching of poetry needs an expanded view which emphasizes student interaction with the text, as well as creation of new texts. In fact, we can say with assurance that there are no official entrances to or exits from the reading of, responding to, or writing of poetry; therefore, as teachers, we would do well to explore as many options as possible for promoting students' direct engagement with poetry if we want to make poetry a part of their lives.

Because we believe that a need for broader perspectives on the teaching of poetry exists, we have put together this collection of essays from poets, teacher-poets, and regular classroom teachers to demonstrate the rich resources available for making poetry a more pleasant and meaningful experience for young readers.

The collection focuses on the needs of the young adult reader, because it is at this level that the resources seem to be most lacking. At the elementary school level, there often seems to be a rich environment for promoting active involvement with poetry. Oral reading of poems, acting out of poems, building poetry collections, talking with poets, and listening to poetry and music all happen on a regular basis. As a result, elementary pupils tend to view poetry as a very natural part of their classroom experiences. Yet when the transitions to high school and college occur, students' pleasure and interest in poetry noticeably decline.

Research on the reader's response to literature suggests one reason for this decline. Many times the reading of a text is oversimplified. For example, in *Literature and the Reader: Research in Response to Literature, Reading Interests and the Teaching of Literature* (Urbana, IL: National Council of Teachers of English, 1972), Alan Purves and Richard Beach show that readers are not only moved by what they read but also are changed, not just intellectually but in their attitudes as well. Purves and Beach believe that understanding and liking are associated and that readers tend to be more interested in content than form. Louise Rosenblatt, first in *Literature as Exploration* (New York: Noble and Noble 1968) and then again in *The Reader, The Text, The Poem* (Carbondale, IL: Southern Illinois University Press, 1978), contends that a special transaction occurs between an individual and a text and that only through this transaction is the poem "produced"; the result of the transaction is dominated as much by the process of reading as by the text on the page. Norman Holland in *Poems as Persons* (New York: W. W. Norton 1973) believes that poetry in particular depends heavily on what the reader brings subjectively to the reading process. These views suggest that responding to a poem is a multifaceted experience that calls for more exploration in the classroom.

As a guiding principle, then, for the selection of essays, we looked for insights into how poems are created and then how they might be presented to students. We looked for ideas that stressed active response on the part of students and that demonstrated that engagement with poetry in and out of the classroom can be a varied, pleasurable, intellectual experience. We have divided the collection into three sections to highlight the varied approaches and resources through which this active response and broadened perspective may be developed.

First, we have attempted to provide some perspectives on what poetry is and how it comes into existence. Such knowledge is imperative if readers are to comprehend fully how poems begin and how poets view their work. To obtain such perspectives, we went to practicing poets and asked them to share some of their thoughts and feelings about poetry and the writing of it. We believe the voices of these poets as they talk about their work will ring true for teachers. The pieces in this section offer insights into the creative process which can be shared with students, helping to underscore how totally absorbed poets are in the activity of making meaning, of writing. Teachers also will find in these poets' accounts of their work ample reinforcement for stressing the value of poetry to their students.

But this is not simply a collection of poets talking about their craft. Although such conversations serve as a useful starting point, there also has to be an emphasis upon classroom approaches that make poetry accessible to students. For this information, we went to classroom teachers who have been successful in engaging students directly with poetry, both as readers and as writers. The result is a potpourri of techniques and approaches: engaging remedial students with poetry; connecting the writing of poetry with the writing process; unlocking the meaning of poems; dramatizing poetry; understanding the significance of meter, rhythm, tone, voice, and mood; ways of responding to students' poetry.

Finally, we include a section on innovative approaches and resources that will prove helpful to teachers looking for ways to extend the reading, the study, and the writing of poetry beyond the conventional sources usually found in the classroom: computers and poetry, an unusual yet growing area of interest; connections between art and poetry, a rich area for development; and resources for selecting and exploring cultural diversity in poetry.

The ideas and approaches in all of these three sections are practical and meant to provide powerful transitions to the classroom. Readers will quickly perceive that no single approach to the teaching of poetry is being advanced, only the idea that engagement with poetry should be an active, not passive, experience and that helping students to reach that goal should be the objective of all literature teachers. We hope only that *Poets' Perspectives* will prove a useful resource and possibly even an inspiration that will lead its readers to approach the teaching of poetry with renewed interest, confidence, and enthusiasm.

CRD & SAJ

Perspectives

Introduction

The poem on the page—where did it come from? How did it begin? Students and teachers approaching the reading, writing, and studying of poetry often fail to comprehend what lies behind the words that suggest a poem on the printed page. It is what happens between the creation and product that needs to be grasped if what is read is to be appreciated. We need a clearer understanding of the process that leads to the expression of an idea or feeling in a poem. As X. J. Kennedy says:

> Students need to take a longer view of life, need to perceive that there is common sense in preparing themselves for the unexpected. To cope with a switch of careers, or to accept an unforeseen opportunity, they need general and basic language skills. Far more useful than acquiring a corpus of technical information is building a sensitivity to words. Here is where poetry offers rewards.

The poets in this section mention a variety of sources and feelings for their poetry. Not surprisingly, each agrees that poems tend to grow from one's experiences and the perspectives that one develops about those experiences. A poem actually may start anywhere; for Marge Piercy, it might begin in the middle of reading *Natural History* magazine or the *Farmer's Almanac*; for Marvin Bell, a poem may be started by a visit to a certain place, such as the home of Emily Dickinson. Diane Wakoski often finds her stimulus through color; Tess Gallagher through childhood memories; Carolyn McElroy through associations with shoes. The sources of poetry are infinite.

But not everyone seems able to take advantage always of the rich source material that exists. Marge Piercy suggests that the poet has to learn "how to flow, how to push yourself, how to reach that cone of concentration ... when all the voices in the head are one voice." And Marvin Bell indicates that "writing poetry is not a way of saying only

3

what one already has the words for, but a way of saying what one didn't know one knew."

How does one actually write a poem? There is some similarity among the poets in this section on their perspectives toward the act of writing, although the particular rituals to get through "hard places" and the specific strategies for shaping ideas may vary. Some poems come quickly, a rush of words and emotion leading to expression; others seem to incubate for varying periods of time, sometimes becoming partially expressed only to stop short until some idea or incident triggers a return to the draft and completion.

It is understandable, therefore, that most poems do not come out the first time in a clear, organized fashion. Frequently, as Nancy Eimers and William Olsen suggest, the poet is on a voyage of discovery and does not know until near the end of the voyage what form the final version will take. Often a poem will start out in one direction or form and finish in a completely different form and location. In between, a considerable amount of shifting of words, of phrases, of whole sections may occur, suggesting that poets often engage in as much revision as many prose writers do.

But what are the implications for teaching that may be drawn from these poets' perspectives on poetry? Aside from endorsing the obvious — students should read as much poetry as possible — all of the poets believe strongly in the benefits of having students and teachers attempt to write poetry. The writing may not always be successful. Philip Levine, for example, says, "I'm never brutal with people who don't have talent. It seems to me utterly pointless. You are only brutal with people who need it. I don't encourage them or discourage them, but I am tough on people who can bear it. The better they are, the tougher you are."

Successful writing takes serious commitment. To demonstrate that commitment, Marie Nelson shares drafts of her poetry with students, showing them how a poem grows through multiple drafts, and suggesting that students, too, will need to pursue their ideas in a similar way. Philip Billings suggests that beginning poets need to "have the courage of their obsessions'." "They will want to write about their convictions, instead. They'll want to say Uncle Ray was sweet; don't let them; get them to tell you about the pungent odor from some kind of plant that always makes them remember Uncle Ray's backyard."

The goal is not necessarily to produce superior poets; in fact, often the results of students' first attempts will be anything but superior poetry. However, the experience of having wrestled with some of the same problems as these poets have will tend to make students more appreciative readers of poetry and more sensitive to what good poets can accomplish.

1

The Usefulness of Poetry

X. J. Kennedy

Of what practical use is the study of poetry? Students will rarely come right out and ask you, but they'll want to know. The question is worth raising in class, and in the following notes I should like to suggest two ways to answer it.

Students are aware — overly aware, maybe — that their studies are supposed to lead to career goals. In the minds of many, a young person puts in time, like a coin in a slot, and eventually receives a gold-edged degree or diploma, exchangeable for a safe and happy future in some career. It is well to throw a little cold sleet on this assumption. Ellen Goodman, one of my favorite newspaper columnists, lately provided some in a piece called "Steering Clear of the One True Course." Goodman's point was that students don't *know* for sure the course of their future lives and seldom end up in the professions to which they first aspire. The U.S. Department of Labor has estimated that the average person, in the course of a working life, changes jobs or professions at least four times. Lately, at the University of Vermont, I heard a guidance man report a survey of the school's English majors of 20 years ago. Few were doing what might have been expected of them. Some, to be sure, had entered the professions of words — as writers and teachers. But one former student of Milton had turned out to be an airline pilot. Another was now the proprietor of a pet shop, while still another had ended up as a vice-president of the Chase Bank. Had they known that they would reach these startling destinations, the students would have been wise, I suspect, to study English anyway.

Students need to take a longer view of life, need to perceive that there is common sense in preparing themselves for the unexpected. To cope with a switch of careers, or to accept an unforeseen opportunity, they need general and basic language skills. Far more useful than acquiring a corpus of technical information is building a sensitivity to words. Here is where poetry offers rewards.

It would be folly to estimate the value of poetry in dollar signs, but in truth, there are quite tangible benefits that poetry imparts. People, one crusty old IBM executive once remarked, don't usually fail in business because they don't know their jobs; they fail or have to be dismissed because they can't understand other people. Unable to imagine themselves inside the skin of a co-worker or a customer, they make bad decisions and arouse resentment. Poetry helps us travel beyond ourselves. Poems can help Whites glimpse what it is like to be Black, and the other way around. For any White venturing forth into the world at large, I should think a familiarity with the poems of Langston Hughes, Dudley Randall, Gwendolyn Brooks, and Sterling A. Brown indispensable. Poems show a man how a woman thinks, and vice versa. While not sure I understand women completely, I thank the poems of Adrienne Rich, Anne Sexton, and Emily Dickinson for helping me to glimmers of comprehension. For the city dweller, poetry affords insight into the mind of someone from the country or a small town. It enables the young to see through the eyes of the old. In "Sailing to Byzantium," Yeats conveys his sense of being an aged scarecrow, with flesh and faculties falling away, and a fierce desire in his heart for immortality. Poems of such caliber expand both our minds and our sympathies.

In another obvious way, poems have practical usefulness. As Mark Twain said, the difference between the right word and the almost right word is like the difference between the lightning and the lightning bug. And that is what poems make us sense: the choice of words that will make our explanations and our arguments memorable. The ability to write and speak is perhaps the most valuable of safety nets in the student's future tightrope-walk through life. To read a few poems and to learn them by heart will do more, I suspect, than many hours of workbook drill and vocabulary memorization.

2

Inviting the Muse*

Marge Piercy

Here is Henry Thoreau from his journal for October 26, 1853, although he is talking about spring. "That afternoon the dream of the toads rang through the elms by Little River and affected the thoughts of men, though they were not conscious that they heard it. How watchful we must be to keep the crystal well that we are made, clear!"

Writing poems can be divided crudely into three kinds of labor: beginning and getting well and hard into it; pushing through inner barriers and finding the correct form; drawing back and judging what you have done and what is still to be done or redone. This essay is about the first stage, learning how to flow, how to push yourself, how to reach that cone of concentration I experience at its best as a tower of light, when all the voices in the head are one voice.

I do not know how to teach that, although concentration can be learned and worked on the same as flattening stomach muscles or swimming farther. You could perhaps set someone to studying a rock or a leaf or a bird—perhaps a warbler. Nothing requires more concentration than trying to observe a warbler up in the leafy maze of a summer tree. If I were really and truly teaching poetry, I would probably drive everybody crazy by sending them off to notice the shades of sand on a beach.

Of course observation isn't concentration, but learning to do one brings on the ability to do the other. My mother taught me to observe. A woman who had not been allowed to finish the tenth grade, she had some extraordinary ideas about how to raise very young children. Later when I was grown out of dependency and highly imperfect, she had trouble with me and could not endure my puberty. However, when I was little enough to fit comfortably into her arms and lap, we played unusual games. She had contempt for people who did not

7

observe, who did not notice, and she would require me to remember the houses we passed going to the store or play mental hide and seek in other people's houses that we had visited. We would give each other three random objects or words to make stories around. We would try to guess the stories of people we saw on the bus and would argue to prove or disprove each other's theories.

I suppose such training might have produced what she wanted, a sharply observant person like herself, a reporter's mentality, a little Sherlock Holmes in Shirley Temple guise. What it produced in me was observation suffused with imagination, since our life was on the whole skimpy, hard, surrounded by violence outdoors and containing familial violence within, a typical patriarchal working-class family in inner-city Detroit. Blacks and whites fought; the Polish and Blacks who lived across Tireman (a street) fought the Irish who went to parochial school. The neighborhood offered the kind of stable family life that writers like Christopher Lasch, beating the dolly of the new narcissism, love to harken back to. Although husbands sometimes took off and not infrequently had girlfriends on the side, women almost never walked out of their homes. Wife beating was common, child beating just as common; drunkenness, drug abuse, rape, and molestation of children occurred on every block, but families went on from generation to generation. In such a neighborhood where the whites comprised Polish, Irish, a few Italian and German Catholics, some remaining Wasps and some newly arrived Appalachian families (I divide the Appalachian Wasps from the others because they were often Celts, and because they were looked down on by everybody as hillbillies and provided some of my closest friends), being a Jew was walking around with a kick-me sign. I'd say the level of tolerance for lesbians was higher than that for Jews. You learn to observe street action and people's muscular tensions and involuntary tics rather closely.

Detroit sprawls there, willfully ugly mile after flat smoggy mile; yet what saves it are trees. Every abandoned vacant lot becomes a jungle in a couple of years. Our tiny backyard was rampant with tomatoes, beans, herbs, lettuce, onions, Swiss chard. One of the earliest poems I wrote and still like is subtly about sex and overtly about peonies, pansies, iris, mock orange, wisteria, hollyhocks along the alley fence, black-eyed susans, golden-glow whose stems were red with spider mites, golden chrysanthemums, a lilac bush by the compost pile. Nothing to me will ever be more beautiful than the flowers in that yard, except my mother when I was young.

You learn to sink roots into your childhood and feed on it, twist it, wring it, use it again and again. Sometimes one daub of childhood mud can set a whole poem right or save a character. It's not always a matter of writing about your family, although at times we will do that. You use your childhood again and again in poems about totally other things. For one thing, you learn how to use that rush of energy and how to make sure your use transcends the often trivial and ludicrous associations you are touching and drawing power from.

Some poets get going, get the flow by reading other poets. You learn whose writing moves you to your own, whether it's Whitman or the King James version of the Bible or Rukeyser or Neruda in Spanish or in translation. Actually I've never met anyone who got going by reading poetry in any other language than the one they were working in, but I'm curious if anybody does. On the other hand, I have met a number of poets who use work in translation to prime themselves. It is a priming act we're talking about. You get the words and rhythms going through you and you begin to align yourself. It has disadvantages, of course; if you are the least impressionable you may produce involuntary pastiche. You may find yourself churning out imagery that is bookishly exotic, imagery culled from others and bearing the imprint of being on loan like clothes that fit badly. Some poets intentionally use poetry of another time to prime themselves, to minimize the unintentional fertilization.

This priming can happen by accident. Oftentimes I am reading poetry and suddenly a poem starts, that change in the brain, maybe words, maybe an image, maybe an idea. It need not even be poetry. That quotation from Thoreau that begins this essay instigated a poem called "Toad dreams." I remember starting a poem in the middle of reading a *Natural History* magazine or the *Farmer's Almanac*.

I think of that instigation as having a peculiar radiance; that is, the idea, the image, the rhythm, the phrase — radiates. I find myself wanting to attend to it. I may not know at once; often I may not find out for several drafts, what that meaning, that implication, that web of associations and train of utterances will be or even in what direction it is leading me. Sometimes the original moment radiates in many directions and my problem is sorting out the direction to pursue first or exclusively.

At that point, if concentration is not forthcoming, the whole possibility may be blown. If you can lose a novel by talking it out, you can easily destroy a poem by not paying attention. I have lost many poems that way; I must lose one a week because I can't get to a typewriter or even to a piece of paper fast enough — sometimes can't break through to silence, to solitude, to a closed door. I am not good at working at the cafe tables, as Sartre was supposed to do, although I have written on planes often enough. Even then I work only when I have a bit of space — never while wedged in the middle seat. I need at least a seat between me and any other person to work on a plane. At home, I need a closed door.

Poems can be aborted by answering the phone at the wrong moment. They can be aborted when an alien rhythm forces itself in or the wrong other words are juxtaposed. I cannot work with a radio on loud enough to hear the words, or a television, or music with words playing. I have trouble working at all with music on, for the rhythms are much too insistent. I know other writers who work to music, but I cannot do so. Rhythm is extremely important to me in building the line and the poem; any other insistent rhythm interferes. Irregular rhythms — hammering on a construction site nearby — have little effect.

I had a friend in Brooklyn who used to work with wax plugs in her ears, but I find that difficult. I talk my poems aloud and my voice roaring in my head gives me a headache. However, I pass on this method as it may do the trick for you. I know another writer who uses a white noise machine — usually purchased to help you sleep. I used to run an air conditioner to screen the noises from outside the apartment, when it seemed to me that every window opening onto the center of our block in Adelphi had a radio or a TV or both turned to top decibel.

Often I begin a poem simply by paying attention to myself, by finding what is stirring in there. I need a quiet moment. I try to use the routine of waking to bring me to work, whether into a novel I am working on or into poetry. I work best in the morning, although I started out believing myself to be a night person. I changed over during the 60s when the one quiet time I was assured of was before the rest of the anti-war movement in New York was awake. I learned to get out of bed and to use waking to move toward work.

Without the pressure on me now to work before friends are stirring, I get up more leisurely but I use the time. I always do some exercises in the morning and I take a morning bath. All of that routine I use to become thoroughly awake but retain some of the connectedness, some of the rich associativeness, of dreaming sleep. I don't want to shed that dark energy of dreams, not lose that concentration and involvement in the clutter of the day. I don't think of it quite as self-involvement. I remember when a relationship that had been part of my life for 17 years was breaking up, I would wake very early after three or four hours sleep and lie in anxiety and pain. Nonetheless by the time I rose through my morning schedule, when I came to the typewriter, I was clear of my immediate anguish and fussing and ready to turn them into work or to write about something entirely different.

I am not saying every writer should get up, eat a good breakfast, take a hot bath and do exercises without talking much to anyone, and then she will write richly. I am trying to say that you must learn how to prepare in a daily way for the combination of concentration and receptivity, a clearing which is also going down into yourself and also putting antennae out. One thing I can not do and work well is worry about something in my life. If I sit at the typewriter fussing about where the money to pay the real estate taxes is coming from or whether my lover loves me more or less today, whether I am spending too much money on oil this winter, whether the decision taken at the MORAL meeting was correct, I will not find my concentration. I can carry emotions to my typewriter but I must be ready to use and transmute them. They must already be a little apart. It is not exactly "emotion recollected in tranquility" I mean, although for 25 years I have contemplated that phrase with increasing respect. I often feel the emotion but with less ego, less anxiety than in ordinary life. The emotion is becoming energy, the pain, the regret, the anger, the pleasure. I suppose whenever I find my life too much more fascinating than work, I work less and less well. I certainly write fiction poorly in these stretches. I produce some poems, often decent ones, but my output is down.

Such periods are not frequent because I love to write more than almost anything — not essays, to be honest, but poems and novels. I am still writing in letters to friends this week that I am immensely relieved that I have finally shipped off my novel *Braided Lives* in its last draft to my publisher. I do, in fact, feel as if an elephant had risen daintily from its perch on my chest and ambled away. Free, free at last, oh free! Of course it will return soon enough all pencilled over with the comments of some copy editor enamored of commas and semicolons. Comes back again as galleys. But essentially it is gone, finished.

Then yesterday afternoon Woody and I were chatting about the next novel I am planning to start when I finish the next volume of poetry. Say, December? It is June now. He made a suggestion as I was mulling over something about the novel and I fell on it immediately and began chewing it, worrying it. It was just right. In the evening in the car on the way to see a movie two towns away, we began chatting again about my next novel until I shrieked that we must stop it, because I cannot get to it before December.

I try to put on with other writers how much I suffer at this excruciating martyrdom and all that posing we are expected to do, but the simple truth is I love to write and I think it an enormous con that I actually get paid for doing it. After all, I did it for 10 years without pay.

Find out when you work best and arrange the days that you have to write or the hours you have, to channel yourself into full concentration. If like Sylvia Plath you have only from four a.m. till the babies wake, if you have only from six a.m. till nine a.m. as I did in New York, if you have only weekends or only Sundays or only afternoons from three-thirty to five-thirty, you have to figure out the funnel that works for you: the set of habitual acts that shuts out distraction and ego noise, shuts out your household, your family, and brings you quickly to the state of prime concentration.

Whatever habits you develop as a writer, your ability to work can not depend on them. I went from writing late afternoons and evenings to writing mornings because that was the only time I could be sure of. I used to smoke all the time I wrote. I imagined I could not write without the smoke from a cigarette curling around me. Then my lungs gave out. I had to die or learn to live without smoking. Given that choice I abandoned smoking rather fast. I can't say my productivity was amazing the couple of years afterwards, but that was mostly because I had chronic bronchitis and it was a while before I was not sick at least 50 percent of the time with too high a fever to work. I have had to give up alcohol at times and to give up coffee, my keenest addiction of all, for periods, and work goes on whatever I am giving up, so long as I have enough strength to make it to the typewriter and sit there.

You can permit yourself any indulgence to get going, so long as you can have it — Cuban cigars, the best espresso or Earl Grey tea, Grandma Hogfat's Pismire Tea, a smelly old jacket — but you have to be able to figure out just what is ritual and what is necessity. I really need silence and to be let alone during the first draft. I like having a typewriter but can produce a first draft of poetry without it; I cannot write prose without a typewriter as I write too slowly by hand. My handwriting is barely legible to me. All the other props are ritual. I have my sacred rocks, my window of tree, my edge-notched card memory annex, my bird fetish necklace hanging over the typewriter, my Olympia standard powered by hand, my reference works on near-by shelves, my cats coming and going, my good coffee downstairs where I am forced to go and straighten my back on the hour as I should. But I have written in vastly less comfort and doubtless will do so again. Don't talk yourself into needing a cork-lined room, although if someone gives it to you, fine. Do ask the price.

For many years I felt an intense and negotiable gratitude to my second husband because, while I had supported myself from age 18 and was doing part-time jobs, at a certain point he offered me five years without having to work at shit jobs, to establish myself as a writer. I took the offer and by the end of five years was making a decent income — decent by my standards, compared to what I earned as part-time secretary, artist's model, telephone operator, store clerk and so on.

Not until I was looking at my own output over the years since I began writing poetry seriously and began my first (dreadful) novel at 15, did I ever realize that I was less productive during those years of being supported than before or since. Women have to be very cautious with gift horses. We feel guilty. Traditional roles press us back and down. When I stayed home I was a writer in my eyes but a housewife in the world's and largely in my husband's view. Why wasn't the floor polished? What had I been doing all day?

I began to write at a decent clip again not during two years of traditional wifehood in Brookline but in New York when I was passionately involved in the anti-war movement and working as an organizer at least six hours a day and sometimes twelve.

I am not saying we work best if we use up a lot of our lives doing other work. Some poets do; few prose writers do. It depends on the type of other work in part; I think the less that other work has to do with writing, with writers, with words, the better. I understand the temptation young writers have to take jobs associated with writing. Sometimes it's the only affirmation available to you that you are a writer in the often many years before publication certifies you to the people around you. I don't think I could have resisted writer's residencies if they had been available when I was un- or underpublished. In an ideal world for writers, we would be paid while apprenticing at some minimum wage and then be encouraged to do something entirely different, in work parties digging sewers or putting in gardens or taking care of the dying, at a reasonable wage.

What I am saying is that the choice may be offered to a woman to stay home (where it is much, much nicer than going out to a lousy job) and write because the amount she can earn as a part-time female worker is negligible from the viewpoint of a professional or skilled male wage earner. The offer can help but it also can hinder. You may find yourself doing a full-time job instead without pay and writing in the interstices — just as before except that you may have even less time that is really yours, and you have lost your independent base of income.

Similarly a job teaching can be wonderful because it answers the question, what do you do? If you get hired as a writer after you have published, say, five short stories, you have sudden legitimacy. If you started in workshops and got an MFA, you have more legitimacy. You have items to add to your resume. Of course once you have taken the teaching job, you may have little time to write, especially given the way the academic marketplace is a buyer's market and teaching loads are getting heavier. You're certified a writer, you deal professionally with literature and words, you make better money and are more respectable in middle class society, but you have less time and energy to put into your own writing than you would if you worked as a waiter or secretary.

Actually sitting and writing novel after novel before one gets accepted at last, the way fiction writers usually must do, actually working and working on poems till they're right when hardly anybody publishes them and when they do you're read by two librarians, three editors and six other poets, gives you little to put in your resume. We all make it as we can, and I do a lot of gigs. Unless writers are of draftable age, we are seldom offered money to do something overtly bad like kill somebody or blow up hospitals or burn villages, seldom paid to invent nerve gases or program databases for the CIA. The jobs available to us range from the therapeutic to the mildly helpful to the pure bullshit to the menial and tedious; all of them sometimes prevent us from writing and sometimes enable us to write. Jobs that have nothing to do with writing often provide more stimulation to the gnome inside who starts poems than jobs that involve teaching writing or writing copy.

When I am trying to get going and find myself empty, often the problem is that I desire to write a poem rather than one specific poem. That is the case sometimes when I have been working eight hours a day finishing up a novel and have not had the time to write poems or the mental space that allows them to begin forming. That is when the writer's notebook or whatever equivalent you use (my own memory annex is on edge-notched cards) can, if it is well organized, disgorge those tidbits put in it. I think of those jottings as matches, the images, the poem ideas, the lines that wait resurrection. Often lines that were cut from other poems will in time serve as the instigation for their own proper home. For me the absolute best way to get going is to resort to my memory annex. That summons the Muse, my own muse for sure.

The notion of a muse is less archaic than a lot of vintage mythology because most poets have probably experienced being picked up by the nape of the neck, shaken, and dumped again miles from where their daily life or ordinary preoccupations could have been expected to bring them. *Duende*, Lorca called that possession. Poems that come down like Moses from the mountaintop, that bore their way through my mind, are not better or worse than poems I labor on for two days, two months, or 15 years. Nonetheless I always remember which ones arrived that way. Sometimes in writing I experience myself as other. Not in the sense of the "I" as social artifact, the other that strangers or intimates see, the mask the camera catches off guard. When we see ourselves videotaped, often we experience a sense of nakedness and say, "so that is what I am really like," as if the exterior because we cannot see it is therefore the truth of our lives. Nor do I mean the artifact we construct, the "I" writers, perhaps more than most people, make up out of parts of themselves and parts of their books as camouflage and advertisement.

What I mean is simply that, in writing, the poet sometimes transcends the daily self into something clearer. I have often had the experience of looking up from the typewriter, the page, and feeling complete blankness about who I am — the minutia of my daily life, where I am, why. I have for a moment no sex, no history, no character. Past a certain point I will not hear the phone. I respect that self, that artisan who feels empty of personal concern even when dealing with the stuff of my intimate life. I guess the only times I ever am free of the buzz of self-concern and the sometimes interesting, often boring, reflection of consciousness on itself is during moments when I am writing and moments when I am making love. I overvalue both activities because of the refreshment of quieting the skull to pure attention.

That to me is ecstasy, rapture — being seized as if by a raptor, the eagle in "The Rose and the Eagle" — the loss of the buzz of ego in the intense and joyous contemplation of something, whether a lover, a sensation, the energy, the image, the artifact. The ability to move into the state I called concentration is a needful preliminary to, in the first and commonest case, the work that you gradually build or, in the second and rarer case, the visit from necessity, the poems that fall through you entire and burning like a meteorite.

In a society that values the ability to see visions, such as some of the Plains Indians did, many people will manage to crank out a few visions at least at critical moments in their lives; very few people will not manage a vision at least once. Some will become virtuosos of vision.

In a society where seeing visions is usually punished by imprisonment, torture with electroshock, heavy drugging that destroys coordination and shortens life expectancy, very few people will see visions. Some of those who do so occasionally will learn early on to keep their mouths shut, respect the visions, use them but keep quiet about seeing or hearing what other people say is not there. A few of my poems are founded in specific visions: "Curse of the earth magician on a metal land," which also was the seed of *Dance the Eagle to Sleep*; "The sun" from the tarot card sequence in "Laying down the tower," which was the seed of *Woman on the Edge of Time*.

That a poem is visionary in inception does not mean it comes entire. Actually writing a poem or any other artifact out of a vision is often a great deal of work. The hinge poem, for the month of Beth in "The Lunar Cycle," called "At the well," was a case in point. I first wrote a version of that experience in 1959 when it happened. Here I am finally being able to bring off the poem that is faithful to it in 1979.

To me, no particular value attaches to the genesis of a poem. I am not embarrassed by the sense I have at times of being a conduit through which a poem forces itself and I am not embarrassed by working as long as it takes to build a poem — in the case I just mentioned, 20 years. I write poems for specific occasions, viewing myself as a useful artisan. I have written poems for anti-war rallies, for women's day rallies, for rallies centering on the rights and abuses of mental institution inmates. I have written poems to raise money for the legal defense of political prisoners, for Inez Garcia who shot the man who raped her, for Shoshana Rihm-Pat Swinton who was for many years a political fugitive and finally acquitted of all charges. I wrote a poem for a poster to raise money for Transition House (a shelter for battered women) along with a beautiful graphic by Betsy Warrior, a warrior for women indeed. I wrote a poem to be presented to the Vietnamese delegation at Montreal during meetings with anti-war activists.

Some of those occasional poems (as some of the category that arrive like a fast train) are among my best poems; some are mediocre. Frequently I find the necessity to write a poem for a specific purpose or when an occasion focuses me; perhaps coalesces is a better verb. A charged rod enters the colloidal substance of my consciousness and particles begin to adhere. "For Shoshana-Pat Swinton" is a meditation on feeling oneself active in history that I consider a very strong poem, for instance. I was, of course, to deal with the figure of the political fugitive as a paradigm of certain women's experiences as well as a touchstone for our recent political history in *Vida*; that swirl of ideas and images was obviously rich for me. What doesn't touch you, you can't make poems of.

One last thing I have learned about starting a poem is that if you manage to write down a certain amount when you begin, and failing that, to memorize enough, you will not lose it. If you cannot memorize or scribble that essential sufficient fragment, the poem will dissolve. Sometimes a couple of lines are ample to preserve the impulse till you can give it your full attention. Often it is a started first draft, maybe what will become eventually the first third of the poem, that I carry to my typewriter. But if I can't memorize and record that seed, that match, the instigating factor, then I have lost that particular poem.

Good work habits are nothing more than habits that let you work, that encourage you to pay attention. Focus is most of it: to be fierce and pointed, so that everything else momentarily sloughs away.

Notes

* This chapter is copyright © 1981 by Marge Piercy. Reprinted by permission of the University of Michigan Press. From *Parti-Colored Blocks for a Quilt* by Marge Piercy.

3

To You Readers and Teachers of Poetry[1]

Marvin Bell

Poetry is an emotional approach to thinking, a means to saying what one didn't know one knew, a trust in process. I write by maneuvering toward the sense I make. I begin with something that occurs to me (it may be an image or the start of a story, a scene, a piece of rhetoric attached to a scene, or something else; it may be a phrase or a sentence, one or two or three lines), something that intrigues or moves me and which does not yet make sense or seems partial. In other words, I write toward my ignorance, beginning with whatever surfaces and trusting my interest. I am intuitive while writing first drafts, analytical in revision. I don't plan as much as I recognize, follow, and connect. I think by increments. And I write when moved to: inspiration? need?

The Mystery of Emily Dickinson[2]

Sometimes the weather goes on for days
but you were different. You were divine.
While the others wrote more and longer,
you wrote much more and much shorter.
I held your white dress once: 12 buttons.
In the cupola, the wasps struck glass
as hard to escape as you hit your sound
again and again asking Welcome. No one.

Except for you, it were a trifle:
This morning, not much after dawn,
in level country, not New England's,
through leftovers of summer rain I
went out rag-tag to the curb, only
a sleepy householder at his routine

17

bending to trash, when a young girl
in a white dress your size passed,

so softly!, carrying her shoes. It must be
she surprised me — her barefoot quick-step
and the earliness of the hour, your dress —
or surely I'd have spoken of it sooner.
I should have called to her, but a neighbor
wore that look you see against happiness.
I won't say anything would have happened
unless there was time, and eternity's plenty.

About "The Mystery of Emily Dickinson"

Anyone who has seen a photo of Emily Dickinson (1830–1886), or
read her poems, knows how easy it might have been to fall in love with
her. She was a great and original American poet who wrote almost
1,800 poems — all of them short, most of them very short — but published
only seven during her lifetime. She was delicate and private. As the
years went by, she grew more and more reclusive and took to wearing
only white.

Once, I wangled a private tour of the Dickinson home in Amherst,
Massachusetts. There, I did what there was to do: I looked through the
house, went up the front staircase and down the back one, climbed to
the cupola where wasps were hitting the windows in the heat, and
visited her bedroom (which was also her writing room). Suddenly, my
host reached into the closet and brought forth one of the white dresses
she had worn, which he let me hold. I sized her up. One way to
measure was to count the buttons. Afterwards, there were family
photo albums to view, and I picked a violet from the lawn before
leaving.

Of course it's somewhat silly! *Of course* I was probably out to
make the experience Important, though that is not usually my approach.
Of course I hoped to manage a poem set at Emily's home.

(When the Emily Dickinson postage stamps appeared, perhaps
four or five years earlier, I bought 100. I had thought to write 100
poems to her, each using one of her lines, and of course I would put a
stamp on each. But I managed only one, an 18-line poem titled "Never
Say Die," which appeared in a book titled *Residue of Song*.)

Home again in Iowa City, I wrote the first stanza of "The Mystery
of Emily Dickinson." It took me a line and a half to get to E. D. It was
an Iowa summer — hot for days. In contrast to the boring oppression of
the heat, and the sameness of a routine life, I placed Emily Dickinson.
I can't say that I thought this out and then wrote it. Rather, one of two
things happened. The first possibility is that I wrote what engaged me

(the endless weather, the sameness, the little joke in line one) and then sought to bend it to events (her life, my visit to her home). The other possibility is that I looked aside from what I most wanted to write about (the visit) so that I could sneak up on it with a viewpoint.

The first eight lines tell what I did there in her house and a few things about her. Having written them, I was stuck. There really wasn't any more to say about the visit. That one stanza sat around with other drafts of poems, odd lines and miscellaneous stanzas for months.

It was still summer, though, when I woke one morning at sun-up. It must have been about 5:30 a.m. My wife and two sons were visiting her parents on a farm in southern Illinois, and it was garbage day. I couldn't go back to sleep and decided to take the garbage cans to the curb. I put them out on a sidewalk still drying from a light rain, in that cool, crisp air one feels and smells at such times, not fully awake in it, when suddenly there appeared a young girl in a white dress, carrying her shoes, padding quickly past, hardly disturbing the air. I turned and went back inside, but I was not through with her.

Later that day, looking again at my one stanza about Emily Dickinson, to which there was nothing to add about Emily Dickinson, I knew I would have to go elsewhere in the poem to extend it. There was also, now, the sudden vision of the girl at an odd hour in an odd manner, and I connected the two. I knew that one was like the other, that my feelings toward one were based on my feelings toward the other. Surely, the white dress might have been the same dress!

From there on, it was easy. I was working with material I could apprehend in the presence of a clear emotion. The poem went down the page, describing the time and terrain, myself and the girl, my reticence and desire—whatever occurred to me with clarity, in order.

The final sentence in the poem employs one of Emily Dickinson's favorite words, "eternity." And of course the sentence is ambiguous. Does "eternity's plenty" mean "the plenty of eternity" or "eternity is plenty?" The former reading suggests that nothing could have happened except in an endless amount of time. But the latter reading suggests that there is always eternity and it will be plenty. I think Emily would have liked that ending and thought it doubly true.

I could play with many small discoveries that took up residence in this poem. E. D.'s "asking Welcome" in stanza one is answered by no one while in stanza three I fail to call the girl. I don't even speak of it right away. I am, like Emily, bent by public opinion and proper behavior, silent in public, expressive in private. Who is that young girl? What is Emily to me except she reappear?

Sometimes, poetry affords the poet permission. "The Mystery of Emily Dickinson" afforded me permission to feel something for that girl who carried her shoes past me on the wet sidewalk at dawn. The poem afforded me permission to take her seriously — as seriously as I take Emily Dickinson. It afforded me permission to counter the distance between us with song and idea. It afforded me the *freedom* to do all of this and more. In the end, poetry is rooted in freedom: the freedom to say anything and then to be responsible to it. What has one confessed? The answer is always there in the poem.

To an Adolescent Weeping Willow[3]

I don't know what you think you're doing,
sweeping the ground. You
do it so easily, backhanded, forehanded.
You hardly bend. Really, you sway.
What can it mean
when a thing is so easy?

I threw dirt on my father's floor.
Not dirt, but a chopped green
dirt which picked up dirt.

I pushed the pushbroom.
I oiled the wooden floor of the store.

He bent over and lifted the coal
into the coalstove. With the back of the shovel
he came down on the rat just topping the bin
and into the fire.

What do you think? — Did he sway?
Did he kiss a rock for luck?
Did he soak up water
and climb into light and turn and turn?

Did he weep and weep in the yard?

Yes, I think he did. Yes,
now I think he did.

So, Willow, you come sweep my floor.
I have no store.
I have a yard. A big yard.

I have a song to weep.
I have a cry.
You who rose up from the dirt,
because I put you there
and like to walk my head in under
your earliest feathery branches —
what can it mean
when a thing is so easy?

It means you are a boy.

About "To an Adolescent Weeping Willow"

My father was an immigrant from the Ukraine who supported us by means of a small five-and-ten in a small town on the south shore of eastern Long Island. At first, the store was heated by coal, and its basement inhabited by rats. I often swept up at closing time. I would scatter a green "something" on the wooden floor to help pick up dirt. Then I would push a wide broom down the aisles, trying not to sweep up customers. Afterwards, I would sprinkle the floor with linseed oil to keep it from drying out.

My father died while I was in my first year of graduate school. I had yet to begin to write poetry seriously. I had married young and would soon have a son. When the marriage ended, I would keep the baby.

Marrying changes your life a little, but having a child changes your life a lot and for good. You become conscious of the difference between the parent and the one who is dependent.

Over the years, I also became "the tree poet" — a title awarded to me by a radio interviewer who noticed that the five poems used during our conversation contained four trees: a mulberry, an elm, a gingko, and a pine. (I have also written about a wild cherry tree and, more recently, a downtown banyan tree in Honolulu. Of course, the trees serve subjects besides themselves.)

Poets are always looking into nature to see if it is a mirror. My poems have often made a distinction between what nature is and the uses we make of it. In "To an Adolescent Weeping Willow," I talk to a young willow in my back yard in Iowa. Like any weeping willow, it is graceful and sweeps the ground. I'm unwilling to let it go at that, and I ask it what it thinks it's doing and what it means when a thing is so easy.

When the question is first posed, there is no answer. If I had known the answer, there would have been no need for the poem. Instead, I associate the sweeping motions of the willow and the dirt in which it grows with my sweeping up in the store and the green "dirt" which was a part of it.

Having said that much, a difference arises. Poetry often develops out of a need (willingness?) to question what one has just said. My first sense of changing direction comes with a mention of my father's tasks — harder than my own.

Then I continue to challenge the willow. What do you think, I ask it, Did my father live like you? Did he do what you do? Yes, now I think he did. Now that I am myself his age and a parent, I more fully comprehend his life.

But what *does* it mean when a thing is so easy? It means you are a boy. It means you are only a boy. By means of my challenge to the

willow, and the necessity in poetry to pay attention and to connect, I
come to say — almost to blurt out — the truth: that an adolescent, for all
the pleasure he provides the parent, does not know the parent's life.

To You Teachers of Poetry

Most students are probably reassured to be told a few things right at
the start. One of these is that writing poetry is not a way of saying
only what one already has the words for, but a way of saying what one
didn't know one knew. This is true of everything about poetry, including
meter and rhyme. While meter and rhyme create specific effects of
expression, they are there in the poem because the poet wanted to be
led, somewhat, by the language into saying things previously unex-
pressed, at least by him or her. We do this all the time in lively
conversation, and it might be argued (I'll argue it!) that good essays
are written the same way.

Students are also reassured to see that contemporary poems are
written in the language of their time. Indeed, it could be argued that
the history of poetry (and perhaps of any art) is in large measure the
history of poets finding ways (daring) to put into their poems both
content and styles formerly thought "unpoetic." Poets are often
seemingly crude, vulgar, casual, personal, emotional, or critical, and
this presents a problem in teaching poetry where offense might be
taken. This is a shame because the very essence of much first-rate
poetry is its ability to think twice, to qualify the conventional wisdom,
to say, "Yes, but ...." or "Why not?" — skills basic to education.

Finally, students ought to be told that neither a semester nor a
year is enough to encompass the astonishing variety in American
poetry, let alone in poetry from other languages and cultures.

Why study poetry at all? It doesn't have to be because the student
is specifically interested in poetry. Rather, one might study poetry
simply to learn to read: not simply to cover the words but to understand
deeply. Poetry is perfect for learning to read well and to think clearly
(the same thing?) because it insists on slow reading and sustained
attention, because in it the words themselves are presumed to matter
beyond the information they carry in common with "synonyms," because
it offers great variety in language and organization in short forms,
because it engages the imagination and heart as well as the lungs and
brain, and because there are no rules in art except those the work of
art establishes as it goes. Beyond that, the best poetry is a synthesis of
form and content that articulates the truth of our lives — what it feels
like and all the things we think at once.

Writing is not as much a matter of intention as a matter of effect.
Often we say, "What did the poet mean by this or that?" The question

might be better phrased, "What is the effect of this or that?" Because writing is a great adventure, in which we are free to be only what we are and everything that we are, the poet is not just a formulator, but a discoverer. In poetry, all the discoveries are brought back and exhibited there in the poem. The willing reader can make them too, again and again.

Notes

1. Copyright © 1981 by Marvin Bell. Reprinted by permission of the author.

2. From *Stars Which See, Stars Which Do Not See*, By Marvin Bell Atheneum Publishers. Copyright © 1977 by Marvin Bell.

3. From *These Green-Going-to-Yellow*, by Marvin Bell, Atheneum Publishers. Copyright © 1981 by Marvin Bell.

4

Color Is a Poet's Tool[1]

Diane Wakoski

In a poem called "What you should know to be a poet," Gary Snyder says that, basically, poets have to know everything, but he starts with this catalogue:

> all you can about animals as persons.
> the names of trees and flowers and weeds.
> names of stars, and the movements of the planets and the moon.
>
> your own six senses, with a watchful and elegant mind.
>
> at least one kind of traditional magic:
> divination, astrology, the *book of changes*, the tarot;[2]

As a young writer I agreed with Snyder that poets had to know everything, but I didn't quite understand how one conveyed that knowledge in poems. I loved the wisdom of Shakespeare on the subjects of love and aging and beauty in his sonnets, but when I tried to write that way, I simply sounded pompous or corny. And his images never made me see pictures. They were abstractions which gave me ideas, but when I tried with similar images of the moon or sun or stars or trees, sketched as they are in Shakespeare, I simply was trite, banal, more clichéd even than I was in ordinary talk.

What I needed, then, was some system for presenting this material in poems. And it was a combination of poets and poetry which assaulted me during my first two years of college, teaching me about images, surrealism, big metaphors, incantation. And it was reading poems and imitating them which finally led to my own prosody and craft.

A poem that inspired me deeply and continues to move me is Lorca's "Somnambule Ballad." Of course I read this in translation. In fact it was because a student friend of mine, Michael Rossman, was passionately and diligently translating Lorca's gypsy poems that I was introduced to this work. The poem offered me so much that was exciting. And more, so much that was new to me at the time. I don't think repetition or incantation were part of my tradition. And the poetry I had read and most enjoyed was not ecstatic poetry, so the use of the intensely lyrical repetition, "Green, how much I want you green./ Green wind. Green branches." thrilled me. And the use of repetition as an organizing device, as well as a means of conveying passionate feeling, excited my desire to try the same.

Because I am a visually oriented person, poems that used vivid imagistic description appealed enormously to me. But I had not, at that time, read a great deal of poetry that did this. Heavy in our curriculum were poems of narrative, or lyric poems which barely touched the visual world, or did so as Shakespeare's sonnets did, with the mind rather than the painterly eye. I am sure the use of color as an organizing device was one of the aspects of this poem which implanted in me so firmly and which gave me permission to continue to use color for the rest of my life, not as decoration, but as a device for organizing a poem.

In the "Somnambule Ballad," Lorca uses the folk tradition of the gypsy world along with twentieth-century surrealist images, and they come together surprisingly well. The simplification of images, and symbolic speech, which is in all folk poetry and painting ("Your white shirt bears/ three hundred dark roses," or "eyes of cold silver," or "I want to change/ my horse for your house,/ my saddle for your mirror,/ my knife for your blanket."), meshes well with the surreal images such as calling the girl "green flesh, hair of green," or referring to "the fish of darkness/ that opens the road of dawn," or referring to the stars as "a thousand crystal tambourines" which were "piercing the dawn."[3]

Taking this poem into my heart entirely, and accepting the gift of its structures, I wrote a whole group of college poems in which I tried to make the world respond to my visions of color. The most successful of these was a poem using blue. In it, my love of the music of Debussy, of early Chinese poems which I had just begun to read, of this Lorca poem, all combined with my own desperately unhappy adolescent life. My longing for love I could not seem to find. My desire for lovers who did not desire me. And a wish for a world of the past, more structured, more orderly, and perhaps more royal or elegant. The poem was a dramatic monologue in which I spoke as the "blue jester" whose lady is royal and throws him out at dawn because he isn't good enough for the world to know that he's her lover. Speaking in the voice of the man rejected by the woman, I think I felt freer than if I had tried to speak in my own desperate adolescent girl's voice then. But I knew well the theme of lost love, as every 20-year-old does, and the lost love of the

"Somnambule Ballad" glittering through its images, repeated by its
refrain, embodied by the color green, inspired me to use those devices
to talk about my own life through the story of the blue jester.

About five years later I was again to use color to organize another
of my best poems. Probably each year of my life since I discovered
this Lorca poem, I have written at least one poem in which color has
been the primary organizing structure. Often I have tried different
techniques, but always the color domination has worked best when I
am attempting a theme of lost love, as was presented in my early
model. A poem that I must have discovered at about the same time in
my undergraduate life that I began to read Lorca was/is Wallace
Stevens' "Domination of Black." This poem uses the image of blackness
to present a dramatic feeling about death or closure. Perhaps in my
mind this reinforced the power of color being associated with pain or
with loss or grief. For I think it is almost always true that the most
successful color poems I write are explorations of those themes.

In the following poem, I was again attempting to talk about lost
love.

The Pink Dress[4]

I could not wear that pink dress tonight.
The velvet one
lace tinting the cuffs with all
the coffee
of longing. My bare shoulder
slipping whiter
than foam
out of the night to remind me
of my own
vulnerability.

I could not wear that pink dress tonight
because it is a dress
that slips memories like
the hands
of obscene strangers
all over my body.
And in my fatigue I could not fight away the images
and their mean touching.
I couldn't wear that pink dress,
the velvet one you had made for me,
all year, you know.

I thought I would tonight because
once again
you have let me enter your house

and look at myself
some mornings
in your mirrors.
            But
I could not wear that pink dress tonight
because it reminded me
of everything
that hurts.
It reminded me of a whole year
during which
I wandered,
a gypsy,
and could not come into your house.
It reminded me of the picture of a blond girl
you took with you to Vermont
and shared your woods with.
The pretty face you left over your bed to stare
at me
and remind me
each night
that you preferred her face to mine,
and which you left there to stare at me
even when you saw how it
broke me,
my calm,
like a stick smashing across my own
plain lonesome face,
and a face which you only
took down
from your wall
after I had mutilated it
and pushed pins into it to get those smug
smiling eyes off my cold
winter
body.

I couldn't wear that pink dress tonight
because it reminded me
of the girl who made it,
whom you slept with,
last year while I was sitting in hotel rooms
wondering why I had to live
with a face
so stony no man could love it.

I could not wear that pink dress
because it reminded me
of how I camp on your doorstep now,

still a gypsy,
still a colorful imaginative beggar
in my pink dress,
building a fire in the landowner's
woods, and my own fierceness
that deserts me
when a man
no, when you,
show a little care and concern
for my presence.

I could not wear that pink dress tonight.
It betrayed all that was strong in me.
The leather boots I wear to stomp through the world
and remind everyone
of the silver and gold and diamonds
from fairy tales
glittering in their lives.
And of the heavy responsibility
we all must bear
just being so joyfully alive
just letting the blood take its own course
in intact vessels
in veins.
That pink dress betrayed my one favorite image
— the motorcyclist riding along the highway
   independent
   alone
   exhilarated with movement
   a blackbird
   more beautiful than any white ones.

But I went off
not wearing the pink dress,
thinking how much I love you
and how if a woman loves a man who does not love her,
it is, as some good poet said,
a pain in the ass.
For both of them.

I went off thinking about all the girls
you preferred to me.
Leaving behind that dress,
remembering one of the colors
of pain
Remembering that my needs
affront you,
my face is not beautiful to you;
you would not share your woods with me.

And the irony
of my images.
That you are the motorcycle rider.
Not I.
I am perhaps,
at best,
the pink dress
thrown against the back
of the chair.
The dress I could not wear
tonight.

In this poem, the obvious narration of lost love is implemented through the image of the pink dress. To me, the idea that women are symbolized by pink has always been hateful. Perhaps because pink is a pastel color, an off shade, a dilution of the primary and powerful color red. Red, of course, is the color of blood and is often used to represent anger. In my poem, the pink dress becomes that dilution of person that a woman is to a man in our culture. Since red would be the color of blood, there is something of the stain of blood, death, and pain about this dream which is the diluted color of blood. And the diluted color of anger.

In "The Pink Dress" I wanted the idea of the color to represent again the emotions I was experiencing, this time not through a verbal pun, but through the symbols of the color itself. In fact, the whole poem works with symbol. The dress itself is a symbol for woman as she is seen by most men, a decorative object, and as she chooses to present herself through her clothes. She is no more than the dress. So both the dress itself and its color, pink, are working as symbols throughout the poem.

Symbol and image are two of the major tools of figurative language. They are a vivid and real part of anyone's life and can be used most powerfully, I think, when they come naturally out of the matrix of one's life. I knew this, theoretically, when I was young and first starting to write, but I did not know how to apply what I knew until I began to discover how to talk personally about my own life in ways that were not obscure or embarrassingly intimate. It was the wonderful examples of poets who also had a painterly, visual vision of the world, like Garcia Lorca and Wallace Stevens, who led me away from cliché, banal language, and trite phrases, permitting me to talk somewhat originally about the clichéd, banal, and trite subject of lost love and the pain of rejection which was to become a major theme in my work. Perhaps "The Pink Dress" can be used by students as a model for writing poems that use organizational devices that they might not have thought of previously, in particular, color.

Notes

1. Copyright © 1981 by Diane Wakoski. Reprinted by permission of Black Sparrow Press.

2. Gary Snyder, *Regarding Wave*. Copyright © 1970 by Gary Snyder. Reprinted by permission.

3. Copyright © 1955 by New Directions Publishing Corp. Reprinted by permission of New Directions.

4. From *The Motorcycle Betrayal Poems*, Simon and Schuster, 1971.

5

"3 A.M. Kitchen: My Father Talking" — Writing in Another Voice

Tess Gallagher

As a child we've all tried on other voices, probably because there is simply an innate pleasure in trying on the sounds of the world. The young aren't embarrassed to cluck like hens in the chicken yard, or to lean their heads over fences and moo, or to gallop onto the porch and into the livingroom neighing and pawing the rug.

As children we spoke back to the world's creatures "as if" we could be understood, "as if" our approximation of their languages would somehow magically break the code of our differences. And who's to say we didn't have conversations with those silent companions of childhood — rocks, trees, stray feathers, ants, snakes, cave-spirits, river currents, even the dirt itself as we shaped it into castles whose corridors rang with commands and secret messages.

Once in Tokyo a boy named Kei, the four-year-old son of my Japanese editor, stood confidently before me and delivered a long, excited soliloquy in Japanese, a language of which I possess only a few phrases and sentences. He'd heard me speaking English to his mother and father, but he assumed quite naturally that if he spoke to me I'd understand. Language wasn't a barrier to him, it was fluid, a kind of democratic rain that fell out of the air when people opened their mouths and spoke. I said something excitely back to him in English. Suddenly language wasn't enough and he ran to the huge king-sized bed in my suite at the Imperial Hotel and began to leap and bounce up and down. "He's pretending he's Superman," his mother, Masako, explained. Kei raised his arms in a soaring pose and kicked off into the skies of Tokyo.

When I try to puzzle out why I became a poet instead of a jet pilot, a longshoreman, or a tug boat captain, I realize that, like Kei, I'd wished to have adventure and a sense of power and freedom. Access to the professions I've named had largely been denied me as a young woman growing up in a time when these were considered "male professions." But I also wanted to be more than "useful." Sure, it would be fine to save people in distress a la Superman. But like that Japanese boy, his arms outstretched on my bed as if carried through the air with an invisible cape flowing out behind him — being able to "leap tall buildings in a single bound" was somehow at the heart of everything. I'm talking about the imagination.

As a poet, I had hoped language itself would propel me through imagined and actual universes toward a connectedness with creatures and nature, as well as with the people and places I loved. Becoming a poet was a choice against the exclusions and humiliations most people experience daily in their use of language. I have never given up the wish to speak for an imagined world in which our very separations become felt and articulated.

One time early in my life as a poet I returned on one of my many visits to my parents' home. I did those distracted things anyone does when they go back to the place and people they've love and left for the wider world. I sifted the traces of my absence and tried to learn freshly who these people were who'd raised and nurtured me. I recall myself now as a kind of sleepwalker who would snap awake at intervals to some recognition I couldn't express.

I had gone away to college. It had changed my language. I spoke English correctly, but those emotional currents that lived in the way English was misspoken by my parents had a beautiful, true power for me. The poem "3 a.m. Kitchen: My Father Talking" was written, in some sense, out of the wish to speak directly *as* my father so that his sound, his voice tone, his vocabulary and signature in tempo and nuance, even his silences would be present for everyone. In one stroke I wanted to *be* him and to *give* him.

I had been gradually realizing that to be a poet was a kind of entrustment, a gift that wasn't just my private shadow game, but which could empower those whose lives would ordinarily not gain stature or recognition. Giving my father poetically powerful speech was also an attempt to make him a part of the country's literature. It was to challenge the prevailing intellectual assumption, which still largely persists in spite of important writers like Raymond Carver, that only those lives which were "educated" were worth dignifying in poetry or story. Oh, Robert Frost could write "The Death of the Hired Man," but he would do so in the voices of the farm people for whom this man worked, not in that hired man's own voice. I wanted to present my father in his full dignity speaking his eighth-grade English, but with his soul so exposed and available that we couldn't avoid being affected at a deep level by what he said.

My father had come from itinerant farms in Oklahoma. He was one of the oldest of seven children, and as was often the case in these families, he had to quit school at the age of thirteen to work in the fields picking cotton, baling hay, or planting the garden which sustained the family. He'd been born in an Indian dugout in New Mexico and his mother would tell me of my Great-grandmother Owens, who was related to the famous Chief Black Hawk. I have never investigated this heritage, but something of a people who dug their houses into the earth clings even now to my memory of my father. He had a mournful, disinherited presence and was capable of sitting for hours smoking cigarettes — the working man's slow suicide — drinking coffee, and staring off into his thoughts. If you spoke to him he would answer in monosyllables or simply take a sip of his coffee, a drag on his cigarette, and look at you as if from a hopeless distance one shouldn't even pretend to cross.

When my father was drinking or playing cards, this reticence fell away. He would slash about in whatever language, foul or fair, came to his tongue. There was a desperation and vigor that outreached anything I could pitifully call poetry. He moved my heart those times. He stopped being simply my father and represented those working-class lives whose toil stays just that: toil. The struggles of these people go unhonored and mostly unrewarded in the general onrush of the American passion for getting and spending. I love the way my first poet-teacher, Theodore Roethke, put it: "Money, money, money. Water, water, water."

By the time of the visit I've mentioned, my father had somehow transcended the mirage upon which the American dream had been hastily constructed — that what one had to do was to work hard and life would be sweet, all would be given. What my father had experienced was that hard work led to more hard work, and he could easily see that those who had the advantage of education arrived by another, less wearisome path. He didn't pretend to be satisfied with trading time for cash on the docks where he worked as a winch-driver. A winch-driver has the responsibility of running a crane-like machine on a ship being loaded above the heads of the other dock workers. It was a job full of tension and dangers since everything from logs to huge rolls of raw paper were maneuvered in a sling from dockside to ship. The safety of his friends was his daily responsibility for hours on end.

He never spoke of this or complained in those sober, solitary times at home. But when he drank, the anguish and sense of having lost track of what it was all for became not just his personal cry, but the cry of any life asking that most basic of questions: what redeems a life from the fear of its having been wasted?

The night before I was to return to my studies in Seattle on the visit I've mentioned, my father came home very early in the morning after a card game at the Chinook Tavern, one of those frontier taverns which has now been turned into a Chinese restaurant. He'd been drinking and gambling, the two demons that made my mother's life hell and which had sent his children scurrying for cover all through childhood. He came home wanting to eat and talk, and since it was my last night home for a while, I got up to be with him.

My father asked if I would fix him some eggs and bacon, which I set about doing. While I was cooking he began to put his life before me, his history through places and jobs which had brought him west from Oklahoma during the post-depression days to the far northwest Olympic Peninsula, where he'd begun logging with my mother as his partner. There had been pleasures too in those early days, an abundance of fish which had dwindled greatly by the time of our kitchen conversation.

The account my father gave of his life in those early morning hours when we were alone seemed at once simple and profound. There was no answer, of course, to the tyranny of the ten- to fourteen-hour days he had sometimes worked to provide food and shelter for his family. Playing cards was his way of balancing the scale, of scoffing at the very money he made, money which represented an exchange of time for labor which he seemed to realize would never be fair, no matter what necessities it provided.

But I wasn't thinking any of these things as my father spoke. I only realized the next morning as I got onto the bus for Seattle and said goodbye to my father and mother, that his voice had lodged so strongly in me I was compelled to record it. I remember finding some scraps of paper in my jacket pocket and writing the words that would become this poem.

In writing it I didn't worry at all about whether or not I was writing poetry. I just paid attention to the sound of my father's voice in my head. I entered his voice there on that bus moving away from him and it's possible that my father became something he had never expected or wanted to be: a poet, someone who speaks intimately and uncompromisingly of what is in their heart, and who believes against odds, like my young Japanese friend Kei, that they will be heard in the only language they have.

For my part there was the immediate pleasure of being my own father, in a sense, for a short while. By writing the poem I could enact him and look back at the world from inside this life which had engendered me. Now that my father has been dead many years, I remember the mild signs of his shy, but certain enjoyment of this poem when I read it to him. No doubt about it, he knew he'd entered another realm where his life might touch people he'd never see or know.

To take another voice can give a poet insight and fresh music. It can allow one to become another sex, another age, another class. It can translate the very inarticulateness of our loves and struggles to receive each other. In writing this poem, I closed a huge gap between myself and my father. He came to believe that maybe his oldest daughter wasn't wasting her life, and that in the process, something of his own life had been briefly redeemed in this strange language which would allow even him to speak, the language of poetry. I can easily say this is one of the most important poems I've ever written, if only for the memory of my father smoking and listening to me read it aloud to him in that same kitchen on another early morning before we sat down to eggs and bacon, while the rest of the house slept on.

3 A.M. Kitchen: My Father Talking

For years it was land working me, oil fields,
cotton fields, then I got some land. I
worked it. Them days you could just about
make a living. I was logging.

Then I sent to Missouri. Momma
come out. We got married.
We got some kids. Five kids.
That kept us going.

We bought some land near the water.
It was cheap then. The water
was right there. You just looked out
the window. It never left the window.

I bought a boat. Fourteen footer.
There was fish out there then.
You remember, we used to catch
six, eight fish, clean them right
out in the yard. I could of fished to China.

I quit the woods. One day just
walked out, took off my corks, said that's
it. I went to the docks.
I was driving winch. You had to watch
to see nothing fell out of the sling. If
you killed somebody you'd
never forget it. All

those years I was just working
I was on edge, every day. Just working.

You kids. I could tell you
a lot. But I won't.

It's winter. I play a lot of cards
down at the tavern. Your mother.
I have to think of excuses
to get out of the house. You're
wasting your time, she says. You're wasting
your money.

You don't have no idea, Threasie.
I run out of things
to work for. Hell, why shouldn't I
play cards? Threasie,
some days now I just don't know.

6

When the Shoe Never Fits: Myth In the Modern Mode

Colleen J. McElroy

Long before Imelda Marcos scandalized the world by reportedly using political contributions to purchase scores of shoes, shoes were, for me, quite political. I have triangular, three-quarter feet — my shoe size a B width at the front and AA at the back, the length having grown progressively with age from six and one-quarter to seven and three-quarters to a final eight and one-quarter. This places me, literally, outside of most shoes. Despite the wondrous shoemaking machine of black inventor Jan Matzeliger, my feet won't fit the forms of a factory-built last, and shoe manufacturers are not interested in nonstandard feet. So I grew without "... the right fit of merchant's shoe/or style to match my mental picture of elegant slipper ...."[1] And it is only natural that my poems, usually addressing subjects outside of the mainstream anyway, should take on shoes.

Originally however, I was more interested in feet, thinking that they, after all, were the culprits. In early poems where feet were mentioned, it is with my envy over the perfect foot, arched and sized to fit a regular shoe.

I dream desert feet — sand encrusted
onyx that seem to have been sculpted
from the earth's tears — or the fame
of dancers' feet — arches blistered
like a cocksman's bow and soles
scarred like a gypsy bandit from my love
of flying into sheer leaps of little death
all dancers come to know —
at night I count my toes and wonder

37

how those artichokes of pain
can so blithely bear my past[2]

There, I took on the view of victim, at the mercy of feet that
dreadfully refused to fit the meanest of shoes. My poems offered an
apology, the narrative voice worked with the "fine whip of her own
tongue," as Erica Jong says in "Alcestis on the Poetry Circuit."

She must wear tight shoes
so she always remembers her bondage.
She must never forget
she is rooted in the ground.[3]

Society's bondage I understood long before Black History Month
evolved out of Negro History Day/Week, but I had not questioned its
reference to anything as causal as a shoe. When I began those questions, I
turned the apology into an apologus, the plea into myth. It was an easy
step, totally befitting a poet, and the details were right there, at my
feet so to speak: a lost shoe on a highway, the fragile princess (these
days in the 'Burbs), Eliot's Mrs. Porter, and those tiny baby shoes,
carefully crafted for little fingers that have no intention of keeping
dainty shoes in place. The myths existed as much a part of this world
as Cinderella's prince was to the world of English kings and royalty. I
like telling my students that there was a time when poets had real jobs,
when they sang the praises of the heroes and villains of a culture,
brought home the news to the tribe, answered the unanswerable questions of life and death. Poets were the griots, the soothsayers, the
seers, the shaman — and stories were created as answers to questions:
Who are we? and Where are we going? and Why? The whole point of
some myths is to answer questions — and to set examples, codes of
conduct, with those answers. Early poets ventured to answer complex
questions: What happens to the sun at night? and Where does the
world end? So my question, at first glance, seemed easy: What is it
with this business of shoes? However, that was quickly complicated by
a second question: Black and female with three-quarter feet, what
examples can I follow? Whatever ease I might have imagined initially
was dispelled with that second question. And a third, and fourth. In
the end, I wrote six poems to create my apologus of shoes.

The most wonderful aspect of mythmaking is the element of
surprise that naturally exists in any situation, especially those we have
come to take for granted. Poems arise out of causal discoveries and
unexpected connections. The first poem of the series began with the
sighting of a shoe on a highway in northern California, a lone shoe in
six lanes of fast traffic with cars veering away from it. Was it a clue?
Something dropped like a breadcrumb trail in the woods? And why

always one shoe, left sad and footless while we run for the hills? The
mythopoeia of the single shoe centered that first poem.

A Pied

one shoe on the roadway presents
its own riddle of so much left
unsaid regardless of the condition:
scoured, unpolished and crumpled
like a drunk forever missing the next step
the tongue bent inward like some church
gossip who has said finally too much
and snapped that last accusation in public
the absence of laces or any restraints
and how everyone passing lurches away
from any entanglement
all roads at some time or other
have held a single shoe — the forlorn
reminder of someone careless enough to be trapped
like a teenager in the wash of fast travel
the incongruous one shoe out of step
without foot or wheels or movement
yet so commonplace as to almost
be forgotten by what is missing:
the left leg dangling bare
the child crying to be forgiven or the family
car careening on its mission of terror

one shoe on the road leaves it all
unsaid — the something that lies
without comment or recognition
in the heaviest of traffic or mid-lane
and turned sideways near the center
strip as if waiting for someone
to answer its description
if, as my father would say, the shoe fits
but this thing, so ordinary, cannot be
explained so easily like those strips
of rubber from burst tires
we'd soon as not remember how anyone
like a shoe may be lost in a crowd
or how part of what we know to be our lives
can become a stray digit or decimal point
an unrelated member of a set
yet any child from a divorce can tell
you how it feels to be abandoned midstream
while the family makes a fast break
for the nearest off-ramp — and we all

know of the countless armies left
scattered like shoes in the traffic of war
along roads where city families once
took their Sunday country outings

but one shoe without ballroom or battleground
can never question the hurry of passing
it bends finally into its own loneliness
and unanswered questions of what might have happened
to its owner or what horror has befallen the other shoe[4]

That poem incorporated some sense of the timelessness myths present. The sudden appearance of the shoe on the road allowed me to explore how we can become so accustomed to the unexpected, the lost shoe. How we are both startled by its appearance, yet take its presence for granted. Everyone recognized the image of a lone shoe on the road, but bend the image a little — disrupt the continuity by adding the unexpected — and the ordinary becomes the extraordinary. Still, this poem merely opened the door to the possibilities of myths. Connecting poems in a series is the discovery of how those images, like loose threads in a tapestry, can help complete the mythopoeia.

In the course of writing these poems, I discovered many people laughed at the mention of shoes. There were murmurs of recognition regarding "the tongue bent inward like some church/gossip who has said finally too much . . ." and even more laughter when the shoe was presented as ". . . waiting for someone/to answer its description/if, as my father would say, the shoe fits . . ." Historians even say Jan Metzeliger, the inventor, was "quick to see the funny side of things," so I followed those threads, undermining, as I went, some of the standard myths of shoes.

Never Depend on a Shoo-in Candidate

the prince was a boob who couldn't remember the broad's face
his only clue was a shoe
and then the struggle to remember which foot
and she, taking the advice of her sisters, fell for the trap
as if life were romance of a woman's peculiar parts
some spineless tapping of toes
against a fast running clock
for which some poor dolt could put the whole kingdom in hock
let's take a hard look at this softhearted myth
here is the prince, standing by the door where his footman
kneels, pillow extended
and those sisters, plotting the ugliness of consequences
while she offers the only ticket that could walk her out of here
a foot too shallow to be the business end of anything
all this needs is a banner reading: What's wrong with this picture?
then someone smart enough to offer the answer

and that's where I come in
not with the chance to try on the boot, no matter how glittery
for this black foot I hold will bear no disguise
even a fairy wand from a lazy godmother could not smoothe
a structure so obviously built for Serengeti or Sahara
once in London's airport, I saw my Sudanese kinfolk swathed
in furs: their feet, like mine, flat as boards
but not a prince to greet them as crowds parted before them
the life they preserved was held fast by their own charms
and charwoman or dancer, this is our common share

there is much to be said for a birth without silver
spoon or satin pump
and nothing to be gained by expecting a prince
or the myth of stardust and false words
tossed in the casual magic of a few moments
the whole of this kingdom is a jungle
where mating is mere coincidence of castles built
to crumble around the keeper of the keys
sisters who, too often, are trustworthy only with open envy
trying their damndest to start another myth
to ferret out the easy life
of golden apples, fine clothes and special books
a uterine world where the prince promises to protect them[5]

This was my first probe of the mythogenesis of shoes. Would you
believe some fool who danced with you all night and couldn't remember
your name or your face, then, the morning after, walked up to you
with some old used shoe, talking about marriage? The irony is obvious.
That is exactly what is expected of women who blindly follow codes of
behavior because "everyone does." We know the story. We know that
as mundane as the world might seem, its little absurdities creep into
our lives and shape our behaviors. Even in the fast wash of a technological world, mythos creates and dictates what we know, and many
women, falling into absurd behaviors on the promise of much less than
kingdoms, are reduced to the sum of famous body parts — a face, legs,
a foot, even the tongue "that arch-guard of memory . . .", and the shoe
a symbol of her sexuality: the small shoe of the virgin bride, the full
shoe of the old woman with too many children.

The shoe is always a conditional symbol — we are expected to fit it,
not the other way around. I had to shake myself free of the legendary
shoe that would not accept my foot. I was still too near that apology
for ill-fitting feet, near memories, perhaps, of buying shoes as a child
in 1944 when the X-ray picture of a shoe store fluoroscope showed me
the bones of my feet dancing like Halloween skeletons. As the step-
sisters discovered, old myths rarely allow for differences. If the shoe
doesn't fit, the promise is null and void: ". . . once in London's airport,
I saw my Sudanese kinfolk swathed/in furs: their feet, like mine, flat as

boards/but not a prince to greet them as crowds parted before them . . . ."
Through that image, I recalled a time when black folks could not try
on shoes in a white store. Now slipping my foot into a shoe cupped in a
salesman's hands avenges my grandmother, and tells me more about
my past than any Cinderella myth. This became the emotive substance
of my mythos.

> under that machine even cheap shoes could seem handmade
> and when mama approved of how they had grown bone dainty
>
> she peeled off dollar bills: one for my father in Normandy
> one for an uncle in the Pacific or a cousin's government check
> the money folded as tight as those new shoes which dressed
>
> me in eyelets that could not see and tongues tucked
> away from naked light . . .[6]

In the third poem of the series, I concentrated on shaping my
personal mythopoeia. As poet, mythmaker, I took up the threads of
my tapestry where mythical promises did not follow traditional story
lines of royalty and kingdoms. In a recent reading, the Chilean author
Isabel Allende cautioned the audience not to believe the notion that
magic realism happens only in Latin America. "The magic is here,"
she said. I could not agree with her more. Poets thrive on the dualism
of reality and magic, and all landscapes have elements of surrealism.
Call them up and they readily appear: a kingdom that is a jungle and
constantly in hock, armies scattered like shoes, young girls fighting the
pull of fast running clocks and the promise of stardust. Poets summon
these images with a turn of phrase, the pattern and rhythm of language.
For while the myths of our realities are held by images, it is music that
lends magic to the poem. Music allows us to extend the poem in much
the same way a dancer extends ordinary movements of arms and legs
into fluid motions, or an artist plays upon the nuances of color.

The tone or sensuality of "Confessions of a Woman Who Sucks
Baby Toes" is held in its rhythm and melody. The images are important,
but it is sonics that ride the crest of this poem.

> a child's bare feet still seeks my weakness
> (yes, I await my grandchildren with bated breath)
> babies are best before they discover what's under-
> foot and while each lick is still a giggle
> and goodbye with no feelings hurt—when pure
> pleasure of the foot delights like moist grapes
> when the sun makes us all too lazy to speak
> and we lie on our backs, honeycombed in sweet
> grass that sticks like onion skin and brushes
> the base of our naked feet in whispers—
> like a sheet caressing the rise of a bare

hip under the musty itch of night — the cup
of body so like the inside curve of a foot
arched, yet hidden — always there
incandescent with desire[7]

The pace is rushed, a breathiness pulled even faster by an infusion
of lip sounds — bare, babies, backs, base, body — and narrow vowels —
still, like, delights, lie, skin, hip, cup — ending with the more sibilant
words — incandescent and desire. The accentual pattern of the lines
and the rush of the stanza in a breath-pause with minimal punctuation,
function like a raised eyebrow, a whisper, the movement of a hand to a
lock of hair. This thread was embroidered differently from the other
parts of the tapestry, yet the same elements of mythos were present. In
its own way, the details of sonics in those lines prompted me to savor
an ornate sense of imagery and magic realism.

Sweet with Wonder My Feet Upon Air

my mother said these feet weren't made for walking
just sedan chairs and palanquins, plenty of sunlight
and pheasant under glass, the feathers still intact
but here I am trapped in a world of shoes, my toes
mutating faster than the timing of any evolutionary clock
mama said: What did you do before you were born
stand in line twice for long legs then take leftover feet
but I've no real complaint against feet that serve me well
bearing up under the weight of such foolishness as heels
and sandals, sling pumps of single gold threads and husbands
and the feet themselves do not lack their own peculiar charm
albeit flat, they are regular and carry the memory of cadence
in a dance, they can pass themselves off as winged
and in bed, they languish and purr like virtual pussy cats
but afoot, they are not

it is difficult to define the actual cause
birth defect: *reluctant feet* does not seem appropriate
for if foot followed function, my family would still be
in the Sudan, rubbing their toes
Hannibal would have set down on that Mediterranean shore
left foot in hand, and let those elephants drown
and Cleopatra, bless her heart, would never have walked
as far as that asp, barge or not
my people have walked miles, shackled one to the other
on feet more horrendous than mine
and my first full-time job of shaving grandma's corns
surely revealed my genetic origins
since I won't swim and can't fly, I must walk
because as my daddy said: These feet won't fit no limb
and crawling is only for coming into this world

unlike Eliot's Mrs. Porter, my mother would not wash
my feet in soda water whenever the moon
asked me to dance nimble on the sweet air
so I disguise these dainty crocodiles I tread on now
for who better than I to badmouth my feet
while I gather what little cover I can hope for
I don't ask much — the extreme unction
of pure expense and comfort will do as I set
out to collect shoe after shoe in the ultimate search
for my own little handsewn, fur-lined jewel of uncommon
measure or mirrors to draw your vision to eyes or ears
before I resort to the wonder of Redwing triple A lifts
and limp like a salesman into the sunset with my burden
singing: Flatfoot floosie with the floy-floy
my closet behind me lined with boxes of leather and canvas

the three-inch, two-inch torture chambers of blunted
and narrow toes — my personal Borgia inventory
my only hope of growing finally beautiful with shoes[8]

How far I had come from the apology of my first shoe/foot images!
In "Sweet With Wonder ..." I sing, chortle, celebrate differences. I
allow the images to arise out of the music of language, not just the
coincidence of discovery. In doing so, I was ready to consider myself
free of the accursed memory of irregular feet. Then I encountered
another mythmaker, a young Native American poet who came up to
me after a reading and said: "Remember me? I was at your last
reading where you read the shoe poems."

"Yes," I said. "On the way home, I saw a shoe on the road," he
continued. "A few yards later, I saw another shoe. I got out of my car
and tried them on. They fit. I'm wearing them now."

I backed up two steps. This is what happens when your myths
begin to haunt you, I thought, promising myself, at that moment, to
avoid shoe poems. But promises are the stuff of myth, and no poet can
resist the wonder of a poem offered as a gift. So I returned to the
series — this time concentrating on a male narrative voice. But having
begun this peculiar tapestry with a woman's perspective, its focus held
true, and in one final moment of surprise, the voice would not shift
gender. Thankfully, my poet friend understands both the fragility of
poems and the stuff of myths. The final poem takes up the last bit of
stitching — moving from chance encounter, to my personal mythos, to
the challenge of female acceptance of a prince wandering out there,
shoe in hand, hoping for happily-ever-after.

The Indian Discoverer on the Dark Continent of Shoes

if legends appeared every day of the week
we would have no patience with coincidence

but having heard my poems on shoes, you offer
me this tale of finding two in a country where folks
never expect the likes of us to find one line of poetry —
much less two shoes — you rock on your heels and Black
Foot to Sudanese delight in the telling as if this
could make us all believers in possibilities — as if
a poem could lead you to that turn in the woods where shoes,
tossed like breadcrumbs or left by some fleetfooted prince
hurrying to the woodchopper's hut, beckon to the innocent

for, by truth, those of us who are transplanted
should not have stopped for such a transient gift
we know you can't put just any shoe on any foot

yet, you wanderer of lost tribes, offer me, lost
forever from my tribal culture, the gift of recovered thick
soled sneakers, which you say, *lay at cross purposes*
tongues bedraggled like injured cottonmouths or moccasins
waiting on the road for who knows what spells to be broken
and I watch you wear them like gloves, rocking on your heels
as you tell me how comfortable you feel
inside someone else's mystery, your own history scattered
along more roads than this country's maps will ever offer
I cringe, knowing even in dreams, the shoe is an uncomfortable
thing, for fit or not, each confirms a prison
surely, every shoe carries its mark of past life
and despite their casual discovery, Indian or African
there must have been reasons for two to be lost

listen to the small cries when the outer skin
succumbs to weather — or the right learns
to speak sharply to the left, mimicking
some half-forgotten owner, some other wanderer, who
getting up out of shapes and sorts, said perhaps
run my bath, take those mice from the portico
that pumpkin is an eyesore sitting all bruised
like that in morning-after sunlight
  then rocking back on her heels, she picked up
  the shoes, bright as used keys
  and tossed them through her captor's window[9]

Perhaps I have only begun. Perhaps there is more to come. Oh,
feet: don't fail me now.

Notes

1. "For Want of a Male a Shoe Was Lost," copyright © 1990 by Colleen
McElroy. All McElroy poems in this chapter are taken from *What Madness
Brought Me Here: New and Selected Poems, 1968–88* by Colleen McElroy,
Wesleyan University Press, University Press of New England.

7

Philip Levine on Teachng Poetry: An Interview

Sally A. Jacobsen

Sally Jacobsen: How would you get young people interested in poetry?

Philip Levine: My experience is with high school kids and college kids, but I really don't see any difference between the people I deal with and anybody else. So I suppose the answer is simply to present them with the wealth of poetry, trying to use relevant poetry as much as I can. I try to read it just as well as I can, to show them how it works without being too much of a pedant, suggest they write it — showing their work alongside a professional poem — and see what happens. I think some people will take to it and some won't. Poetry is not for everybody. It's been my experience that nothing seems to be for everybody, nothing worth having; people are different.

Jacobsen: What does the poet say to a teacher of poetry who *doesn't* write? How do you overcome the gulf of ignorance between you and people who haven't had that experience?

Levine: I suppose what the poet says to a teacher of poetry who doesn't write is "good luck." I think that most people who love poetry, who live with it, try to write it. I don't think that the experience of writing mediocre poetry is all that different from writing good poetry or bad poetry. It seems to me that I am just as ignorant as any other passionate reader of poetry when the two of us sit down to read Ben Johnson or James Wright — that there is a "gulf of ignorance." There is the experience and confidence of writing, so there is a sense sometimes of certain strategies, of certain methods, but I think that only works with poetry in the same cast as the kind I write. It seems to me that when I sit down and read a poem by Rilke or Stevens, who don't work the way I do, except for the narrative structure, relation of imagery, the way the lines and structure are arranged, written strategies, I don't have much advantage over anyone else.

Jacobsen: T. S. Eliot recommended sixteen or seventeen as the optimum age for students to read Shelley. Which poems of yours would you like to be read by students of that age and why?

Levine: It would seem to me that all of my poems would be accessible to a bright person of sixteen or seventeen, given that the opportunity is presented for that person to know the essentials. If the poem is about a particular event, they have to know the event; if the poem is about certain kinds of conditions in the thirties that I happen to be writing about, they have to know what those conditions are; or if the poem makes a reference to people living in Spain in the thirties, they have to know about the Civil War. Anybody could present that to them. I hope my poems are available to bright seventeen-year-olds.

Jacobsen: My fifteen-year-old daughter enjoyed *Not This Pig*. She liked "Animals Are Passing from Our Lives," "To a Child Trapped in a Barber Shop," and "The Cemetery at Academy, California" — especially the idealistic, in-tune-with-nature ending.

But is there an optimum age for which one should wait before challenging students with ambiguity, so as to avoid their feeling "dumb" when the poem stumps them? Didn't you have some students susceptible to that feeling when you were first at Columbia? Or at California State at Fresno? Or should one begin as early as possible teaching that poems are puzzles to which the reader contributes some of the meaning?

Levine: I don't think poems are puzzles. I do think readers contribute a great deal of meaning. Of course I had students at Columbia, at Fresno, and at Tufts who did feel "dumb" and will continue to feel dumb, because they *are* dumb in the face of the poem. Other people are dumb in the face of something else — the season, their sexuality, growing corn, driving an automobile. I am not sure that there is an optimum age for which one should wait. I wouldn't teach Wallace Stevens to a ten-year-old; it would just be a waste of time. I don't know how old students have to be to read Shakespeare. They have to be old enough to be familiar with the kind of sentence structure, that kind of syntax — if you have to be constantly breaking a sentence down into little components the students can deal with, they are not going to get the poetry. In other words, students must have a capability of the English language that matches the difficulty or lack of difficulty of poems.

Jacobsen: You say in your book, *Don't Ask*, that schools should educate people to make meaningful choices about how they live — and that you dislike teaching where a school isn't committed to that. Should poetry, too, be relevant in that way?

Levine: Of course it should, if it chooses to be. There are plenty of us who choose that.

Jacobsen: You recommend reading Keats's letters as well as his poems for students. Because the letters show that the poetry grew out of an experience of "life as tough as it is." What other poets do you recommend for students who want to write, to widen their horizons?

Levine: I think a much overlooked poet in America is Kenneth Patchen — a very powerful political poet, a beautiful poet of love, and a poet who wrote about ecology before the word existed. I certainly would introduce Rilke's letters; unfortunately in translation they seem to be very formal — they probably were, from one middle European to another. I would present the political poetry of Latin America and Spain by Garcia Lorca, Miguel Hernandez, Rafael Alberti. The poetry of Allen Lewis, the political poetry of Jon Silkin in our time, as well as other poetry. I teach James Wright to young people; I teach Ginsberg. Students find him dated. I teach William Carlos Williams, Thomas Wyatt, Edward Thomas, Dylan Thomas. D. H. Lawrence is one of my favorites; Denise Levertov, Emily Dickinson, Walt Whitman.

Jacobsen: You said in *Don't Ask* that you would like to have been able to believe you "stopped the war with your little poems" — that you "turned this country right around." What political poets and poems now, twenty years later, do you think students should read?

Levine: I think there are very few good poems that aren't political. A poem which is about the beauty of love, after all, is political. We exist in a time where sexual love has been dragged into such things as the presidency, the right to enjoy sexual love, the right to have air that is uncorrupted — all political questions. So when poetry deals with any kind of atmosphere, internal or external, we are entering into a very political sphere; we don't have to say, "Don't go to war, don't fight, don't kill." There are the more obviously political poets — Rexroth, Kenneth Patchen, Jim Wright, myself. It seems to me all of us who are writing well are to a degree political poets.

Jacobsen: The "little stories" in your poems, capturing the places you like and the people, are very important. You speak of being obsessed with the universality of what "we all make up together, ... the thing that comes into being because we touch each other's lives and become part of each other" — that you can be "still a young man in Detroit, a woman in California, a guy wandering the roads of Alabama" — that you're many people, living and dead. Do you ever give students the exercise of writing a poem from another specific point of view, and do you think that's a good idea for teenage students?

Levine: Yes, I do. I rarely give assignments, actually, but sometimes, to beginning students, I do — students who need it, really. Once a student writes awhile, she or he perhaps doesn't need it. But without experience they tend to write, "I fell in love, I was lonesome, I'm miserable," etc., etc., and I think it's a very good exercise to get them out of that concern and the vocabulary that accompanies it. I think it would be just as good for teenagers. Of course, some of my students are teenagers.

Jacobsen: Are you "brutal with mediocre poems"?

Levine: I'm never brutal with people who don't have talent. It seems to me utterly pointless. You are only brutal with people who need it. I don't encourage them or discourage them, but I am tough on people who can bear it. The better they are, the tougher you are.

Jacobsen: How could one make demands on even younger students without their feeling the teacher was brutal?

Levine: I don't know — that is very tricky. It seems to me that the younger the kids are — not so much younger, but the less experienced they are — the more I encourage them. I don't know what's there, so I have to do a lot of encouraging. I won't talk about a problem unless I have something good to say.

Jacobsen: How does one get students to make greater demands of themselves?

Levine: They begin to read their poems with an eye to an audience, and at the same time they begin to see poems by other students in new ways. They see their vices and they see their virtues. I also introduce to them "real poems" by mature poets, and I think that does a great deal to raise their standards.

Jacobsen: What practical tips for becoming established would you offer unknown poets convinced of the value of their work — or teachers who recognize such talent?

Levine: I'm not in the business of giving tips. But my advice to most people is, "Stay out of the marketplace as long as you can. There is a time when you should try to publish — if you don't you become embittered." I could imagine I would have become embittered if I'd had to wait another ten years. At forty I published a "real" book. It did me a lot of good not to be published too early.

Jacobsen: Could you talk a little about "writing as an act of discovery?" Writing through a conventional "you" to the point where you "break into something fresh, and start from there and throw the rest away?" It seems that would be a very useful idea to teach student writers. How do you get them to recognize that point?

Levine: I would say largely that you don't. I am not sure that happens very often to student writers. I don't think that breaking into something fresh and throwing the rest away happens without discipline. However, I think you can talk to young poets and young writers about the level of the "trite" in their work, how often the characters and situations, the dramas, are just loose borrowing from the popular arts, from junk, from television, from bad popular songs. They don't really believe in this stuff and know perfectly well that the stuff they are seeing on television is unreal; that is, it does not involve people they care about, the people they really know. It really does not involve anybody except the kind of celebrity who is in *People* magazine. I think they go for these things like I go for similar junk, for release, and for the pure foolish entertainment that we all seem to need and love. When their work involves that sort of thing you can say, "Hey, you don't believe in that junk. What are you putting it in your poetry for?"

From that sense I think you can get them to throw a lot away. You can get young kids, as they go through emotions about love, to turn to themselves rather than to require *you* to suddenly enter the room of their imagination. I really believe that.

As for myself, when you talk about writing as an act of discovery, it's hard for me to talk about; it happens in a kind of a flash. Frequently I begin writing in a sort of mechanical, I might even say, stupefied way. I sit down in the usual place with the usual pen and pad of paper, and I start making scratchings. I may even start writing lines—none of it is particularly awe-inspiring—a poem, or what I think is a poem. It seems that, when I write at my best, a point comes at which I take something I put on that page, or something that passes through my mind because of this sort of wasted effort (which is, in fact, not wasted), which triggers a deeper layer of awareness or emotion, and then I just turn away from everything and proceed toward whatever direction that new thing is taking. Sometimes I'll write a whole draft of a poem and it may sit around for a few days; I'll look at it and then I'll see that there is a life, vitality, integrity, intensity in some passage, and I'll just banish the rest and pursue the implications of that unfulfilled portion that is so much livelier, so much more intense, more imaginative.

I think that took me a long time to learn to do, so I wouldn't bring something like that up to young writers. I do bring up to students in my class the need to follow the hints of their imaginations and to become, as quickly as possible, dissatisfied with the kinds of conscious aims that one sits down to write with. They tend to write the poem of ideas, of social service, the right poem with the right attitudes, the most boring thing imaginable, when the real self is somewhere gasping for breath or calling for a voice of his or her own. So, very quickly, I say to them, "Hey, this is why this is dead. Why don't you follow this?"

"Yeah, but my intention is to write a poem of this kind."

I say, "Well, forget that intention. Listen to the poem you are writing, don't listen to that conscious voice, that obligatory 'daddy' that says, 'No, thou must not do this.' Listen to what your imagination is really doing."

Jacobsen: You mentioned once in an interview that it is important to avoid being seduced by one's own writing, and elsewhere you have indicated that writers tend to fall back with a "sigh of fulfillment as if writing something were a big meal they'd just finished." How do you keep the young from being mesmerized by their own writing?

Levine: It's much easier to keep the young from being mesmerized by their writing, and I wish that, when I was young, I'd had friends who had been capable of it. By and large, when I was in my twenties, most of the people I showed my work to said, "Oh, it's so awesomely gorgeous," and it wasn't. It took me years to see, "Hey, my friends don't know enough and they're not tough enough." They weren't sure of themselves and they didn't know as much about writing as I do. Later on I made friends who had more confidence, friends who knew more about poetry; they were tougher on me.

So I think that function that my friends performed I can perform for students. They respect me; they know I know a lot; they may not even *like* me all the time; they get angry at me — that's not the problem. My problem is not to be their friend. I'm not in a classroom to make loving friends; I'm not there to seduce the girls or have the boys admire me; I'm there to help them with their writing and, in order to do that, sometimes I have to risk being disliked by them. When I get a gifted person who repeats him or herself over and over, I say, "Hey look, we know you can do this, and while you think it's extraordinary, I think it's just okey-dokey." I have to put next to it what I think *is* extraordinary and say, "Hey, wake up." There are some people who can't take it; they shouldn't be in classrooms and after a while they aren't. They get upset, they create scenes, and sometimes people who know the truth resist it most fiercely — those are the difficult ones. But I've been in a teaching situation with some awfully good people who got very angry and wound up in the long run being awfully good writers. They struggled, they fought, but in the long run they really did take the criticism. So it can be a painful process. I've been told I was a son-of-a-bitch; I didn't feel that bad about it. I didn't start teaching till I was in my thirties, so I had the advantage of knowing that these kids could behave in infantile ways. I could too. So they didn't love me that day.

Jacobsen: How do you prod yourself?

Levine: The problem of doing it for myself is much harder. I think if I have had any success the secret is that I have been writing—I've had poems in reserve. I was talking to a man the other day whose manuscript I looked at—it was perhaps sixty pages long; he's perhaps thirty. He writes seriously; he's a slow worker; he got a late start; and here he is, thirty years old, and he's got sixty pages of poems. I suggested the sixty ought to be cut down to about thirty because there were about thirty rather interesting pages and thirty very conventional or badly written pages. He was a little upset. Something got him to go back to my criticism, and the second time around he found more value in it and began to throw out. Also, the fact that he was writing new work and could add eight or ten pages meant he could take eight or ten pages out. Then he took more out. He finally ended up cutting as much as I had suggested to him—maybe even more. One of the reasons he was able to do this was that he did have new work that he could bank his hopes on. I think that, since I have written almost continuously all these years. I've been able to throw a lot of stuff away because I *had* a lot of stuff. I think if you write a poem every two months, it's awfully tough to throw it away. If you are writing constantly and trying, and the work is coming, you have some faith that the lines you wrote yesterday will not be the last—that since you wrote yesterday and you wrote Tuesday and Friday, it's likely that you'll get some more. You're going to be able to be tougher and harder on what you did.

However, there is always that deep, unkillable desire to love what you've done. "No memory of having starred/Atones for later disregard./Or keeps the end from being hard," says Frost in a wonderful poem. All those early successes that you have as a writer don't matter that much if you're not having recent successes. And sometimes you seduce yourself into believing that what you are doing is the best you can do when it isn't. Sometimes your writing is not as good as it could be because you *need* it too badly. One of the advantages of being a poet, and living by and large as poets do, not off their poetry but off something else they do, is that they don't need it to make a living; so at least it doesn't suffer that. You can throw it away because you aren't going to starve, because it never made the difference between your eating and starving anyway. I still try hard to prod myself, and I still find that a lot of what I write is not going to get in any published pages. I dismiss a great many of my poems. Whitman says, "Dismiss whatever insults your own soul." Well, I don't think I have the courage to do that in terms, say, of the institutions I teach in — to most of them I should say, "School dismissed," but at least I think I am able to do it quite often with my own writing. I say, "You're dismissed."

8

Poetry and Travel

William Olsen
Nancy Eimers

Think of the long trip home.
Should we have stayed at home and thought of here?
Elizabeth Bishop

As teaching poets at the same university, we have found it helpful to share ideas about classroom teaching, poetry exercises, and, of course, poetry itself. Often we give our Poetry Writing classes the same writing exercises and assignments and compare the results. What we have both discovered is that some of the most successful assignments have had to do with the issue of travel. This issue became the subject of our article.

How do two people "co-write" an article? To avoid looking over each other's shoulders, we decided first to *depart* from the conventional essay: each of us would write separately *toward* the issue of travel in poetry writing and teaching. Once having *arrived* at our common *destination*, together we would present our travel assignments. It seemed that the vocabulary of travel was already creeping irresistibly into our discussion. Departures, distances. Arrivals, destinations. Our meanderings have taken different directions but are, we hope, clearly related, the first discussion, by William Olsen, more "theoretical," the other, by Nancy Eimers, more "practical" in approach. They are followed by two travel assignments.

Where does a poem begin?
This must be one of the most stultifying of all first questions about poetry. The pleasures of process notwithstanding, part of us always feels we have to have something to write about. You may not come to

the terrain of the poem with a map or an itinerary or anything more than the free-floating urgencies of the day. Maybe you read first (this is what I do: it subdues some of the pressure of being "creative," it reminds me that I indeed do have a vocabulary, and on the good days, when I am reading well, it transports me beyond the distractions of self-doubt and ambition). You jot down lines, phrases, verbal figure-eights, the awkward little notations toward the poem that starts out in obscurity. Each time you start a new poem, you are beginning all over again. You are writing as if for the very first time, inventing the poem and in a sense re-inventing all of poetry. You recognize your enthusiasm to be a little arrogant, but that's okay, that's forgivable. You are a beginner again, and as John Berryman said, if beginners were good critics of themselves they wouldn't be able to let stand a single line.

Say one of these lines or phrases holds enough fascination to take you along with it into a poem. Before long you are on your way, irretrievably if you are lucky enough to get good and lost at the start. No doubt the sheer joy of playing with language got you where you find yourself. But what if something made you choose that first line of your first draft? Very possibly something real, something from your experience or touching upon your experience made those first few words win your interest. I'm talking about the cosmic stuff, the shadow of a grasshopper on your driveway at dusk, the streetlights that come out every night because it's hard to see, the fireflies that dodge the first raindrops, the fact that you've never seen a raindrop hit a firefly. You began inside language and ended up outside in the world. That first forgivable line invented travel as well as poetry.

You have also re-invented your solitude. But why wax poetic over solitude? Solitude has only the one gift to offer: it gets you on your way.

Each mortal thing does one thing and the same,
Doles out that being indoors each one dwells.

Thus spaketh Gerard Manley Hopkins.

A good poem gets us mortal things outside of ourselves — outdoors. It begets its details by granting other things their thingness, their "being indoors," and it does this, weirdly, not by grasping to its details, but by letting them go, to have their own existence apart from that of the poet. It gets details out there, where they have presence and danger and pull. That lovely little poem by William Carlos Williams about the red wheelbarrow glazed with rain water beside the white chickens must have happened because Williams was fortunate enough for an instant to get outdoors, even if he was just looking out his window. Whatever personal significance that red wheelbarrow had for him he had to let go, let that mortal thing dole out its being indoors.

His poem records both the time it took for him to look intensely at a red wheelbarrow and the split-second it took for him to let it go.

Once again I am talking about the evasive stuff of subject matter, though it may be that subject matter finds us. One thing that makes writing poetry seem hard is the sheer effort of displacement: your very physical surroundings must dissolve before you begin. I sit down to my desk in Kalamazoo, Michigan, to begin a poem, and I end up outside a small town in Mexico on the Gulf of California, fifteen years ago, twenty-one years old:

> where I and two others wade a half-mile out,
> up to our waists nightfishing with spears, our flashlights
> making wet spotlights only water steps into.

I have traveled beyond my room, toward Mexico, and Mexico has met me halfway. The windowed maples knocking about in the sunlight are now killing their hours in the moonlight. My house has moved to its usual nightly place under its buzzing streetlight. Great spaces have been crossed. My three lines may never accrete a poem, but they have a few interesting motions, and they got me outdoors.

Here is another axiom, this time Thomas Wolfe, an American, on Americans. I paraphrase: *the great paradox about Americans is that they feel stable and fixed only when they are in motion.* That sounds about right to me. And you can reverse that axiom, too: when we are not in motion, when the brakes grip and the wheels slow and our thoughts stop turning over, somehow we feel unstable, unfixed.

Consider this James Wright poem, a poem about feeling uprooted in the very place one finds oneself, in this case at home, behind a desk:

> Outside Fargo, North Dakota
>
> Along the sprawled body of the derailed
>   Great Northern freight car,
> I strike a match slowly and lift it slowly.
> No wind.
>
> Beyond town, three heavy white horses
> Wade all the way to their shoulders
> In a silo shadow.
>
> Suddenly the freight car lurches.
> The door slams back, a man with a flashlight
> Calls me good evening.
> I nod as I write good evening, lonely
> And sick for home.[1]

Every thing in this poem is either set into motion—the lit match lifted up into the darkness, the three heavy white horses, the lurching freight car, the door that slams back, the train dick with the flashlight—or it is fixed, arrested, derailed like the carcass of the Great Northern Freight train. The "I," too, seems to have no place to go, no wind to shake his match, no more company than a call from the train dick. Finally the poet reveals to us, and more importantly to himself, that he has never really left his office where he is writing. Yet he finds himself fooled into nodding to a mere flicker of a remembered man. He ends up *sick for home*. And everyone who has experienced enough of James Wright's beautiful poems about his industry-ravaged Ohio knows in his or her bones this physical sickness of the longing to go home again.

But the poet *is* at home as he is writing this. He allows himself to be displaced, to become a memory of himself stranded outside Fargo, North Dakota, lost to solitude. Then in the second stanza the *self* seems to dissolve altogether, and the poem travels outside the point of view of the self and relinquishes a visual—*white, silo shadow*—and tactile—*heavy, wide, shoulders*—presence of the three horses. These horses are traveling, too. And not toward the "I." And then suddenly there is the closer motion of the lurching freight car, then the brief human presence of the train dick, then a human greeting, which turns out to be a goodbye. Just as suddenly there is the poet, doomed to the instability of self-consciousness because he is doomed not to be in motion. It turns out he has gotten nowhere. And this feeling of getting nowhere is not some bright literary idea but a sickening, physical feeling, a bodily loneliness, and almost incommunicable. Yet what distances are traveled here. No images here are still-life images. We travel, for instance, from the gasp of the lit match to the glare of the flashlight. Such connections flash out across stanzas to perforate and populate the blackness. There are other lonelinesses out there, and they are in motion. So the poet's loneliness has created for itself some huge space to move around in, and now he can utter his loneliness without its crushing him.

The problem with analyzing poems is that analysis makes writing seem impossible. Anyone who had the *intention* of saying all that I found for myself in this eleven-line poem would have to be nearly superhuman, or a little bit crazy. But as a reader I'll gladly take this chance of overreaching, at home for myself or in the classroom for my students. The poem is no great finish to a man, Whitman said, but only a beginning. Without our flailing, headlong responses to it the poem is just words lined up on the page, flush left. The audience-response theorists now tell us the poem isn't even completed until the reader has responded to it. But you don't need any theory, you only need common sense to tell you how valuable good models are to the beginning poet—and all poets are beginning poets. If sometimes students think poetry is about hypotheticals, about high ideas, about anything but earthly experience, this must owe to their not having read any poetry:

because for that person who has read no poetry, poetry literally lies outside earthly experience.

The truly sustaining thing for me about the James Wright poem is how and with what ease it shows the process of writing poetry to be an out-of-the-body experience, even as it restores us to ourselves.

Here is part of a poem called "Travelling," by David Lee, one of my students. I'll let it have my last word on poetry and traveling:

Without a car I drive past a friend's familiar
brick house
with its lone motorcycle and still lit
front porch light,
and the celery flats, the flooded fields
on either side of River Road
with the flat-red ramshackle pole-barns
sided with dented tin
and the automobile graveyards, the cars up on blocks,
doorless and empty (in the pivotal light
they look as if they're weeping),...
while far ahead in the just-beginning-to-rise
heat, a period
turns into a gnat
turns into three flapping crows
turns into a dead raccoon,
eyes open and belly up,
having died where the world funnels into
a miles-long archway of blowing trees:
oaks and maples and basswoods reach out over the road
as you enter the light-flecked tunnel.
The open fields
snap in long horizontal distances
back toward the horizon,
because now you're really moving,
travelling,
speeding through the green, flickering light,
arriving, and having already arrived.

The easiest thing to do within a poem is to stay put. Travel is just one subject matter. It has this advantage: it goes. (W. O.)

... to the creator there is no poverty and no poor indifferent place.

                                              Rilke

It was while traveling that I first learned about keeping a journal. In high school I'd kept a diary, off and on, for the sheer pleasure of possessing a spiritual autobiography. I would read back over it, wafting through my feelings and moods as if through pastel tissues lifted, layer by layer, from an old cedar chest. Looking back years later, what I found was effusive but not very pleasurable. Some entries were so heartfelt they had left their impressions on several layers of paper. But actual contents had not gone as deep. What I felt when Todd's brother died. What I felt when Jack walked Cathy down the hall. What I felt: the physical world of facts and details had blown away and left me in the Twilight Zone, emotions without time, without dimension. I came to believe that, to borrow from Rilke, my emotions were a poor and indifferent place — precisely because they *had* no place.

One summer I found myself keeping a travel journal when my husband and I drove to Santa Fe. That is, we were driven to Santa Fe by Susan, our friend, who remained at the wheel each day because travel, for her, was an *active* state: she felt compelled at all times to participate. The act of driving was a kind of absolute attention to the details of travel, from the first night's full moon over Blieders Creek near New Braunfels, Texas, to the silvermound — a low, frothy bush — and the long grasses shifting from silver to greenish-pink when the wind blew over them ten miles outside of Santa Fe.

I remember these details because I recorded them. Here are some typical entries:

> Shidoni — sculpture garden with funky tin coyote.
> Penasco, on high road to Taos — Hispanic town with fair where we bought fireworks: Black Cats, Chinese Dragon Fire. Videos dubbed in Spanish in store.
> D. H. Lawrence ranch. Caretaker called Houston "the sinking city."

What strikes me in reading back over these and other entries from that trip is their bareness: uncluttered by articles, sparing of adjectives and verbs, free of commentary or response. As a traveler, I found this meant less fuss with words at the end of each full, tiring day; as a writer, less fuss with foggy emotions that might in time obscure what I'd meant to remember. So I stuck to the awesome particulars perceived by the tired but receptive tourist: "Ghost Ranch — canyon walls striped salmon, yellow, red, brown. Reservoir under some mtns. and bright green fields under canyons." I was overdoing my own detachment, of course — but it freed me to do so.

I used some of these details years later in a travel poem. The "sinking city" became Santa Fe, despite the fact that at the time I had thought it an excellent epitaph for Houston and the way I felt about living there. In the poem, "sinking" had more to do with the fireworks that flared up, then died into ashes and floated back down to earth, and with a local graveyard whose resident souls, under concrete slabs, seemed more of this earth than of heaven. In this same poem I superimposed in the graveyard some baby graves with pinwheel decorations I had seen once in Tucson. It seemed that my separate travels had started informing each other of a grief that I couldn't have understood at the time. Eventually I learned not to limit my journal entries to sheer, stern description. I learned to have fun, to allow myself many freedoms of style, subject matter, and approach. But the greatest freedom was traveling place to place in my journal without excess emotional baggage. The details I carried with me were weighty enough. At home, I took them out of my pockets and looked, and they brought back everything.

In Poetry Writing, the first thing I ask of my students is to keep a kind of "travel journal." I discourage them from diary-keeping — mere chronological recordings of that day's events (a dreary task to be filled out several times a week with no urgency and few surprises) — and, at the other extreme, from those ineffable feelings void of place and time.

What, then? they want to know. What else can you *do* in a journal? What do you *want* from us?

What I want is for them to see their own lives through the eyes of a tourist — in their journals, and, ultimately, in their poetry. I want them to realize that they have traveled far to get here. They may be tired or overwhelmed, but they shouldn't want to miss a single thing. Once you imagine you are seeing things for the first time, how strange, how marvelous to hear that electric guitar talking screechily to itself in the next apartment! How militaristic your five pairs of shoes look, lined up in the closet! Why do you need to draw some weighty conclusion? To choose one delicate representative feeling? Why not let it all simmer instead in its own delightful and terrible strangeness?

I tell them the journal is the place to be attentive to details, insatiably curious and easily mystified. Any poor, indifferent place can become pressurized with specificity, the clogged salt shaker at the Big Boy, tendrils of ash on a desktop, an uptipped grocery cart ... *Details and focus!* I warn them; *You'll get sick of hearing me say that!* And they do. But the richness of details, the emergence of place and of time empower not only their journal entries but, as they eventually discover, the poems that may grow, directly or indirectly, out of the notes of the traveler.

Here is a list of possibilities for journal-keeping:

1. Write down overheard conversations. Park yourself in a booth at Bob's Big Boy and eavesdrop. Record the particulars of the drama of place: what she said, how he answered with silence, what rhythms or emphases each used ("you're a LOUDmouth!"), the

intermittent scurrying of waiters and waitresses. Allow yourself to perceive all the quirks and contrasts and ironies that make up any idle coffee shop conversation.

2. Record striking impressions, colors, details, facts. Don't worry about what you will "do" with them. Enjoy them. Travel back with them into history, public or private: "The colored spotlights in the fountain made me think of my father's letter-opener with its little fake jewels on the handle." "Today I read that the Chinese believed dried sea horses have aphrodisiac properties." Allow yourself sheer fascination, no strings attached. However, if someone starts to hum, if certain particulars switch on some motor, start a poem. See what accumulates.

3. Write down language you enjoy — yours or another writer's words, lines, poems. Language, too, can become a place. A newly discovered word, once heard, surfaces uncannily during the next few days like a curious local custom; a pleasing rhyme (Marianne Moore's favorite Elizabeth Bishop rhyme was many/antennae), an overheard repetition of sounds (*bad break! tough luck!*) — these may awaken your tourist's curiosity to know more, and, knowing, to play and then work with language, its sounds and connotations and rhythms, until you are at home with them.

4. Try an automatic writing exercise. That is, sit down for ten or twenty minutes and write without stopping. Set an alarm clock, if you like the slightly manic orderliness of that. Set no rules for yourself but this one: keep moving your pen on the page. Then read what you have written: have you journeyed anywhere interesting? tapped into a buried subject unexpectedly? learned a new, circuitous route toward subject matter? Have you reached a dead end? Try again.

5. Be alert for the similarities between basically unlike things. Compare the incomparable; write down metaphors and similes that occur to you. If Elizabeth Bishop can compare the skin of a fish to a flowered, peeling wallpaper, you can observe that the flabby posterior of a passing jogger looks like an upside down heart of jello. In poetry, as in travel, resemblances are important. They bring things closer to home, and, perhaps, make home seem more mysterious. They reveal the unusual in the commonplace. Through them, we arrive at inevitable surprise.

6. Let places remind you of other places, details of other details. Allow yourself to become obsessive about this.

On the trip to Santa Fe, I had vivid dreams. Here is one journal entry: "2 dreams — I'm dying. One with Mom, Dad, and Bill downstairs.

One with me having a lung condition that Karen White had had." I did a sketchy, lazy job of recording particulars; even so, what remains *is* specific. Mom, Dad, Bill. Karen White, a woman I knew in grad school. A lung condition (she'd never had one, though her husband's first wife had died of cancer).

Dreams thrive on details: who, where, what. *Why* is not so insistent about itself. The details jar: maybe you're trying to open a bottle with a key, or helping fly a plane by running, Flintstone-style, in your seat. The incongruity of *who* and *what* with *where* is often a great source of tension.

On November 22 last year I dreamed I was talking to President Kennedy on the phone. This was the 25th anniversary of his death, and all week I'd seen TV specials about him. After a weirdly detailed and illogical conversation, I suddenly remembered that he was dead. "Where are you?" I asked in some dread. I heard him laugh and repeat my question to someone in the room with him. (Who on earth? from what place?) Then he said, "I'm a federal judge in Benton Harbor." At this point, my airplane alarm clock went off in the dream, and in real life, and I awoke.

I have never stopped in Benton Harbor, a western Michigan town on the lake, but every time I drive by the Benton Harbor exit on the way to Chicago, I have an eerie feeling, and wonder, why *there*? Why a federal judge in Benton Harbor? And looking at the prosaic sign, white letters on a green backing, I feel some mystery that, to the traveler, underlies the most ordinary of places.

Every semester I ask students to write down and bring in a recent dream. Every semester the results are, in one way, the same: almost every dream has its proliferation of details. A heavy metal album turns into a snake. A car crash on a roadside metamorphoses into a college dorm room. A dead grade school friend walks into a showing of "Honey, I Shrunk the Kids." The details are tantalizingly familiar, but they don't match the place; or the place keeps changing.

Details have tremendous power; anyone who has ever woken suddenly from a happy dream or a nightmare knows the power of details to haunt us. When students read one another their dreams, recorded economically, without fuss, they are struck immediately with how specific they are. Red, silver, an old Corvette, Frank Sinatra turning into somebody's father—what WILD imaginations! But really, the details are often themselves prosaic; it is the way they occur beside one another, or the fact that they crop up in unexpected places, that amazes, that causes joy, uneasiness, fear. Sometimes setting accommodates people from two different times. Or it changes into some other place. Dreams involve all kinds of travel—and if in dreams, why not in poetry? We can travel backward and forward in time; we can leap outward from object to association; we can grope back through place to an earlier self and bring together places that never met on the map (Santa Fe, Houston, Tucson). Our dreams teach us again and again that static details are connected somehow with motion as well as emotion—that through them, we travel to subject matter and thought and meaning we had not anticipated. Dreams teach us that traveling is and should be a matter of constant surprise.

In our everyday lives, we can travel physically back and forth, and we travel, without a choice, without exception, steadily forward in time. We have not yet invented a way to travel back, except in memory and dreams. Poetry travels like dream and memory, hovers at details powerfully and subjectively, travels place to place. It honors place for what it provides us: a point of departure, a place of arrival. (N. E.)

Travel Assignments

Word List

In this exercise, the teacher reads a list of items to the class. If the word is italicized, read the word and ask the students to copy it down. If the word is not italicized, ask the students to free-associate: "Write down the first word you think of when I say *rain*." At times you will ask the students to write down place names, streets, colors, and so on.

Once the lists are completed, have the students quickly cross out any ten words. Pause, and have them cross out ten more words. Now tell the students they are each to write a poem. The only rule: use as many words as possible from the twenty-word list that remains. The rationale behind this assignment is to allow students subconsciously to determine a linguistic realm for a poem. Also, to give students the advantage of a few concrete words and the hovering influence of place.

1) rain
2) city of your birth
3) sadness
4) name the place you'd least like to be in right now
5) unbearable
6) virgin
7) your least favorite color
8) *donkey*
9) *avenue*
10) promise
11) secret
12) *hail*
13) *fluorescent*
14) *apple*
15) cave
16) fly
17) field
18) tornado
19) your most favorite color
20) *sunset*
21) name of the first street you can remember from your hometown

22) *telephone*
23) your favorite season
24) place you'd most like to be
    in right now
25) perfume
26) closet
27) *pigeon*
28) *birch*
29) *violin*
30) *ravage*
31) *splendid*
32) name of your least favorite
    season
33) destiny

34) *knuckles*
35) *burn*
36) *astonishing*
37) hell
38) heaven
39) mother
40) pick a number between 1
    and 10

Travel Poem

As a starting point for a travel poem, use a particular place you have traveled to at some time in your life. Write your poem in a way that locates you there or has you passing through. No matter what location you choose — a city you remember driving through once, a farm, a coffee shop, an airport, a bus station — or what vehicle you find yourself in — a train car, an old Ford, a jet, a bicycle — allow details to materialize powerfully around you. Remembering that all good poetry rises out of obsession, try to do some of the following:

1. Through concrete language and figures of speech, fasten on just those details that obsess you for no reason at all.

2. Say one thing — an admission, a judgment, a complaint — that is difficult for you to say, that never occurred to you before to say.

3. Don't be afraid to depart from the truth.

4. Let a tension arise from some specific thing you do or don't do in the place.

5. Even if you barely know that place, be arrogant and assume familiarity.

6. Put at least some of your details in motion.

7. End with a surprise — an image, an emotional leap, an uncharacteristic understatement — that seems unavoidable.

Notes

1. Reprinted from *Collected Poems* © 1968 by James Wright, Wesleyan University Press by permission of the University Press of New England.

9

Faded Blue Jeans and Wool Turtlenecks:
How One Writer Learned to Trust Poetry to Teach Itself

Marie Wilson Nelson

In 1965 poetry walked in faded blue jeans and wore wool turtlenecks. And it refused to be ignored. Since that time I've never taught a poetry unit. I've never taught poetry lessons. In fact, I've never *taught* poetry at all. My students hear lots of poems, though, and we read, haggle, and respond. When I find a poem I like, I share it, no matter what else we're doing. And when what we're doing brings to mind a poem — my own, a student's, or an established writer's work — I get that poem into my classroom so it can teach itself. That's the only way I work with poetry anymore, and it's something I learned from Bob Ford, during my first year of teaching, back in Greenville, South Carolina, many years ago.

Bob of the blue jeans and black turtlenecks was nineteen at the time, a sophomore at a college in the city where I taught, but he was the first real poetry teacher I ever had (and yes, I *did* major in English). Bob would drop by my house in the evenings with *avant garde* poems he'd found and sit for hours on the mat-covered floor of my tiny first apartment reading his favorite passages to my roommate and me and our friends, involving us in his pleasure at a well-phrased line, ecstatic in his approval when a passage spoke to him. The rest of us, entranced, joined naturally in the talk, pointing out parts we liked or disliked, asking when questions arose, running to college texts to find pieces we were reminded of, discussing how the poets achieved their effects, and speculating about what the poems we read revealed of their lives. Single-handedly Bob created, in the spare comfort I called home, a community of unlikely folk who read, wrote, and talked poetry. And though I tucked them away without showing anyone, I wrote almost fifty poems that year.

The other thing Bob did for me was share the things he wrote. He even wrote poems for me at times, an honor I never returned. I never shared my stuff with him, I don't think. I was too unsure, too new. Bob was the first poet I'd known, the first to *act* like a poet in my presence, at any rate, the first to share his poet self, the first to bring poetry to life. From him I learned that the poems I love are often those I find myself or learn about from friends. And I learned that the desire to read and write poetry, not to mention analyze it or discuss it critically, will develop spontaneously, given the right conditions, even among people who've learned in school to hate or fear poetry.

An Experience-Based Approach to Reading and Writing Poems

I've been reading and writing poetry ever since Bob Ford demonstrated his love affair with poems and poets to me, and my once traditional teaching has never been the same. In classrooms I dip into school anthologies time and again, and I regularly encourage students to do the same, but poetry no longer begins and ends with dead or distant poets. It's living poets, including my students, who bring it to life for me. And my own reading and writing of poems shapes the way I teach.

Some years ago now my friend Sandra Worsham, writer of fine short fiction and an award-winning high school teacher from Milledgeville, Georgia, asked me to speak to a creative writing class of hers. Sandra didn't write poems herself, she informed me, so she wanted a "real poet" to come talk to the group. "How I Write a Poem" was the assigned topic, and I stayed up late the night before, searching for the order in my knowledge of how I write.

Sandra's invitation to bring poetry live into her classroom forced me to adapt the way I usually teach. Patterned on interactions among Bob and my friends and me, my poetry teaching is at once planned and spontaneous—whether it takes place in literature or writing classes. Because I have semester-long blocks of time to play around with, it follows emerging interests and welcomes serendipity. I've read a lot of poems to reading classes too, for short poems are microcosms of the linguistic features that structure less compressed prose. Full of the sorts of language readers have problems with, poems are often just the right length to read and discuss in class. And because they so often deal unabashedly with feelings, it's not hard to find poems with which students will get involved. Students of all shapes and sizes ungrudgingly expore imagery, word choice, syntactic structures, and multiple layers of meaning — when these occur in poems they like (or hate) — if they are also allowed to express honestly how they feel. Students will initiate such explorations themselves — if they have personal reasons for wanting to make sense of a piece.

While preparing to talk with Sandra's high school writers, I tried to remember the kinds of things I say about poetry when my university students struggle with it. My goal was to pull together, from the questions I'm most often asked, a focus for a coherent, 50-minute dialogue. This effort produced many insights about myself as a writer, all of which have since, in turn, affected how I teach. Whether memos, poetry or fiction, letters to friends, or critical essays, careful study of how we write is the most reliable source of guidance we writing teachers can seek. Likewise careful examination of our reading habits is a powerful source of insight about how to help others read. Research tells us what other readers and writers *appear* to do, and theory attempts to enlighten us as to why, but personal knowledge of reading and writing is always accurate.

As long as we remember to respect differences and don't expect all writers and readers to react just like us, experiential knowledge is a dependable guide, for differences among learners are more superficial than profound. For example, five years of studying hundreds of writers in a university program (Nelson 1991), revealed that despite differences at the observable level, the roots of most writing successes and problems were similar. Likenesses lay in writers' need for real-world rewards, in the strong motivation they developed with freedom of choice, in the kinds of conditions rapid improvement required, in the various phases writing cycled through, in the strategies writers used when shaping their ideas, and in the psychological demands writing made on them. Differences lay in the rituals writers used to get through the hard parts (though few failed to rely on some rituals), in the specific structures they used for shaping ideas, and in the way certain phases of writing (revision, for example) tended either toward the more explicit or the more covert.

Though Bob Ford set me on my path to experience-based teaching, my faith in experience as a guide for teaching writing and reading is grounded in more than infatuation with poets and poetry. It's confirmed by research on over one hundred writers who teach (Nelson 1982, 1983). For three years I studied how writers teach writing in middle and secondary schools. I talked to dozens of writers teaching in schools spread across two states, did two- to three-hour interviews with twenty-three of those, observed for a day or two in each of eight classrooms, and spent one term each observing, for three days a week, in the classrooms of the three writers whose teaching was most consistently shaped by their writing experience. In these classrooms, I observed teaching and learning being done and attempted to specify relationships between the two. Personal writing experience, I discovered in the process, was a primary source of insight used by more successful-feeling teachers to help them understand what conditions their students needed to improve. Firsthand knowledge — when tempered by its companion, increased acceptance of writers' idiosyncrasies — never failed the teachers who relied on it. By contrast, those teachers who failed to trust their writing intuitions grew bitter, frustrated, elitist, or cynical when they felt less than successful at helping *all* students succeed.

From my observations another consistent pattern emerged. Those writers who said they felt highly successful teaching writing (and equally important, those who claimed to be most content) were those who *taught writing only as they practiced it.* When firsthand experience conflicted with teaching traditions — like teaching as they themselves had been taught, preparing students for college and tests, or covering "what English teachers are *supposed* to teach" — more successful and less burned-out teachers followed one rule of thumb: All valued experience over tradition as a guide. More basic than specific methods (for details of their teaching varied) was the consistent way these teachers set up for their students the kinds of conditions they themselves needed when writing or learning to write. All avoided what one writer called "the stigma of the grade," found any excuse they could think of to praise student writers' work, established trusting communities whose members felt safe taking risks, supported students in a range of writing purposes, and modeled the role — that of writer — they hoped all students would adopt. Strikingly, all who relied first on writing experience exhibited rapid upward spirals of increasing professional self-confidence and success.

A different pattern characterized *less* satisfied teachers who write. By contrast with their more successful-feeling peers, these writers described discrepancies between how they taught and how they wrote. All taught in ways incompatible with experience, some largely so. And all described feelings of failure, frustration, or burnout regarding their work — except when their teaching assignments included only elite groups. Unlike the upward spirals of those who taught from experience, writers whose methods were inconsistent with firsthand knowledge of writing fell into downward spirals of growing frustration and defeat whether they recognized the inconsistencies or not. Some even left teaching before my study was complete.

Most writers I met fell in between these extremes, however. Some aspects of their teaching were experience-inspired while others were shaped by public (and sometimes professional) expectations of "what

English teachers are *supposed* to do." One of these "schitzy" writers, a poet, was winner of the Davidson Prize, an honor that led to a spate of readings at colleges throughout the northeast. Katie, as I've called her (Nelson 1982), said she taught "traditionally—except for a poetry unit" that she "saved for the end of the year." Assigning both topic and format for most of the writing her students did, she grew bored with repeatedly teaching the same literary selections:

> We write all year, mostly paragraphs and essays. I spent the past six weeks on expository skills, and I'll continue that throughout the year. We read *Huck Finn*, and I assign three paragraphs on three topics. Then we do a paper on *The Great Gatsby* in which I show them how to expand an idea. They should have one paragraph of introduction, one of conclusion, and a body made up of three paragraphs.... (p. 182)

"Do they do any creative writing?" I asked.

> Creative writing? Some of the paragraphs are sort of like that.... We study transitions. You know—describe a scene, lead the reader from one point, around the scene, and back to the beginning. I don't have them write stories or anything like that. If I had a creative writing class, I would do that, but I feel so compelled to do all these other things that I'm going to be held responsible for. (p. 183)

When I asked about poetry, Katie's methods changed, as did her demeanor. She sat up straight, her eyes lit up, and she spoke passionately, illustrating how differently writers treat genres in which they write:

> I feel I have a *very* successful unit teaching poetry. We begin with the images in the poem. ... Then we get into writing poems [and finally I give] what I call a "final experience reading." For example, we read Ferlinghetti's poem "Fortune," about the first loss of innocence, running naked under the fire hoses in the street; then we discuss those times in our own lives—the ones when you know that from there on out it'll never be the same again. Finally, when we are ready, we write poems about it. (pp. 183–184)

> I feel the main thing you can do to a poem is *experience* it. Marianne Moore says a poem should make the hair rise on the back of your neck, and that when it does that, you have "experienced" it. So while I read it, they are to keep the whole thing in mind, and we never say anything [analytical] about it again. It's that important. ... (p. 183)

In the poetry unit Katie taught reading, writing, listening, discussing, and "experiencing" in ways she did not do with other genres she taught. She also modeled the intense feelings she as a poet felt, including respect (for others' work) and vulnerability:

At this point [December, long before the poetry unit] the students don't know that I write, but by the end of the year they'll know. *It gives me the right to tell them about writing.* Since I am a writer myself, the main thing I teach about poetry is that it should be respected and appreciated. [Emphasis mine] (p. 184)

The first year I taught I was *so* afraid. I put off and put off the poetry unit. I wanted so *much* for them to receive poetry without hostility, with appreciation. Now I give my students a pep talk at the beginning of the unit. I tell them, "If you don't like it, you better not let me know." If they ever want to say they don't like something, they have to give their reasons using literary terms. (pp. 184–185)

I don't allow any derogatory remarks! Poetry is so important to me. That's the only way I can deal with teaching it. That's why I talk to them before. All they have to do is accept it as a valuable part of life or understand others who do. Everyone is not expected to like it, but I do expect them to respect the others who pull out poetry and read and read and read. And I mean, I have some of the worst hoodlums in the world just fall in love with it! (p. 185)

Katie dramatizes the conflict between using personal writing and reading experience as a guide and relying on "what English teachers are *supposed* to do." All year Katie the teacher taught essay formulas to rooms full of students who did not know she wrote. At the end of the year, after covering all she felt compelled to teach, Katie the poet came out of hiding to teach poetry. No longer did students read only those classics common at their grade level; Katie offered a "miscellaneous unit" of poets she loved. No longer was Katie's aim the analysis of a prescribed canon; experience with literature had become the goal. Katie's students wrote no more formula essays on assigned topics; during the poetry unit they explored personal experience in search of inspiration for a focused creative response. As Katie's attitude toward course content shifted from obligation to awe, her goals for students shifted as well—from literary analysis and content coverage to experience, appreciation, and self-expression; from the students writing critically about the famed author's works to creating literature of their own. And not only did Katie take more pleasure in her teaching, she felt more successful when she taught this way.

It is not my goal to describe in detail how writers teach, only to emphasize that trusting experience as a guide was the behavior that distinguished greater from lesser success. Studying writers like Katie confirmed what I'd learned long before from Bob Ford—to trust my own reading and writing experience, limited though it was. Let me sketch for you, then, what I learned about myself as a writer while preparing to speak to Sandra's creative writing class. I do so not to add to your already crowded curriculum, but to illustrate the kinds of things we teachers can learn by looking honestly at what we as readers or writers do. You see, I was not then and am not now a widely published poet. Most of the writing I do is of an academic nature, and most of my publishing has been done since I spoke to Sandra's class. For me, reading poetry is a sometime avocation: I read mostly contemporary poets — sporadically, on my own. Even so, students say that my personal involvement with poetry and my vulnerability about sharing the poems I write make poems and poets more approachable for them. There are "poetry epidemics" in every class I teach.

What I Learned About Writing by Studying Myself

What did I learn as I pulled together my knowledge of how I write? And how do I think such personal knowledge can best be taught? I'm not sure how-to knowledge of writing or reading *can* be taught directly, but I have seen awareness of my writing blocks, habits, goals, and attitudes validate for beginners the writing experience they have, particularly when it conflicts with rules they've been drilled on in school. Exposure to the frustrations that more experienced writers go through offers beginners new problem-solving strategies. For example, I can not tell a student how to revise a poem, but I can expand her awareness of alternatives by describing considerations I make in my work or suggesting *the kinds* of revisions I *might* make were her poem mine. She can then decide for herself whether what I do will work for the stage of development she and her piece are at.

I began preparing for Sandra's class by paging through my notebooks, reconstructing the processes by which poems had emerged. I'd always seen myself as an endless reviser. I also knew many poems had been efforts to capture feelings, to learn where they had come from, and to clarify them for myself. I knew my poetry usually stemmed from ambivalence, often about changes taking place in relationships. In fact, I had said as much to my own students many times. One thing I'd never realized, though, was how often my impulse to write had been sparked by reading other poets' work, whether poems by famous writers or poems by friends of mine. In short, I knew many writers used reading to find inspiration, but I hadn't noticed how frequently I do so myself. Since that night of self-study, when I lack inspiration I can seek it in the work of poets who have a strong impact on me. I encourage students to try this strategy as well, and I often read poems aloud to help a class get unstuck. Confident in the knowledge that inspiration grows naturally and that the hunger it leaves in its wake motivates concern for craft, I now accept creative responses as well as analyses of the poems students in my classes read.

The following poem, "Tokyo, 1967," is a poem I like rereading, for writing it synthesized buried feelings about my years in Japan. It began, however, as a somewhat annoyed reaction to one of Richard Brautigan's *June 30th, June 30th* poems, which he wrote during a brief (six-week) pilgrimage to Japan. "A brown cat lies/in front of a Chinese restaurant/in a very narrow lane/in Shinjuku," began Brautigan. "The window of the restaurant is/filled with plastic models/of Chinese food that looks good/enough to eat."* I decided to share my response to Brautigan with Sandra's class to illustrate the creative response principle:

Tokyo, 1967

I remember the fat brown cat of
Shinjuku, lying in the *alley*, Brautigan,
not *lane*, where—damp green stones
littered with bok choi—shreds of hakusai
cling to the piss-streaked portal of the
chinese bar. We could have afforded to
enter of course—it's easy to tell by the
plastic food in the case—but we leaned
against an aloof stonewall in the darkness
and skittered gravel at intruding lions.

I remember the lean brown cat of
Roppongi. We arched backwards together
into the shadows when the glittering
people intruded from the Chinese Restaurant
at the end of the lane. There are Hotel
Edens and porno flicks near the station
and the Shin-Otani and the Frank Lloyd Wright
on the hill, but I have discovered your hands,
here in the darkness. The chauffeur-driven
limousine's eyes are still.

Another thing I hadn't realize about my writing was what differing amounts of work various poems required. Having earned a reputation, even among writer friends, for the amount of in-process, on-page revision I do, I was surprised to discover how many shorter poems had seemingly floated up whole, like shimmering bubbles, to me. Shortly after my visit with Sandra's students, it happened again. Working late one evening, transcribing interviews from research tapes, I stopped for a stiff-backed moment to get a bite to eat. As I stood by the old gas

---

* From *June 30th, June 30th* by Richard Brautigan. Copyright 1977, 1978 by Richard Brautigan. Reprinted by permission of Delacorte Press/Seymour Lawrence, a division of Bantam Doubleday Dell Publishing Group, Inc.

stove, lifting spinach from a bamboo steamer with weathered chopsticks, these lines overtook me and I hurried to write them down.

> Pausing past midnight
> to steam for myself
> a rice-bowl of spinach
> dashed with my chinese sesame
> and her japanese soy,
> I wish that you were here.

Far from the best work I've done, even as short poems go, this gratuitous bubble captured a feeling I could not have preserved in words without images. For a number of years now it's served as a memory of that night for me.

Realizing while reading my notebooks that a number of poems had come from fleeting rather than sustained impulses, I began training myself to notice the feelings to which the roots of such poems could be traced. This practice is most difficult but also most productive when these feelings occur at a normally busy hour and vie with persistent bids — traffic, or children — for attention. Suddenly, I remembered that once, during dinner at a friend's, Tom Liner, a more experienced poet than I, asked the host for paper and pulled out a pen. Three or four times that evening I watched the pen in Tom's hand arc almost imperceptibly back and forth above the page, trying to pick up a poem, like a radar sweep, I thought. Each time, after some moments, a short but polished poem appeared, confirming that for some poems craft can be less self-conscious, less overt. I too must listen carefully to spot and catch my poems — though unlike Tom I often have little warning that one's on the way. And since becoming conscious of creative payoffs for listening, I now suggest that students may want to do the same.

Another type of poem I found as I went through my poetry notebooks falls somewhere between extensive revision and short bursts of inspiration. Sometimes I sense a likeness between unlike people or events, and from that juxtaposition a poem grows. Though such poems may require only three or four drafts to assume a shape, tinkering with images, diction, rhythms, line breaks, and the like may continue for months and cannot be rushed.

Students often show interest in these poems' evolution, perhaps because the amount of revision does not intimidate them, and I've shared "The Mine Shaft," which follows, with classes several times.

The Mine Shaft

> Today I looked into your
> eyes, I saw your face, I
> knew and called your name.

"The Mine Shaft": Draft 1

"The Mine Shaft": Draft 2

"The Mine Shaft": Draft 3

But it was my name, bouncing
back in echoes from the
abandoned mine-shaft of

my former self. And it
was my face, pain twisted
by the rubble-pinned limbs

of time. And the eyes cried
out to me pleading: Come,
shift these boulders that

I may pace in comfort in
the light-streaked tunnels
of my caved-in dreams.

Asked to read some poems and talk about how I write at a summer
Governor's Honors Program for talented Georgia students, I read a
near-final version, then traced this poem's development across drafts
while students followed along with the handwritten copies you see
here. It began with a struggle (Draft 1) to define an emerging metaphor
and a feeling of uncertainty about the tone. Once the first draft was
down, there was a period of regression (Draft 2), during which I wrote

doggedly, though nothing I liked would come. All grasp of form was slipping away, but I kept the poem alive by holding fast to the feelings that had prompted it. The final stage, which even middle school students spot easily, was the reimposition of control, which occurred in Draft 3. I finalized the typed version thirteen years later as I reviewed the page proofs for this article.

Though I have never considered trying to publish it elsewhere, this poem preserves my memory of the burst of empathy that flashed from me to a friend as he struggled through a crisis reminiscent of one I myself had survived. Even though students sometimes feel confused about this poem, it serves an important function for me. The fact that poems save and clarify experience is something I may never have stated explicitly to students, but something that becomes obvious when I share my process with them. They also become aware of specific revisions I've made and — if they find them effective — may try similar strategies. Sometimes they say, for example, that before I shared poetry drafts, they would not have considered trying such-and-such a change. Even those who lack technical terms for the changes I make recognize improvement when they see or hear it. Over time almost all students incorporate some of my revising approaches, whether in their poetry or in their prose.

The last type of poem I include here illustrates the revising end of my writing continuum. These poems go through draft after draft, sometimes resolving the tension that births them within a single week, sometimes requiring months, and in other cases several years. An unfinished poem about a friend's death from cancer some years ago now seems to be evolving in this way. The latest version is far shorter than earlier drafts, for I have tightened and cut and condensed repeatedly to get rid of all direct expressions of pain and replace them with images from memory in an effort to evoke feeling in the reader firsthand. Not until almost a year after Elaine's rainy-day burial in the high-walled Hebrew Cemetery near my home did the piece first begin to feel like it might make a poem, but since then it's been incubating for several years.

Perhaps Elaine's poem will finish itself. Perhaps it won't. Who knows? I suspect it may someday fit a pattern I've seen before — that of remaining incomplete until time juxtaposes it against some future and, for the most part, *unlike* experience. It's poems like this one that keep me humble (and stay my grading pen) when students feel blocked and can't get a piece they've worked hard on to go anywhere. If I'm not willing to publish an unsolved problem piece in this essay, how can I expect students to submit unfinished products for grades?

Much of what I've learned about poems by writing them also helps me improve the academic writing that I do. Just as some poems sit for years waiting to be reworked, this essay has shown me that exposition can do the same. Not only have I fine-tuned the language of this essay, but I have shifted the focus of the piece in several ways. I've added new insights from my expanding experience, inserted findings from my most recent research project, added the Katie material, inserted two new sub-headings, and revised several of the poems that I've included. In fact, I had to restrain myself from adding another section when a new poem materialized while I was revising a draft.

Poetic processes are not discrete, in other words, so teachers need not constrain assignments to single genres. I learn from reading and writing poems, lessons that I apply to prose. Writers develop when writers follow ideas wherever they flow. Sometimes budding poets have pressing ideas that demand prose expression, and not all sophisticated responses to literature appear in prose. In other words, choice and language growth are indivisible. By dividing them I can inhibit creative development in so many students that most will forget they are capable of it.

Related to this issue of indivisibility is the fact that, in the wild, reading and writing exist in symbiotic relationship. As Bob Ford demonstrated so vividly, one volunteers when the other is introduced lovingly. The major difference, since then, between my reading and writing classes is the relative emphasis placed on each activity. As a writer whose poems are often reading-inspired and whose resulting craft-hunger in turn influences what I read, I provide time in all classes for both reading and writing poems, as I believe I must if my students are to do either well.

The poem that follows illustrates this symbiosis. It sprang from the final line of a poem written for me by a friend, one of many ways by which poetry begets poetry. "When the Last Door Slams" survived a process of coming together slowly, over time and through a number of drafts. To the last borrowed line were attracted several images, a cluster of fragments that I sensed from the start were related, though for a while I had no clue as to how. It took about a week to fix relationships among the parts and integrate stray images that would not go away. (It's taken several years to understand why they had to be there.) Altogether, this poem has been through thirty or more revisions, and I've changed it significantly since publishing it the first time.

When the Last Door Slams

When the last door slams behind me
on a taut week's work
and my tired sun flows like honey
on the rearview horizon

out from behind the corners of
my eyes you leap at me
dance in the quiet glint of rooftops
tin on spring grain flashing

glance off the sharp-edged
hollows of my silences
but I cannot find your face.
At speed zone ahead

I downshift for the harrow.
Soon it's cotton dust in my nose
on my tongue, as the blue ridge fades
away. In through twin channels of

stereosong you wash sudden
but I do not know your name
and there's no righthand line
on a dark Georgia road

to protect me from the glare.
What would I give to keep you near
where I might see you stumble
and what could I pay an aged man

to tell me who you are?
Oh, I would make only new mistakes
with you, none of the old ones
but who would I sell my children to?

Helmet and goggle, the one-eyed
Harley takes me from behind
long breath slow coming
then rearing, skirts my vision's

convex lens and roars ahead. Afar
two fan-tailed hawks anchor
competing jack-pines to the sky.
Distances hurt me softly when they fly.

Hardly a poem I'd thinkingly choose to read to high school students. I impulsively stuffed my notebook into an opaque projector to show the extensive and furious drafting process some poems go through. I suppose I thought Sandra's students would note the number of crossouts per line, the messiness in the margins, and let it go at that. I should have known better. Like writers, students rarely show interest in revision for its own sake. They anchor every discussion of writing to content, to author's intentions, for unlike English teachers, they find scant relevance in form alone.

And they are right, of course. Form is a vehicle; without content it does not exist. With neither prompting from me nor coaching from her, Sandra's small-town students approached this poem much like critics, though as writers themselves, all were careful to protect my self-esteem, a courtesy neither all critics nor all English teachers extend. They asked me to read several drafts of this poem for comparison, wanted to verify just what feelings I'd tried to express, were curious to know the literal meanings behind images, wanted to know how and where I'd used poetic license — and why. In this setting they refrained from judging details of my life; instead they struggled to understand how my craft derived from them. They wanted to know if the line breaks related to the meaning, what certain lines meant anyway, and why I chose certain words. And they seemed delighted to hear that I'd lifted the final line — which had rung in my ears for months — from an otherwise forgotten poem by a friend.

My solid identification with that last lonely line had impelled my struggle to write this poem from the start, and the fact that the line carved out a niche for itself in my work makes me more forgiving when my own students copy (or steal from) writers they love. As two-time PEN/Faulkner finalist Dick Bausch told one of my classes: "I beg, steal or borrow whatever I can. All writers do. Just don't get caught."

High school students' interest in a content hardly "relevant" to the typical adolescent's experience brings me to my last point about teaching poetry (or any genre) by relying on reading and writing experience as a guide. Good writing is honest writing. As such it is often revealing, sometimes uncomfortably so. As a writer I must not fall into the trap of hiding my feelings from students I would teach, for that habit is destructive to my work and theirs. Honesty of expression is essential to writing well, regardless of the level at which I (or they) currently perform. Censoring what I say distorts the writer/reader's role, and that role is the source of my credibility where poetry — whether great writers', my own, or students' — is concerned. I don't mean we should share all adult experiences with young readers; I do believe that once writing is shared, censoring can pervert the piece by misshaping students' understanding of how writers work. Modeling honestly is essential if students are to learn from us how reading and writing are successfully done.

Writing is risky business as every student knows, and sharing writing honestly is riskier still. I suspect that's why the most successful writer-teachers I studied worked first to build trusting communities in reading and writing classes. For trust to develop, however, it has to flow both ways. Trust made writing well possible in the classrooms I studied while lack of trust inhibited writing development. Trust made the fellow-writer stance safe for teachers too. And trust was what turned me into a reader and writer of poetry though I rarely understood the poems Bob Ford read. Bob never gave assignments or grades. Nor did he see what I wrote. He just lived, breathed, and reveled in poems until I understood that if they gave him such pleasure, they might delight me too.

So What's Left for Non-Writers Who Want Their Students to Love Poetry?

"But I've written no poems since high school," you tell me, "I'm not a poet at all. I *can't* rely on experience writing poetry as a guide." Then don't "teach" poetry writing, I say (Lesson 1 from your experience). It's probably better not to teach it directly anyway. Instead let the closeted poets hiding in your classes teach you how *not* to reproduce — for them and for their friends — conditions that made you abandon poetry writing when you were in school. Don't require every student to write poems if you yourself don't (Lesson 2). But don't preclude poetry options as responses to literature just because you yourself feel more comfortable writing critiques. Beneath surface differences in these preferences lies a similarity: Neither you nor your student poets feel equally competent in all modes. Just as the trust level needs to be high for you to write poetry (and just as when you attempt poems you may feel vulnerable, and with cause), student writers need to be allowed to lead from strength, building confidence with what they're good at before being challenged where they're weak.

Nurturing budding poets is nothing to be afraid of, for though you're not yet a poet, you can establish a climate in which poets and poetry thrive. You can easily imitate much of what poet-teachers do by taking some risks yourself and sharing some failures with kids. You can show the respect, even awe, you feel for skillful poets. You can invite to your classroom friends and acquaintances who write. You can spend classroom poetry time teaching only poems you love rather than boring students with selections that bore you. You can let poetry study flow back and forth between reading and writing, regardless of the name ("composition" or "literature") of your course. You can accept poetic responses in place of critical essays — and accept critiques or satires or "disasters" in place of poems at times. You can let student writers organize poetry groups *on class time* and help them produce practiced (and recorded) readings of their work. You can ask student poets to talk about "How I Write a Poem," and give credit for work on some poems they've not yet finished (or shared).

If you model honestly whatever writing and reading you do, respond with sensitivity in support of fledgling poets, and ensure that poets and poems get only respect in your class, you'll never need to worry about your failure to teach poetry. Poetry will reward you. Poetry will teach itself.

10

Only a Well-Digger's Teacher[1]

Philip Billings

Richard Hugo, in a long, excellent article in *American Poetry Review* (March/April 1979), wrote on the subject of how to teach poetry-writing. I remember three things from it: one, make them use lead pencils so that they are not in the slightest way encouraged to think of their early-draft words as permanent; two, tell them they had better have some favorite words and use them a lot, unless they are amazingly talented; and, three, coax them to have "the courage of their obsessions." I don't like it when poets can't talk about poetry without every minute quoting some other poet talking about poetry, so I promise not to do it again. But I did want to get that third idea said and credited exactly right because that is the log on the fire I want to poke at here. I want to say what I think Hugo means by "obsessions" and by "courage" and why, in poetry, the one demands the other, and why this is so important for beginning poets and their teachers to realize.

We obviously have different levels of obsession. I am obsessed with truth, with death, and with women. Less generally I am obsessed with the way truth can be so deep and beautiful as to be of no more practical use than a flower, with the deaths of children, and with stubborn, tough old ladies. Specifically, I am obsessed with the (partly imagined) sight of my grandmother lying very much like a baby in a hospital bed made very much like a crib by its safety bars along the sides, pounding her bony fist against one of those bars all night, my father sitting next to her unable to do or say anything about his love that would aid her in her fight against—or was it for—death. I am obsessed with myself, my aging, my hairline. I am obsessed with soft things beneath rough surfaces, with the very real, delicate joys of two-a-day fall football practices, with the sweet smell and cool feel of the grass during 8:00 a.m. push-ups.

It is the third, most exact sort of obsession, I think, that Hugo is talking about. It must be. I didn't feel especially courageous, didn't feel I was risking much of anything, when I told you those first two kinds. It would take courage for most people to say they were *not* obsessed with or at least seriously interested in such "topics." But that third kind: Weren't there things in it that you might find unseemly? Excesses of morbidity, nostalgia, vanity? A person's most particular obsessions, those precise gestures of mind and body he can't help but repeat, give him away in a flash. Even to himself. He hopes no one is watching; he half-wishes he himself weren't. Especially in this age that has so thoroughly refined and propagated for commercial purposes the idea of mass sameness or, if you will, of mass, "normal" obsessions (as with personal hygiene), to admit to idiosyncratic obsessions of almost any sort takes guts. You've singled yourself out. You are eccentric, unhealthy, noncommercial, which is nearly the same as unpatriotic.

To come at the subject another way, I think Richard Hugo advises poets to have the courage of their most particular forms of obsession because my favorite poems, including some of his own, are full of them. They are what people literally read first and remember longest. Ironically, it can often be the best literature students who most consistently forget this. We teachers make them. The good student turns to Keats's "To Autumn," sails through line after line of precise images of the man's obsessions—heavily ripe fruits and vegetables, drowsy afternoon boys, buzzing gnats—then writes in the margin "attempts to accept death." That's probably the nice safe *idea* the teacher will ask for on the next test. Or, if the teacher turns out odd enough to actually ask about images, the good student learns to talk about them as if they were totally conscious devices to convey theme. Keats needed something, again, to symbolize "Beauty: the narcotic power of"; so he went again to his dictionary of literary motifs and found "the fume of poppies." The man who made so sane (and old) a poem couldn't have been *really* hung-up on gorgeous narcotics, could he?

My answer, and I believe Hugo's, is a resounding yes. He not only could but also *should* have been. Writing out of real, personal obsession of some kind, that is. Almost any kind would have served, so long as it was honest. Why? Because that's the major way to write sentences that don't sound quite like anyone else's. It is the source of the intensity that makes images, metaphors, ironies, rhythms, repetitions, and all other verbal tricks spring to genuine life and then stay under control. It is the only material you've got to clothe and thereby make visible those oh-so-popular but elusive "feelings" that everyone knows you go to poetry for. While the proper, disciplined pupil of your eye is focusing on just what it's supposed to in the night sky, the thematically significant constellations, the rowdy, careless peripheral vision catches the biggest, deepest, most mysterious and (thus) interesting stars of all. It does more than catch them, actually; it helps to *make* them.

I can imagine three objections to this obsession-oriented poetic thinking, especially as it might be applied to teaching adolescents. First, there is something else besides specific, obsessive imagery in great poetry, namely, wisdom. General, universal truth asserted in the most appropriate form, whether it be plain or baroque, ingenuous or ironic or whatever—this, too, is something that makes sentences eminently worth reading. It wasn't just Pope or Frost who thought so, either; Mark Strand is always saying wise things like:

> His pursuit was a form of evasion:
> the more he tried to uncover
> the more there was to conceal
> the less he understood.
> If he kept it up,
> he would lose everything.[2]

This is no place to get into the old battles between Romantic and Classic, Imagist and Meditator. I'm not only willing to grant the place of overt wisdom in poetry; in fact, I love and would defend to my figurative death that place. But not in teaching adolescent poets. Wisdom and its concomitant ability to freshen and control abstract truths is something those kids just don't have. When they try for it, what you get is the stuff of warmed-up athletic banquet speeches and disinterred American Legion essay contests. They say what they think you want them to in ways as stuffy and stern and self-righteous as they think your old-fashioned life is. Do I have to give examples? Young people's bodies are wiser than their minds. I can hardly think of any of the overtly wise poetry I love that was written by people under 35.

But, someone might counter, isn't the "courage of your obsessions," the strength and willingness to damn conformity, equally beyond the adolescent grasp? Who more than the teenager literally buys all those commercials, clings more desperately to the crowd's hem, feels more acutely the screws put to him by peers? Kids who sign up to write poetry have already gone out on a limb, because everyone "knows" what poets are like; now you want them to saw it off with real self-revelation in the things they actually write?

I admit the case is a bad one. Something like the old question of whether it's easier to make a handsome boy smart or a smart boy handsome. But (not knowing which of those alternatives it more closely corresponds to) I choose the truth of obsessions in their most particular form over wisdom in its most general. For one thing, there might be a better chance than you think that the very courage that made the kid sign up for or, if it wasn't optional, even pay attention in your poetry-writing class gives evidence of the capability for even more courage when inspired by a good subject or teacher. For another thing, the risk once taken might lead to self-revelation of a positive nature; peer groups often try, after all, to enforce inferior, stupid, or insensitive self-concepts. The exhilaration of finding them wrong can become a life-long habit.

Furthermore, promising young poets often resist genuine involvement in the discipline of writing seriously exactly *because* they have been told that THE POET first and foremost shows forth WISDOM — the very thing their innate honesty and common sense tell them they are fresh out of. If they are hard-boiled enough to suspect that adults come up short in this area, too, then THE POET described only in relation to WISDOM is an even bigger fake than their principal. Faking it in class may be fun for awhile, may even be mandatory, but it finally isn't as good as the real thing you get at the auto-repair shop, ball game, or senior class play. One more consideration. Once teenagers get in tight enough with a crowd, they can get remarkably reckless, loose, crazy. Besides being the most conformity-minded among us, they may also be the most self-conscious; and, when that quality gets turned inside-out in the peer-group's safe confines, they can wear their obsessions like five coats of Clearasil. Maybe the poetry class can eventually turn into a group like that.

The final complaint I can imagine against teaching poetry-writing in this obsession-oriented way is that what you will get is trivial or neurotic or quirky stuff best left to the therapist or the peeping Tom. Who cares, finally, about aberrations? Schools are meant to civilize kids, teach them how best to fit into the common, productive scheme of things, how most thoroughly to blend in with "society." My response to this belief is pretty simple: anyone who believes it whole-heartedly should not teach poetry-writing to anyone. I understand the assumption behind all art to be, simply, that it is not "civilized" (in the sense just described anyway); it is chronically childlike. The single case is always more important than the group norm. The aberration art publicizes proves some other, more important rule. The truth it cherishes is always a little quirky.

But not, finally, limited or trivial, not *merely* personal. That star that the corner of the eye sees better than the pupil does belongs to the whole universe which includes each of us; and each of us helps to make that star. Without us it is dead. Or to choose a more utilitarian metaphor: poetry is water that the whole community needs in order to fully live, and the best way to get at it is just to drill straight down from where you are standing. It takes a good deal of faith, especially at first, but it works every time. If your efforts have brought up nothing but trivial, sick, or incomprehensive sludge so far, it's a simple (though exhausting) matter of trying harder, drilling deeper. If you hit solid rock, you were unlucky this time. Move over a little and try again. The water table is down there somewhere, for sure. Have courage.

First of all, then, teach beginning poets to "have the courage of their obsessions." That's what I'd advise. They will want to write about their convictions, instead. They'll want to say Uncle Ray was sweet; don't let them; get them to tell you about the pungent odor from some kind of plant that always makes them remember Uncle Ray's back yard. They'll want to write about the importance of victory; make them describe instead the sight of the pitch that almost took their head off last summer and that they still have dreams about. Or make them describe the act of having thrown it. They'll insist on saying they're in glorious love or nobody understands them or life is what you make it; ask them what they practice in front of the full-length bedroom mirror, the one on the back of the locked door, every night. If the answer would be *only* embarrassing—don't worry, they would never tell you in 1,000 years. They will want to use rhymes; let them if it doesn't interfere with the truth. (It probably will.)

The biggest draw-back to this "obsessive" method may relate more to the teacher than to the young student. Since kids learn best by example, the teacher him- or herself cannot finally avoid showing the same kind of courage she or he is demanding. I have been playing teacher of this method here and have, therefore, used myself by way of illustration near the beginning to an extent that would otherwise be inappropriate. Let me end out on the same limb by citing one of my poems.

That Log

Ringed full of a sleep
no rounder or longer than the others'
but at least twice as heavy,
that log
was the last one hauled in.
In never got really caught up
in the pale yellow-blue exhibition
that crackled briefly beneath it.
For hours afterwards it shrank and grew
black-gray-white by itself.

Now, just before we click off,
follow as usual the last light up,
then smooth and tuck ourselves finally out,
that log

cracks itself open to the heart
and blooms its own flame.
And that flame
quivers once, then stands:
deep gold-purple, tight with attention,
ready for the long night.

I don't claim a lot for this poem. I wrote it when I was even more of a beginner than I am now. I think now I can do better. But I am not ashamed of it either, and I can't imagine ever being ashamed, because I feel something true to my best self and to something more in it. You may check the poem against the personal obsessions mentioned earlier in order to get a psychologist's eye-view of some of the roots that lead up to this sturdy feeling. That analytical view was not at all mine, however, when I wrote the poem. All I could see was that log. I watched it for hours one night, first out of the corner of my eye, then directly, when I "should" have been doing something else, I forget what. Then I couldn't stop watching it with my mind for days afterwards. Finally I saw a scary white sheet of paper that I could make safe with words that fit that log as well as I could make them fit. When I have shown the poem to writing classes, none seems to have found it trivial or embarrassing. Most seem, miraculously to me still, to have recognized either from experience or from intuition what the poem is about. At the same time, miraculously again, they seem to have learned something new from it. And not primarily about me at all. About real logs. And "real life." A few even thought they learned something about writing poetry.

Notes

1. Reprinted with permission of Atheneum Publishers, an imprint of Macmillan Publishing Co. from *The Story of Our Lives* by Mark Strand. Copyright © 1973 by Mark Strand. Originally appeared in *Poetry*.

2. Reprinted by permission of Mark Strand from "The Untelling," in *The Story of Our Lives* by Mark Strand (New York: Atheneum, 1971, pp. 42–43).

Applications

Introduction

Hearing what poets have to say about their craft and about their feelings for poetry is useful, but there remains the basic problem that all instructors face when they enter a classroom: I have an appreciation and an understanding of poetry but how do I communicate these to young people who, more often than not, resist any thought that poetry might be important to them? Is it important, after all, that nonreaders and nonwriters who so frequently populate our classrooms even know that poetry exists and that it may speak to many of their concerns and wishes? The answer is obviously yes, and the suggestions of how to make this connection appear in this section.

A common thread runs through the discussions of applications which appear in this section: namely, that one of the first things that has to be done in the classroom to help students become interested in poetry is to make it accessible to them. One way of accomplishing this is to help students understand the power of words. For many students, as Tom Liner points out in his anecdotal account of working with low-level students, being able to use words to communicate feelings and ideas is a totally new experience; once the contact with words begins, however, an entire new world begins to appear and students embrace it eagerly. Jim Heynen and Ingrid Wendt share their experiences as poets in the schools, explaining the different techniques they use to introduce language play as the first step toward understanding poetry. Coming to grips with the possibilities of words, of their combinations, and of their meanings can lead gradually to more extended use of language and a greater understanding of the power of language to communicate.

Introducing poetry to students should be done in gradual stages, beginning with language play and then moving on to the intellectual meaning in poems. Denny Wolfe provides a practical approach for systematically building upon language play to make poetry more accessible. James S. Mullican outlines an approach for involving students in unlocking the meaning of a poem, suggesting that many poems remain a kind of riddle until the clues are put together. Mullican shows how this "riddle approach" can be applied easily to classroom study of poetry. Charles R. Duke suggests that the meaning of poetry can be enriched and extended through the medium of creative dramatics; his sequential framework for integrating dramatic techniques with poetry provides the classroom teacher unfamiliar with creative drama, an immediate entrance into a new perspective on responding to and interpreting poetry.

In addition to understanding the role of language and meaning in poetry, students eventually will need to develop an understanding of form. Danny L. Miller suggests the ballad as an accessible form for young adults; as a popular form, the ballad has many connections to today's music and to our enjoyment of narrative. Drawing upon these connections, the ballad becomes a natural vehicle for teaching form. But with form comes also the need to understand meter, rhythm, tone, and voice. R. L. Barth provides an explanation of the more technical aspects students eventually will need to comprehend as they become more sophisticated in their reading and writing of poetry.

Finally, Patrick Bizzaro addresses the issue of evaluation; always a tough issue for teachers and students, the means by which poetry can be critiqued to promote continued improvement often creates an unnecessary tension between student and teacher. Bizzaro shows how different literary theories of criticism—the New Criticism, Reader Response Criticism, and Deconstructionism—can be applied to the reading of students' work. His suggestions that perhaps all three approaches may have their place in the evaluation process as students move from beginning efforts to more sophisticated ones should prove useful to teachers, particularly those in creative writing classes.

11

The Outlaws ... and Jonathan, Smiling

Tom Liner

Fourth Period. Half of Gainesville High School was at lunch, and it sounded like most of them were in the hall outside my room at the end of third wing. My class was coming into the room. Like Jackson Browne singing from the tape player in the corner, I felt like I was "running on empty"—already tired at mid-day, frustrated, worried about this bunch of seniors in a class called Practical Writing. They, and I, knew that meant it was a basic level class for seniors who had trouble with English, especially with writing. All but one of them (who was misscheduled and couldn't get out somehow) had to pass this one to graduate. Most of them had been in trouble with other teachers and the principal, some with the law. They were mostly male, mostly tough and street-wise, mostly negative about school, about themselves, about writing. I had known them only a week, and I was having serious doubts about the structure of the class—an open writing workshop with daily free writing in a journal, sharing my reading aloud, and editing for in-class publishing. I often used the workshop-developmental model with gifted students and average students in elective creative writing classes, but I didn't know if I could make it work for these hard-core "basic" kids.

Yet, they came in smiling. I think they liked being there. I had no way of anticipating it at the time, but my Outlaws, as I called them and still think of them, were to be the most rewarding class I've ever taught. From that bright Friday in January until June, I saw them grow as writers. More importantly, I saw them grow *together*, writing and sharing their writing and themselves in an atmosphere of mutual support and openness. I'm not sure where the magic came from but part of it came from Jonathan, the Outlaws' poet.

93

He came in late, as usual. He was a tall, handsome Black kid, and he always dressed "sharp." He was as street-wise and street-tough as any kid I've known. But beneath that brittle outside was something genuine and vulnerable. Maybe I already sensed it, I don't know. I liked him.

"Jonathan, my man, where've you been?"

His teeth flashed, the loose-jointed walk kept its slow pace to his desk. "Be cool, Brother Liner, the little girls needed some attention."

Instead of getting mad, I laughed. We laughed together and began the bond of trust and acceptance and affection that would reach to the whole class. The ritual greeting at the first of each period was established. I always called Jonathan "my man," he always responded with "Brother Liner." It was never a problem.

I started the class, as I always did, with a 10 to 15 minute free writing. We wrote together before I checked the roll, made assignments, or performed other clerical duties. And I did not allow anything to interrupt the free writing. We were 10 minutes late for one fire drill. Astonished teachers, students with messages, even the assistant principal were told to "come back in 10 minutes, we're writing now."

After the first few days, I'd say, "Give me 10 minutes, gentlemen — and ladies," turn on the music, and sit and write with them as they fell to work. They were some of the most pleasant times I've spent in the classroom. Noisy students in the room were usually silenced by neighbors before I could call them down.

I wrote my first poetry with them in class that Friday. Actually, I started a poem I never finished. Neither form nor subject was prescribed in the free writings. And most of the writing I did and the students did during the semester was prose. Yet, all but one of them, including Allen, who was blind, wrote poetry at one time or another. Only two of these kids had ever written poetry of any kind before, and that was in grammar school. The forms of their writings literally grew out of the flow and substance of the developing writings themselves — with a lot of encouragement and sometimes with a lot of work.

After free writing with them each day, I read aloud what I had just written to them. Good or bad, confused or coherent, I read it straight off the page and talked about where the writing came from, what I thought about it, what I would like to do with it next. Especially I talked about the problems of a writer faced with the blank page and the tentative, difficult, searching, but joyous work of writing. And today I read a rambling free writing that finally turned my eyes to the bright January sky out the windows.

"People need some reason to believe"
— a hard day to get it going, so it goes — in this

writing business, trying to catch a hook and start
something — O, well, there are those days.
   if I were to pick an object that represented *me*
right now, what would it be? How about that coffee cup —
a thing of little value, wearing my "sign" I guess.
I've grown from peace signs to rainbows. Maybe that's
growing?
   What do you want to be when you grow up, Tom?
   I don't know yet. I just like to play.

   jet stream cumulus, fingers of the sky

a nice line, I guess — now what?
   and the cold opened its hand to touch me

Winter song

   the wind rattles in the broom sedge
   jet stream cumulus hold the sun
     in an open hand
   the sky's touch is cold
   wind from the west
       ?

I told them I wasn' t happy with the writing and probably wouldn't
finish the poem. Jonathan was smiling. Then I asked, "OK, anybody
have anything you want to read?" The invitation was usually met with
silence, but today Hub, a White kid who sat by the windows and wrote
turned toward them looking out, read in a halting and almost shy voice
a description of the hill, the gym, and parking lot behind the school. I
remember one phrase about "the light glare on a hundred windshields
hurts," and I remember how quiet the group got when he started
reading. When Hub stopped (his piece was very short) I started to
praise him, but Jonathan beat me to it. "Man, that was *something*!
You sure can *write*!" Hub grinned and looked at me for affirmation.
All I did was nod and say, "Listen to the man."

Jonathan didn't read that Friday, but I felt the class come together
because of his listening ear, his generous spirit, and his smile. Hub
turned into a fine descriptive and narrative writer by the end of the
year, his voice growing stronger in his writing each week. I discovered
Jonathan's writing voice when I read his journal over the weekend.

The sky is grateful ... Daydreaming All day,
Daydreaming All night Wake Up in 4th period,
ready to write ... You feel crazy & you feel
great, Just let your pen move and not Hesistate.

Right On! Right On! Right On! ... The Halls
are Ambitious! ... A Voice here, A Voice there.

Why can't it consume quietness ... The Act of
Togetherness was really there ... Will the
World stand still? ... Thinking. That's what
I'm doing, Thinking ... OOH, What a Crazyful
World. On your toes, on your feet! You've got a
special duty to meet. That's the law around here,
You have to wear your sunglasses and you have to
be on your toes. Why did I put toes first and
sunglasses last?*

I could "hear" him places, and his phrasing struck me. At the end
of his journal for that first week I wrote, "I think you're going to be a
natural poet!"

For the next few weeks, I pushed the Outlaws to read aloud in
class because of the positive feeling in that room when they shared
their writings. Once a week, I pulled them into a circle for a "quick
round," calling on each of them in turn. They could pass or read. I
encouraged. Gradually they began to read. Often I heard Jonathan's
"Hey, Man, read the thing" in those sessions.

They were invited to read after each free writing, but no one was
called on. When someone did volunteer, that was the best reading we
did together. At the end of the second week, Jonathan volunteered his
first poem to the class.

Daydream, Daydream, Daydream
lady, lady, lady, Wondering, Wondering
Wondering, will you be there real soon

As he did with me when I read poetry, I asked him to read it the
second time. It didn't get any better with the second reading, but it
was a start. And his journal that week was open and honest, reaching
to an audience that he was suddenly aware of and had many things to
talk to about. I wrote in his journal that week, "The man can *write!*"

I don't know who the "lady" was in the first poem, but he was in
love and had lost her. A few days after he read in class, I was thinking
about his daydream, and I sketched out a rough daydream sequence of
my own about lost love. When I read the first version to the class, I
told Jonathan, "I'm working on your daydream idea, my man. You've
got me hooked." I spent a couple of days writing with them, putting
this poem together.

Waking Dreams: A Sequence

I paint these pictures on the walls of my mind
and the colors tremble when I touch them

your memory is like singing at the edge of night
in your hands are two perfect white stars

I follow your footsteps in the sand like sunset
but the tide is sleeping where they end

this fire dances yellow in the wind
sparks tangle in the trees like midnight

I keep losing your face in the dark
when your voice goes out like a candle

clouds are walking down the sky
and sleep is easier than dreams

the wind touches the window wanting in
I smile and tell it lonely secrets

my life is an empty room in a deserted house
dust and shadows wait behind the door

children write on the empty walls
I hear them laughing in the mote-still light

I close my hands without touching you
the fire is dying sparks fly up like wings

the clouds are passing I can see the stars

We talked through the drafts together. Jonathan took an overseer's pride in the process. It was his idea, after all. And he wasn't shy about his criticism of the final product. "Man, I don't know about that poem. It just don't get itself together." Then he smiled. "You got better stuff than that, Brother Liner."

He was right. I never published it. But we did talk a lot about writing poetry and the *process* of writing that week.

Meanwhile, he was writing longer poems in his journal and reading them proudly to the class. Most were about girls, but there was also this sensitive exploration of a 19-year-old's feelings about his relationship with his father.

Father

Though capable,
but never,
releasing the tensions
brought about between us,
Or shall I say
Though wanting,
but hesitant to —
To square me away,
To Live,
To forget my past,
To accept me,
        Once Again,

For you have
all of the World's
greatest reasons

It's Love
It really is
Though we hardly confront it,
but often thinking,
Our love
only grows stronger

To say, I love you,
is a phrase
waiting to be heard,
but Afraid to be
    given,

What shall be,
    Will be,
Through thick,
Through thin,
I am his Son,
a Son indeed,

Waiting for my father,
Who is waiting for me.

        Daddy.

I especially like the ending of this poem — "I am his Son,/a Son indeed,/ Waiting for my father,/Who is waiting for me./Daddy." —and what it says about the assumption of manhood and the subtle, often painful, love of sons and fathers.

The class was moving, writing and talking about writing together, and taking a great pride in being writers. During the fourth week, I decided it was time to publish in the class. All of the free writings and other writings had been done in single drafts in their journals. By now, many of them were being read to the group and talked about, and I responded to them in writing each weekend. But we had done no editing.

We managed to publish only twice in Fourth Period, all the dittoed writings eventually going into a small book for each student. Some pieces were written, some printed, and some "two-finger" typed with the indulgence of a friendly typing teacher down on first wing. Spelling and language usage in the journals were exactly what you'd expect in a basic level class of former "nonwriters." Editing was slow and frustrating, for them and for me. I remember one short piece by Chris, a lumbering White kid who liked to fight and whose handwriting was the worst scrawl in class, that went through at least five drafts and five conferences with me before it was finished. I insisted that the published pieces be as good, and as correct, as we could make them. It was the hardest work we did, and probably the most important. Their words in print made them, officially, *writers*.

With the daily free writing continuing and other activities going on, it took us three weeks to publish the first time. Sometime in early March, I wrote this poem in response to something Jonathan had said about the class in his journal.

4th Period

Mid-day passes quickly
in sunlight
Spring rises this morning
and waits for your
smiles

"Man, that's *us!*" he said Monday when he read it, and he insisted I publish it with the class.

But he refused to show me the piece he was preparing for publication. "Now, Jonathan, my man, it better be good. And no mistakes. This is important," I told him when I called him over for an editing conference. "Be cool, Brother Liner, this poem is *bad* [i.e., very good]. It's a *surprise*. Darryl'll help." Some of the others in the class looked up and grinned knowingly. I knew Darryl, the lanky basketball player, spelled almost as badly as Jonathan did. But I left them alone. I had insisted on proofing final "copy" on the dittoes and running them off myself before the pages were punched to include in their books. Somehow, Jonathan and Darryl got to an unguarded duplicating machine. They proudly marched into class a few days later bearing the finished copies.

"This goes in the *front*," Jonathan smiled and handed me the stack of copies. I was surprised all right.

Mr. Liner

From one great poet
to another
From one self-contained youngman
to his brother.

Our lives are alike
in such a way
That we live beside each other
Day by day
The way we live,
The way we laugh,
The way we cry,
Our tears are together
in that single drop

for to let us know
Our brotherhood will not stop

For the Day will come
when we will depart
but until that day
We are heart in heart

Be Cool, Brother Liner

When I read his journal that weekend, I found three carefully worked over drafts of the poem on three successive days. I know he spent hours writing and editing the poem. For many reasons, it makes me feel good when I open a small yellow binder on my desk and see his poem first.

The Outlaws grew together into the spring and lived up to their nickname. Chris got into another fight in the hall. Tony, the long haired rock musician who had been married since he was 14, changed jobs and was having trouble getting to school on time. Alex showed up one day barefooted because the dog had chewed up his shoes. Martie dropped out of school suddenly. I was never told why. Hub was in trouble with the principal again. I think everyone in the room was in danger of not graduating at one time or another. Jonathan seemed to fall in and out of love on a weekly basis, and he spun out poems about all of them.

In early May we were editing and getting ready to publish again. I still reserved time for free writing to start each class. We enjoyed it, for one thing, and they were volunteering to read aloud more all the time. I began writing sketches of each person in the class. I don't know what started it, but my writings were quickly done during the free writing and took the form of impressionistic prose-poems. I tried to write one a day, and I read it to the class and directly to the student. The result was electric! Soon everybody was writing about everybody else in the room, and voluntarily *reading them aloud*. I felt the class hold its collective breath each time one was read. They were all positive, very personal statements, and many were gentle and moving. They asked me to publish my sketches in the last publication. By unspoken agreement, none of theirs was published. They were too personal, and shared best read aloud by the writer to his subject.

Jonathan's smile was never brighter than when I read this one to him.

JONATHAN is my darker brother—"Jonathan, my man,
how are you?"—poets talking living smiling the
day into tomorrow. I will envy you the journey.
You are honest. I write and teach, only two things.

Movement and *yes*-saying, singing is smiling,
running to catch the sun rising.
Jonathan, my man, thanks for the teaching.

A few days later he read a very nice, personal piece to me. But, he said, "I done yours before. It's in the *book*." The finest moment for me in that class came unexpectedly on another sunny Friday, this time in late spring, when Jonathan read his poem to Chris. Their friendship had grown over the semester. Chris was big, boisterous, and White. Jonathan was street-wise and cool, sharp and tough, and Black. And never more beautiful than when he read in a clear, cadenced, and completely sincere voice:

Chris

To be a friend of yours
is to be a friend of many.
The security you give,
the friendliness you share,
the smile you win,
For to be Chris,
shall I say,
is to be champion in many ways.
For the things you do,
you will never know,
For the thing you share
is to accept us all.
I do not face you
as a different race.

Instead I face you wrapped within
closed tight the texture
of my own receiving face

Chris, through the tough
time and times we've both seen

Through the extent we've made
our Mothers be a Mother,
Shall I not be halted to say

I simply love you as
my Brother, Brother.

"Jonathan, my man," I said when I could trust my voice, "you make me proud."

They all made me proud. Except for Martie, all the Outlaws graduated. And scattered. Most are working, or I hope they are. A few are in college and probably having a hard time of it. Maybe their pride and new confidence will keep them going. I haven't heard from

Jonathan. He was thinking about college, but he knew it would be very difficult, both academically and financially. I hope he's still falling in love and still writing poetry.

I was going to include a series of *do's* and *don'ts* about teaching poetry to "basic" kids, but that doesn't feel right now. I hope the "rules" of sharing the experience of writing, accepting the young struggling writer, growing together in a caring and safe community of writers, and reaching up for something we didn't think we could do but are proud we did—I hope these *basic* rules of writing and teaching writing are expressed in my relationship with and my love for the Fourth Period Outlaws and Jonathan, my *Man*.

Notes

* Excerpts from the journal and other writings of Jonathan Butts, Gainesville, GA, are published with his permission.

12

Shimmering Chartreuse

Jim Heynen

Let us be realistic about teaching poetry to young people. Part of teaching for most of you is survival — financial and personal. When the black dog of poverty is not at your heels, you are facing a classroom of potentially diffusive energy that threatens bedlam at any moment. You think of ways to stay ahead of your students, to anticipate their disruptive and sometimes cynical moves. Still, for many of you, teaching poetry is a way of trying to salvage lives and minds and potential talents, of somehow finding a path toward beauty through all of the brambles. A few of you may be in a precious setting with well-disciplined, dedicated, and gifted students. Your task is not easy either, since you have to guard against complacency, against the easy divisions of life and art, against a kind of honor student decadence. But most of you are in some way on the defensive. Because you are nevertheless still possessed with love and dedication, you read essays like this one and believe you can effect change, that both you and your students can grow through the dynamics of the classroom. Thank God for you. I hope in some way I can help you.

For several years I directed a poetry workshop program for gifted students. After a few years of the program, I realized that the best young poets were consistently coming in clusters from certain teachers. I began to wonder if, instead of providing workshops for gifted students, we were simply confirming the results of gifted teachers.

One obvious conclusion was that the writing of good poetry can be taught. However, I began to wonder how we might recognize potential in students who do not participate in such programs. I sent out a questionnaire to scores of American poets asking them to characterize the young poet whom they thought would be potentially good. I assumed that many of the poets would recall their own childhood obsessions, and I am sure many of them did. The sampling was quite representative, including Pulitzer Prize and National Book Award winners, as well as young poets just starting to publish nationally.

What characterizes the potentially gifted poet? By far the most frequent response had to do with "delight with the language." Answers took the form of such phrases as "likes to play with words," and "is interested in words for their own sake." Other answers which tallied high were (a) broad reading interests and habits and (b) a general curiosity about the world. Interestingly, hardly any of the poets surveyed said anything about feelings or sensitivity. This survey confirmed some of my hunches and made me feel more comfortable about my own inclinations. I like to have fun in the classroom, and the survey seemed to suggest that my predilection for using language games just might be all right.

I remember well a one-week visiting poetry engagement I had in a Washington suburban school where this predilection worked to my advantage, as well as to that of the students. I am not sure how typical the high school classes were that I visited, but there seemed to be an extraordinarily high level of frivolous obsessions over hair and clothing styles, over cars, over "in" parties, over recreational drugs, and over social cliques. So much snobbery and so little reason for it, I thought. My label as "poet" was one strike against me, since, among other things, it obviously meant that I did not make much money and that I probably did not have very much power in the world. I read them some poems by teenagers. I wrote poems on the blackboard, impromptu, on any topic they wanted. They were clearly impressed, the way they might be by someone who did card tricks, but they were not turned on to poetry. Noticing that the classroom was filled with cliques, many of them mildly hostile toward each other, I told them to rearrange themselves in the room so that they would be with their best friends and to form into groups I called committees. The teacher cringed seeing the likes getting together into conglomerates of like energy. I then told them that each of the committees was assigned the task of providing a list of new color names for next year's line of lipsticks to come out from some prestigious cosmetics company.

The assignment was no more — or less — than a competitive word game, and one which accepted all the baser social and snobbish qualities of the group. Of course there were the "dead-frog greens" from the smiling-tough males and the "pleasant peaches" from the 1950s-nice females. But then there was the "shimmering chartreuse" group, a basically ambivalent and sassy committee of young women who, I guessed, had tried every teenage fad by the time they were 15 and had come out the other side bored. This assignment was clearly for them and they came out, by my pronouncement, the glittering and excited winners.

Sizing up the group, I made my committee word assignments which would at some point give every group a chance to shine. Advertising slogans for motorcycles. Bumper stickers on a wide range of topics. Ironic (real or imagined) road signs. The delight in language was fantastic.

At some point, the "playing with words" guideline will fall short, but if you are in a classroom setting where attitudes toward writing and poetry are still major obstacles, you will feel more comfortable with the seemingly trivial word games which may come to mind or which you may find in any number of writing handbooks.

The following days in that suburban school, I had no trouble building on the good spirit created by the competitive word games. One day we wrote country-western songs. Most of them parodies, of course. Round-robin. I supplied first lines ("Checkerboard square on the table — your move"; "I'm a little dog caught in the kennel of your heart"; "Your coat hanger left a twang in the closet when you left me"; etc.) and would help bring a song back on track — or off track — if it seemed to be getting lost. Five songs were circulating simultaneously around the room, and I had one going on the blackboard that students could work on when the circulating songs were not in front of them. Whoever came up with the next line for the song on the board simply ran to the front and wrote it down. There would actually be a scramble of people rushing to put the next line on the board. We wrote rock lyrics the day after that. The students were indeed turned on, and the assignments produced some big class hits.

The transition from word play had begun. Already I could see hints of the new and more mature form emerging: personal touches in the song, real feelings and experiences crouching within the cliched images from contemporary rock songs. For some, of course, the transition from the rather frivolous activities will never progress into serious attempts at their own poetry. For others, the word games are simply a delightful aside to what is already a commitment to using language toward more personally meaningful and even ambitious ends. But the shimmering chartreuses! And their counterparts, male and female! These are the ones who challenge the teacher in me and who make my idealistic vapors rise! And I suppose these students are "most students."

This may sound outrageous, but if you can help that mass of students see the relationship between words and power, you may be opening the doors to more personal and committed writing. Much of the success of the word games is owing to the students' sense of having a creative power and control with words. Competitive word games — especially ones hinting at a commercial market — emphasize even more the possible relationship between words and power in society. And I do not think I am being carelessly out-of-touch with youth when I nearly equate *money* and *power*. Bending a rather base motive just a little, you can assign poems in which students have the power to effect change. For example, any variety of poems which call for transformations or directives: How to ... or Instructions for.... This chain of a subtle shifts and variations can go on *ad infinitum*. It can lead to rewriting fairy tales in verse as several contemporary poets have done; it can lead to poems about the love affair that might have turned out differently; it can lead to rewriting parents into people the students wish they had been. Most primitive cultures knew that the word, that poetry, is power. Once we return to that realization, we also realize just how "heavy" word games can be, for by acquainting and delighting students with the weaponry of words we are equipping them with the kind of power that none of us will ultimately be able to do without.

Following is a How to ... poem which I wrote and which I have often used with students as a transition from the word games to a more personal poetry. It has in it the kind of word play they may have come to enjoy, and yet it also has a kind of menacing power: the reader can feel at some point that he or she is the tourist controlled by the world created by the poem. (One of the many good responses to this poem was one entitled "Student Guide: How You Can Tell For Sure When A Teacher Is In A Bad Mood".)

Tourist Guide: How You Can Tell for Sure You're in South Dakota[1]

You drive down Main Street
of the first town you come to.

There's a traffic light.
Always. Prestige.

When it sees you coming,
it turns red.

You stop and you're exposed,
and you know it.

A thin cowboy's rabid dog
eyes you from the pool hall.

Then a thick old man
thumps down from the curb.

He's in front of your car
when the light turns green.

Something slow meets your eye.
An eye meets your eye.

You smile.
It doesn't.

You start to drive away.
The whole world stalls.

Glancing over what I have presented thus far, I see that I have espoused an approach to teaching poetry from the outside in. Starting with words and forms and working toward the students' felt experience. Very well. But I can imagine someone achieving similar ends with a totally reverse approach! Indeed, I can recall an argument among teachers of poetry which broke down into two camps: those who would start by encouraging self-expression and those who were more inclined toward emphasizing ways of writing, or technique. I was acquainted with the results of some of the teaching from both camps and knew that some teachers had students who wrote beautiful poetry from a premise which was pretty close to *just write what you feel*! These teachers made extensive use of journal writing, automatic writing, meditation, dream recording, and other methods of probing the inner self. The technique camp were more intrigued by my approach. [Though I use all the other methods too when I have time (shh).] Alas, the two camps do in some way represent that old distinction between the poet as maker and the poet as seer, as craftsman or visionary. But I do not believe that distinction has ever been very useful for the making of poems or even for the instruction and inspiration of young poets. Truth is, many poems of vision or substantial ideas have been written by poets concentrating on form, and many formally interesting and exquisite creations have accompanied the poet's concentration on subject. One may hold one concern more consciously in focus in one poem or another, but the other side will be there, even if at a subconscious level. And who would dare to say whether it is the conscious or subconscious energy that provides the greater contribution to the process of creating a poem?

What I am saying, really, is that the debate is a silly one. When it comes to successful teaching of poetry to young people, the only intelligent and, probably, workable decision is to go with one's own passions and what one perceives to be the passions of the students. That is, finally, what I do when I go to the classroom and it is, finally, what I would encourage others to do. A personal, passionate involvement with poetry, whether the teacher writes poetry or not, is perhaps the most essential prerequisite to successful teaching of it. Rather than using someone else's gimmicks and formulas out of a fear of one's own inexperience or whatever, the act of teaching poetry writing or reading should be very much like the act of writing a poem: a steady alertness and allegiance to the moment and to one's inner vibrancy. And whatever ideals give rise to that vibrancy are ones that you will have to trust. At some point that trust may be as basic as accepting who you are. I accept my ideals and passions, even if I do have to make fun of them to keep from being consumed by them. My hot air. But it keeps me aloft. If my approach seems wrong for you, I hope you trust your own passions — and fly with them.

Notes

1. "Tourist Guide: How You Can Tell for Sure When You're in South Dakota" appeared originally in *South Dakota Review*. Reprinted by permission of the author and *South Dakota Review*.

13

First Attempts:
Free Association into Free Verse

Ingrid Wendt

clock

The word stands alone, its letters large and confident, near the top of the chalkboard with plenty of space all around. You, the teacher, have just put it there, and your class of fourth- or ninth- or twelfth-grade students (or even adults) has paper and pencils ready, desks cleared of everything else. They're expecting to write a poem, but a poem different, you've promised, from anything they've ever written before—a kind of experiment in thinking as poets often think—in letting ideas flow unhindered; in writing quickly without a thought (at the moment) to punctuation, spelling, neat penmanship, making sense; without any of the self-censoring mental devices that keep us from writing as fast as we can or from trusting our own spontaneity. Today you've told your students to forget, for a while, all other poems they've ever read or tried to write. Today they'll be writing "chain poems."

"Clock," you say and point to the board, chalk in hand, having volunteered to write an example. "What does the word 'clock' remind you of? What one single word comes into your mind? The first one."

"Time," someone says, and someone else, "tick tock." Slowly at first, answers start to leap out: "grandfather," "mouse," "alarm," "minutes." There's no right answer, you encourage, and no wrong one (unless it belongs to someone else).

clock
time

You write another word under the first: "time" in this case, instead of other answers, because it was the first word volunteered, not because

109

it's the best. There is no best. No worst. Word choice doesn't even
have to make sense. (But you could also have used the last word
offered, or the second, or third; as a teacher you know how a little
classroom structure goes a long way.)

What's next? (You've guessed it.) "What does 'time' bring to
mind?"

"Lunch." "Late." "Machine." "Magazine." And so on, until everyone knows what's expected, what to do—until everyone has gotten
involved and there's a list on the board something like this:

> clock
> time
> lunch
> awful
> monster
> movies
> popcorn

But it could have looked like this:

> clock
> tick tock
> cake walk
> carnival
> Ferris wheel
> umbrella
> rain

or this:

> clock
> grandfather
> old
> shoe
> hole
> well
> deep

You try a few more lists on the board, for illustration. Not poems yet,
you admit, but chains of words, each word like a link connected to
words just below and above.

Notice (you point out) how the topics keep changing: how the first
word doesn't really relate to words farther on down the line. It's
almost like dreaming. (Who dreams? you ask. At night? In the day?)
You start out with one idea or one picture in your mind; before you
know it, you're off the subject. One thought leads into another, one
picture changes to something else. Who knows what will happen?

And isn't that part of the fun — of dreaming, of thinking, of seeing a movie or reading a story — where the unexpected is bound to occur? Variety, anticipation, surprise all hold our attention. The same thing can happen, in a different way, in poems, which makes them a pleasure to read and (believe it or not) sometimes even to write.

Moving now toward individual work, each student gets ready to write his or her own list, just like the ones on the board, this time using a different first word — most likely a noun, and a noun that is "open" enough to avoid predictable, dead-ended responses. Everyone, furthermore, starts with the same word, making it not only fair but allowing you to point out that everyone *is* unique: Everyone will almost certainly end up with a word different from everyone else. (Maybe our minds are like filing cabinets, storing similar images, memories, words and ideas, but organized each in a personal way.)

Getting ready to copy the word you put on the board, younger students might first draw a short black line near the top of the page, as close to center as possible. This is where the first word will go, and the rest of the list — underneath — as many as six or eight or ten words. More than that, for older students. But not many more. You'll want to set limits.

And while they are writing, you're busy, too. You're writing as fast as you can on the chalkboard, filling in spaces around the original "chain," so when students look up at the end of their lists, they'll see something like this:

When my grandfather clock ate
            the time and I missed
            my lunch, I
        felt as awful as
            a monster
        at the movies when no one
    will share popcorn with him.

It looks like a poem. It sounds like a poem. No one would call it great, but that isn't the point. The point is that again, as in making the chain, you've shown how it's possible to write something off the top of your head — something you hadn't planned to say. There's lots of stuff in your head, you tell your students. Some of it's bound to be good, and surprises are interesting. How will you know what might happen unless you try?

In fact, this same chain could have produced an entirely different poem. For illustration, you might erase everything you've written except for the original chain, and ask students to help fill in the blanks this time with their own words — maybe one sentence per line, instead of one long sentence. Possibilities can go on as long as attention spans, until each student has turned back to his or her own paper, filling in around the chains, producing what looks, sounds, and feels like a poem. Here's one example of what happened with the word "fence" in a fifth-grade class at Dunn School in Eugene, Oregon:

The fence sits
byastick,guarding
the garden of
bluegrapeschanging
to wine over
chilled ice.
Peaches burn to
acityofraspberries.

Don't fence me in,
for the gate is locked, and there
is no other door.
Not even a window to look through.
Let me see. Help me recover
from blindness. I have
no imagination.

The fence
trapped someone.
Don't be afraid, even
though you're care-
less like a monkey
swinging on a swing
in the park
on the playground.

Compounding such variety by 20 or more "chain poems" from the same class, each starting with the word "fence," the point has been made by the students themselves: they *can* write something that resembles a poem; they *can each* be original, mainly by being themselves. Engaged right from the first in a nonthreatening, noncompetitive, indeed a playful writing exercise, everyone "wins." With exceptions too few to mention, everyone who is able to write, at whatever level of proficiency, is able to do this assignment (which is one of the reasons that in my role as visiting poet I make this the first assignment each time I meet several dozen new classes each year). Likewise, I believe that every teacher — at whatever grade level, with whatever background he or she has or hasn't had in poetry — can have fun with it in the classroom (another reason for the editorial "you" of the preceding pages). You can do it and introduce poetry in a way that's both instructive and entertaining.

Fun is one of two main objectives here: fun for both teacher and student, writing the poems and reading (or hearing them read) aloud, noting the many directions thoughts can go, even when they've started all in the same place. *Later* you and the students can recognize room for improvement. *Later* they will care enough, it is hoped, about their work to want to learn to revise, to learn technique, to correct their spelling, to make a "neat sheet" out of their "sloppy copy." In fact, within a very few classroom meetings I approach other things: musical language, rhythms, patterns of repetition, metaphor, and other formal techniques. But first, students have had a chance to discover some of the reasons for learning these things; they've discovered that they have something to write about, even when they think they haven't.

And perhaps this discovery, made early enough, or strongly enough, will help prevent some of the agonies, some of the stumbles we as teachers no doubt have experienced in our own writing careers: the uncertainties and self-doubts about the merits of our ideas; the feeling that we can't begin to write until we know exactly what we're going to say; and what we think of to say has already been said before. (Sound familiar?)

Frustrated once myself (and not just for the first time), I found myself one day with unexpected free time, private space, a restless urge to write a poem, any poem — and with nothing to write about. Nothing came to mind. At least nothing I thought was any good — until finally, out of desperation and a need to do something, I started to follow the advice I'd been giving my class (of college students, at that time), and I wrote down the objects of my attention: the things that were keeping me from writing, the things immediately around me that were so ingrained in my total feelings of the moment I couldn't ignore them. I fully expected to throw away what I wrote, thinking I was just using my words as catharsis, and that the "real" poem would come after I'd cleared my head. It came. But not in the way I expected, for not only did the list of frustrations show some unity, some cohesion in imagery, but it led into the theme of the "real" poem itself.

Feeling Dry

To want to write, but to lack words.
More accurately, to lack some
thing to feel.

This unpainted
desk, cars outside
proving themselves on the hill,
smoke from burning fields
slipping unnoticed under the sun
until someone drowns
in his own breath.

To listen for some wind.

To feel responsible for listening
and to be unmoved, an air sock
limp as an unfilled dunce's cap
waiting some change in the weather,
something full as the river
you fished last weekend
without luck

and then swimming saw
the whitefish
grazing on stones

the flickering trout steady
as mobiles suspended
on more levels
than you thought water
could contain.

What I hadn't expected when I began to write was that I'd remember the river experience — a very real, very beautiful time which I'd wanted to write about when I was living it but hadn't the words right then, or the approach, and so had let it go by. In fact, I didn't think of writing about it again until I'd written the phrase "something full as ...," which itself came directly from the image of the "unfilled dunce's cap." I wanted an image that would be the opposite of empty; I needed an example from my immediate experience. It was natural to remember the river.

But again, what wasn't planned (indeed I wasn't conscious of it until teaching the poem, some months later) was that the image of the river, with the accompanying images of fishing, swimming, and seeing the fish (something that really happened), would turn out to be so appropriately symbolic of the creative act itself. Trying so hard to get a fish, to catch one with my "blind" line, and failing to get one, I'd concluded there weren't any there. But having donned face mask and snorkel, and letting myself drift with the current down the Middle Fork of the Willamette River, I was both surprised and chagrined: How could I have been so wrong? (How could I also have thought, writing, I had nothing "to feel"?)

Learning to write quickly, to take notes as fast as I think, to give whatever pops into my mind a chance to enlighten the rest (by comparison or juxtaposition), has been perhaps the single most difficult thing for me to learn about writing. Every time I write I still have to remind myself it's all right to proceed even when I sometimes don't know what I'm saying, to use the margins, to scribble if necessary, to trust stray thoughts, even if off the subject, because (who knows?) they might just be valuable. And in this I suspect I'm not alone. Judging from conversations with friends and statements made by other writers, I've discovered that many things can get in the way of the creative process. Until one is free to drift with the current, to see the many levels "water can contain," it's unlikely we'll see any fish.

Perhaps even more important than fun, then, is this second objective in writing "chain poems": to learn that writing can be truly an "act of discovery"; and that if we can just relax enough to let ourselves *be* ourselves — to trust our sometimes wildly erratic impulses, getting off the subject and following tangents when necessary — we'll usually find something to say. That something might be funny, or serious, or sad; ordinary or sparkling. But it probably wouldn't be found by adhering to an outline or knowing in advance what the poem was going to be about or "to mean."

Different from what most of us have been taught to teach, writing poems depends somewhat on forgetting the rules, on not struggling to do it the "right" way, to say the "right" things. Not that technique isn't important, nor that form and function don't often go together; often I find that technique leads me into using certain words, which in turn prompt new ideas, and so on, happily! But I would prefer to let technique act in the service of words, rather than let it control them. To let students discover that by finding their own things to say, they might someday find ways to say them better: to learn, first, to trust themselves — which, I discover, having written all this so far, I find is what I'm really writing about.

14

Poetry and the Composing Process:
A Whole Language Approach

Denny Wolfe

According to legend, Robert Frost once sat in the back of a one-room schoolhouse in New England, listening to a teacher "teach" his "Stopping by Woods on a Snowy Evening." By "teach," I mean dissect and particularize the poem's elements. At the end of the lesson, the teacher — breathless, smug, and content — said to the poet, "Now, Mr. Frost, tell us what you really meant by that last stanza." Frost reportedly rose from his seat, stretched, hesitated dramatically, and declared, "What I *really* meant was that it was time for my little horse and me to get the hell out of there." At least Frost was invited to respond. That's much better treatment than most students probably received in that classroom. Yet instruction in poetry must be response-centered if teachers are ever to penetrate the prejudices which students hold toward the genre.

Further, students must be led to see how and why some people actually spend agonizing hours writing poetry, as well as how and why some people actually spend equally agonizing hours reading what poets write. And they must be led to see that the reward for the agony is delight, ultimate and serene. Obviously, in the beginning, instruction should emphasize the delight and minimize the agony. But honesty must prevail, and if the teaching approach goes right, students will move on their own, at their own individual paces and levels of readiness, from delight to agony and — we must hope — back again to delight. The best chance we have to help students end with delight is to establish a process for teaching that reflects the way real poets construct poems and the way real readers read them.

The Composing Process

In the figure shown is a pattern, followed by discussion, which illustrates such a process.

I doubt seriously that Wordsworth bounded out of bed one morning in the English Lake Country, ran downstairs and announced to his sister Dorothy that his "heart leaps up" each time he "beholds a rainbow in the sky." And, even if it did happen that way, I'll wager that Wordsworth didn't say such a thing without ever having seen a rainbow. It is significant to recall how he defined poetry in the Preface to *Lyrical Ballads*: ". . . the spontaneous overflow of powerful feelings; it takes its origin from emotion *recollected in tranquility*" (italics mine). The writing of a poem begins, then, with an *experience*—an event, an encounter, an engagement, a connection, a discovery, a dilemma. In short, the writing of a poem begins with a *stimulus*. The stimulus is at the core of the way the composing goes and the way instruction should go. It is the first phase in moving students toward composing poems, as well as toward reading them.

A clear charge to teachers, therefore, is to create an experience which can stimulate the student's thought, feeling, and imagination. As an example, a teacher might ask students to rise from their seats, stand in a comfortable posture, close their eyes, and relax. They must think of nothing—perhaps a blank movie screen will do. The teacher suggests that they concentrate on relaxing their toes, ankles, calves, thighs, upper torsos, necks, and shoulders (much tension gets stored there), their fingers, forearms, biceps. They must begin to feel numb, floating free. "Now," they are told, "concentrate all your psychic energy into your *left* thumb. . . . You *are* your thumb. The rest of you is gone. All that is left is your thumb, and that's you. Now, open your eyes and pair off with a partner." At this point the teacher suggests several encounters: "Meet the other person as a friend." (Some students will forget they are their thumbs, so they must be reminded.) "Meet the other person as a boxer, a wrestler, a slithering snake, a blind person, a flesh-eating plant, a robot, a fish, an invisible person, a lover." At this point the students may sit down. The stimulus has been provided.

In the second phase, students are asked to *reflect* on the experience — to *recollect in tranquility*. They must recall the encounters and think of what they did and felt. They must remember which encounter they felt most strongly about, or which one perhaps triggered a thought or memory worth pursuing further.

The students are almost ready for the next phase in the process. So far, two crucial steps have been taken: (1) the teacher has provided the *stimulus*, and (2) the students have begun to respond to it and to *reflect* on how it made them feel. Before students move to the third phase in the process, however, the teacher provides a bit of "direct" instruction about haiku poetry, pointing to its structural requirements of three verses with a 5−7−5 syllable count in the sequence of lines, for a total of 17 syllables in the poem. The teacher should also mention certain characteristics of the content in haiku, i.e., what the haiku poet is attempting to achieve. There are almost invariably two or more images which somehow merge to create a sense of universal harmony and unity as an overall effect of the poem. Perhaps the most famous haiku poem in Japan, which Japanese people know as well as Americans know nursery rhymes, goes this way in translation (the English does not contain the 5−7−5 syllable count):

> Old pond
> Frog leaps in
> Splashing water

Amy Lowell's "Staying in My Room" is an example of American haiku, which does conform to the 5−7−5 syllable count, and there are many others for students to see. Several excellent sources include: R. H. Blyth (ed.), *A History of Haiku* (Tokyo: The Hokuseido Press, 1963); Harold G. Henderson (ed.), *An Introduction to Haiku* (Garden City, NY: Doubleday, 1958); *Issa, The Year of My Life*, trans. by Hobuyuki Yuasa (Los Angeles: University of California Press, 1972); and Kenneth Yasuda, *The Japanese Haiku* (Bloomington, IN: Indiana University Press, 1975).

The third phase of the process has to do with *selection*. The teacher has assigned the form. Each student will write a haiku (obviously, other forms could be used: cinquain, concrete poetry, "guided" poetry, based on phrases to complete or short questions to answer—many options exist; I am using haiku as an example to define the process approach). The students must select an image from the several encounters with their thumbs: friend, boxer, wrestler, snake, blind person, flesh-eating plant, robot, invisible person, lover. Who knows where the images will lead? The actual poems which students write may contain no direct references at all to the specific stimulus. The stimulus may serve strictly as a mnemonic device, triggering a memory of another experience, real or imagined.

Phase four is a *zero draft*, a jotting down of possible images, phrases, comparisons, descriptive words—in short, a "bank" to draw on for the first draft. The zero draft may be a series of questions, a sketch, or an outline. It may be a word association game that the student plays with himself or herself—perhaps written as a "cluster" with a "core" word or words (images, really) placed in the center of a blank page and associative words encircling it. (My diagram of the process I am describing might be viewed as an exercise in "clustering.") Then the associative words may lead to still more associations, until the student discovers some direction for the next phase.

In the fifth phase, students write their *first drafts*, attending to both the structural and content requirements of the haiku form. Line by line, students will be making diction choices which may be changed as they go to conform to syllable counts and to achieve the harmony of images which the haiku demands. Revision often occurs during the drafting process itself—it is not always a separate and distinct phase.

The sixth phase calls for a *peer review*. Students exchange poems with their partners in the "thumbs exercise." As they read each other's drafts, they are to make at least one complimentary comment and at least one suggestion for possible strengthening of the drafts. The quality and amount of feedback one gets largely depend upon questions the writer asks of the peer reviewer. The teacher should ask students to consider diction choices particularly, noting Coleridge's famous distinction between prose and poetry: *prose*, words in their best order: *poetry*, the best words in their best order.

The seventh phase is for *revision*. Students get their poems back and consider the feedback they have received. The feedback comes both from peer reviewers and from the writer's own continual reflection. The writer will reconsider the stimulus, the tentative selection of images he or she has made, and the "bank" created by the zero draft. The writer always functions as executive decision maker; that is, only the writer can decide which feedback to use and how to use it in making revisions.

As a *culminating activity*, in the eighth phase, the teacher asks for
several volunteers to write their haiku poems on the chalkboard. An
added "wrinkle," though, is that the volunteers are instructed to leave
out every third word, drawing lines to equal length in the spaces left by
the omitted words. Once the poems appear on the board, the class
attempts to supply the missing words in oral discussions of the poems.
This activity enables students to "publish" their work, enlarge their
vocabularies, further recognize the importance of revision, further
engage in critical and creative thinking, and — certainly not least — begin
to appreciate the craft of making poems. After a discussion of each
poem, the writer reveals his or her own answers to the missing words.
The writer is the lone "authority" as to the "truth" of the missing
words.

Haiku poems that secondary students have written when I have
conducted this activity include the following samples:

My self met her self.
Wrestled playfully awhile,
Suddenly to love.
                    (ninth grader)

Photosynthesis
Spectrum of light invading,
Making the world green.
                    (tenth grader)

Serpents entangled,
Slithering for advantage,
Conquering their fears.
                    (eleventh grader)

Venus sits waiting;
A lightning bug approaches—
The strongest survives.
                    (twelfth grader)

Man making robots
To do his labor for him—
Just one soul to share.
                    (twelfth grader)

Engaging students in the practice of making poems as a prerequisite
to reading them can combat the difficulties I cited at the beginning.
Students who write poems can learn to relate to poets, thereby breaking down prejudicial stereotypes which have made poets seem dilet-
tantish and unfathomable. And teachers, discovering that their students
can and will actually write poems, may not be so inclined to begin
instruction reductively. Finally, poems which students write do not
seem to abhor instruction. Like Frost in the New England classroom,

the poet is present to express his or her own "truths" and to untangle confused intentions. From a writing approach to the teaching of poems, teachers can lead students toward higher levels of meaning-making with poetry in the classroom.

15

Solving the Poetry Riddle

James S. Mullican

Too many young people profess to hate poetry. As children they loved nursery rhymes and stories in rhythmic, rhyming verse, and as adolescents and young adults they retain their affection for verse in popular songs. Yet in the English classroom they profess to hate poetry. For these young people, poetry consists largely of "deep meanings" understood only by teachers. Many of these young people don't like what one of my students called the "shredding of poetry" for the purpose of sifting out that last bit of meaning in a poem. I'm sure that this student and many others like her would agree with Wordsworth that too often we "murder to dissect."

We can, I am sure, lure some of our students into a renewed liking for poetry by returning, with appropriate adaptations, to their childhood loves. We can read to them narrative poems and light verse. We probably should do more of this kind of exercise, since a good story, rollicking rhythm and rhyme, and humor are attractive qualities in many poems, and students should be made aware of these qualities. Not all poems are "deep."

Yet too much lightness can be a cop-out. Experienced teachers know that much of the best poetry is complex, subtle, and difficult and that some of the pleasure of reading poetry resides in wrenching meaning from complex, dense, and puzzling poetry. We teachers would like to share our enjoyment of excellent poetry with our students, and we would like to assist our students in gaining the skills necessary to read such poetry. Our problem is to find ways of presenting such poetry in a pleasing, nonthreatening manner. One solution that I have discovered is to present poems explicitly as riddles. I begin by reading aloud some of the riddle poems in May Swenson's *Poems To Solve* (New York: Charles Scribner's Sons, 1966). After reading each poem aloud, I ask students to suggest answers to the riddle and "prove" their solutions by citing specific words in the poem. Sometimes I stop after a few lines and ask if anyone can solve the riddle before hearing the entire poem. I find that after a little practice both high school and college students become quite adept at solving these poetry riddles.

My next step is to present several other poems that are not explicit riddles but that have puzzling aspects that need to be solved. For example, I ask who are the narrators in Wolcott Gibb's "Declaration of Independence," in John Crowe Ransom's "Blue Girls," and in Theodore Roethke's "My Papa's Waltz." Sometimes solving the riddle consists of supplying titles to poems whose titles I have omitted: Plath's "Mushrooms," Yeats's "Father and Child," Tennyson's "The Eagle," and Langston Hughes's "Mother to Son" have proved excellent for this exercise. I cite these examples because they are rather well-known, but I find some of my best poetry riddles in current magazines. Somehow poems seem more real and relevant to students when they are located in current magazines. For several years, for example, I used Richard Peck's "Nancy" (*Saturday Review* [June 21, 1969]: 6) as a riddle or puzzle; students tried to discover who Nancy was (an alienated high school or college student), who the narrator was (a teacher), and what dramatic action was implied in the poem (a confrontation based on "relevance" and "the generation gap"). Students in the early 70s found much to empathize with in the antiestablishment protagonist portrayed in the poem. By the mid-70s, however, I found students required "historical" background to understand the poem, and its day in my classroom was done. An advantage of using magazines is that they permit us to exploit the interests of the day; unfortunately, the occasional nature of many of these poems condemns even the best of them to obsolescence.

After the foregoing exercises, students are ready to become involved in locating riddle poems. I ask students, in groups of three, to search out poems, not usually taught in school, which they find puzzling in some way. Sufficient copies are to be brought to class so that everyone can have a copy. I've found that having three students lead the discussion diffuses responsibility among the students and relieves the pressure on them. The selectors are at least potentially more expert concerning their poem than anyone else in the classroom, including the teacher, since only the selectors have had certain access to the poem before class.

Once three high school students in our honors seminar brought Sylvia Plath's poem, "Metaphors," from *The Collected Poems of Sylvia Plath* (New York: Harper & Row, 1981) to class. This poem proved perfect for my purposes, since it explicitly proclaims itself a riddle. The class struggled through the poem, admiring the imagery but not solving the riddle, until someone suggested tentatively: "Could the narrator of the poem be pregnant?" Once the question was asked, the answer was obvious, and many students joined in to show how each detail fit in with the suggested solution. Someone pointed out that even the nine syllables in "I'm a riddle in nine syllables" were not arbitrary, since they corresponded with the nine months of human gestation. Then someone discovered that there are nine lines in the poem and nine syllables in each line.

In setting up the ground rules for solving poetry riddles, I have found Laurence Perrine's "The Nature of Proof in the Interpretation of Poetry" (*English Journal*, 51 [September 1962]: 393–98) most helpful. Perrine contends that we should consider all the details in a poem as data in demonstrating proof for any interpretation. Any solution to a poetic riddle must account for all the details in a poem; the interpretation that accounts for all the details in the simplest way is the best. Class discussion thus has a rational basis and a norm for testing the validity of answers.

After the experience of working with poetic riddles in the classroom, I discovered an article that offers some reasons why this approach can be successful: S. I. Sackett's "Poetry and Folklore: Some Points of Affinity" (*Journal of American Folklore*, 77 [April/June 1964]: 142–53). In this article, Sackett contends that the appeal of metaphor stems from its nature as a riddle, something that all cultures find attractive. We enjoy solving riddles because "It is only human for us to feel pleased with ourselves for having solved a problem." Approaching the poem as riddle, according to Sackett, can also induce the reader to cooperate in the enactment of a poem: "Through the use of metaphor, the poet brings the reader into the poetic process as a participant, and the reader must guess the metaphor before he can read the poem with any degree of comprehension." By regarding some poems — or parts of poems — as riddles, Sackett has located at least one source of the enjoyment of complex poetry: reading such poetry is "a natural human activity deriving from natural human impulses and appealing to natural human instincts." If Sackett is correct — and I think that he is — treating some poems as riddles is not merely using sugar to make the medicine go down. Decoding the metaphor — or solving the riddle — is the essence of reading and enjoying some poetry.

My proposals for teaching poetry riddles are modest: (1) use the more familiar and more attractive term: a riddle is less intimidating than a deep meaning; (2) begin with riddles that students can solve and work gradually toward more difficult poetry; and (3) involve students in locating and solving poetic riddles, giving them the opportunity to become the experts.

As teachers and students work toward meaning through questioning, probing, offering tentative solutions, making errors and correcting them, they solve more than the riddle before them. They come to understand something of the reading process and the ways in which we arrive at meaning, using the poem, as I. A. Richards suggested, as "a machine to think with." In the process, we can all rediscover another pleasure of childhood, solving riddles.

16

Dramatizing the Shape and Sound of Poetry

Charles R. Duke

Not surprisingly, poetry usually does not rank among the favorite types of literature for adolescents or for adults. Part of the reason for this may well be how we have presented poetry in the classroom.

Many students have not had the opportunity to fully savor the shape and sounds of poetry nor have they had a chance to fully engage the text. More frequently we as teachers have approached the teaching of poetry as if it were a trip through a foreign land. Just as newcomers to a land often find the natives' dialect strange, we assume that students will find the language of poetry strange; hence, an interpreter, the teacher, provides the necessary translation.

We know enough now about the reading process, however, to realize that such interpretive trips may be rewarding for the teacher but for young adolescents they primarily just reinforce the notion that poetry is something far removed from their everyday lives. Clearly we need to find ways that will help students enter the world of poetry to discover for themselves what rewarding experiences can be found there.

One approach for this purpose can be found in using various aspects of creative dramatics to unlock the poetic text. Creative drama refers to an "improvisational . . . . . process-centered form of drama in which participants are guided by a leader to imagine, enact, and reflect upon human experiences" (McCaslin 1985).

Whenever we turn to creative dramatics as a learning process, however, we must remember that unless students understand the process, they will need help in making connections between its elements and the poetry they read. What follows, then, is an approach for

126

integrating creative dramatics techniques with the study of literature, specifically poetry. Although this process takes time to implement, once students understand the power of drama, they will quickly become accustomed to using it as a natural process in understanding many kinds of literature.

Setting the Stage

Because dramatization in any form requires concentration, students need practice in finding a point of concentration (POC) and using it effectively. A simple strategy, developed originally by Viola Spolin (1963) as a warm-up technique for actors, can be done with almost any age group. Called "mirrors," the activity requires students to pair off and to work silently with each other. Basically, the partners face each other, with one designated as the initiator of the action, the other the mirror. The initiator begins a series of slow movements with hands, arms, face, entire body; the mirror reflects these movements. The objective is to become so synchronized in movement and so focused in concentration that the role of initiator and mirror can be switched back and forth between partners without interruption or oral communication. This activity should go on only long enough for students to feel comfortable with each other's movements. The teacher may wish to "side coach" at times, reminding the students to concentrate, not to talk, and to keep their movements slow and abstract.

Once students seem to be synchronized with each other's movements, they should be encouraged to discuss how they felt, what they observed, what was simple, what was difficult. To internalize the principle of point of concentration, students need to reflect on what they have been doing. After such a discussion, they can again turn to their partners and this time silently observe each other, trying to take in as many details as possible—clothing, hairstyle, jewelry, eye color, shoes, etc. Once students think they have a sharp mental image of their partners, they should turn their backs to each other and make three subtle changes in their own appearance; this might include putting a ring on another finger, unbuttoning one button, tucking a shirt in which had been on the outside, etc. After making the changes, students face their partners again and take turns attempting to identify the alterations in each other's appearance.

Without discussion following this activity, students then should sit at their desks and as rapidly as possible, without looking back at their partners, record as much specific detail as possible about each other. Side coaching here may prove helpful, reminding students to think of colors, position, etc. Students should be observed closely and when they seem to be having great difficulty listing additional details, they should be asked to draw a line at the bottom of their lists and then look at their partners one more time; any details they have missed, they should add to their lists below the line.

Upon completion of the listing, students should have the opportunity to comment on what kinds of details they were able to recall, which they overlooked, if any order emerged in their listing. Did they, for example, start with the head and work to the toes? Start with the feet and work to the head? Encourage students to reflect on why they approached the task as they did.

Following the discussion, students can then listen to the following two paragraphs, concentrating on identifying differences between the two:

A. Sally Jones has blonde hair, blue eyes, and stands about 5'4" tall. She wears wire-rimmed glasses and has a thin gold chain around her neck. Her ears are large, her nose small, and her mouth about average. She is wearing a white blouse, open at the neck, a large red belt, and designer jeans. Her shoes have high, pointed heels and no back. There is a high school ring on her fourth finger of the right hand and a large ornate silver ring (it looks Mexican) on the middle of her left hand.

B. Joe Smith looks tired. The medium-length brown hair that only partly covers his head is lifeless and thinning. His gray eyes are only half open, and his lower lids sag down beside his large, pockmarked nose. His large mouth literally droops at the corners. His face is quite pale. Joe is wearing scuffed brown loafers, baggy tan corduroy pants, and a faded blue flannel shirt, only partly tucked in.

Students will quickly identify the major difference between the two paragraphs—a matter of focus. Where Sally is described in catalog fashion, the details about Joe all contribute to a dominant impression. Students usually agree that concentrating the details on a single image tends to leave a stronger impression with the reader or listener. At this point, students can be invited to develop their own paragraphs of description, drawing upon the items in their lists, and be encouraged to make these descriptions as detailed and as focused as possible, since they will be exchanging their drafts with their partners for reaction.

Establishing Context

After students seem to have grasped the principle of POC, they are ready to move on to an understanding about the importance of context for meaning. Students should be placed in groups of five or six, with each group being provided a single word; some which work particularly well include *happiness*, *sadness*, *patriotism*, *friendliness*, *love*, *joy*, *liberty*, and *suspicion*. Each group is charged with the task of deciding how best to represent as many meanings of this word as they can nonverbally. Because most students have at least heard of the game charades, they usually grasp the principle of the activity quickly. They should talk in their groups about how to arrange their bodies, facial expressions, use of space, etc., in such a way that other people might be able to determine what word is being represented. Five to ten minutes is usually sufficient planning time.

Each group is asked to set itself up at the front of the class; upon the signal "freeze," the group assumes and holds its positions for a minute; then the rest of the class is asked to determine what word is being represented. Discussion should focus on what elements of nonverbal expression helped the class identify the word. Each group takes a turn in this process. If each tableau is videotaped, the discussion can become more detailed.

To help students understand more about the importance of how each individual may or may not bring a special context to a word, several groups may be given the same word. Discussion can also center on symbols that may have been created by the groups such as a representation of the Statue of Liberty to suggest liberty. Students need to realize that if they had not seen pictures of the statue, they might not have that context for what they saw. These tableaus, then, help to reinforce how important the context is which viewers — and readers — may bring to the page and how important it may be for an author to select symbols familiar to a large number of readers.

Following the tableau discussion, students can then develop active tableaus with oral text. This activity may be done in class or students can be given the necessary instructions and then make preparations outside of class time. Again students work in groups of five to eight and are provided with copies of a poem such as the following by George Cooper (Sechrist 1946) where images and a sequence of action predominate.

The Wonderful Weaver

There's a wonderful weaver
　High up in the air,
And he weaves a white mantle
　For cold earth to wear
With the wind for his shuttle,
　The cloud for his loom,
How he weaves, how he weaves,
　In the light, in the gloom.
Oh, with finest of laces
　He decks bush and tree,

On the bare, flinty meadows
　　A cover lays he.
Then a quaint cap he places
　　On pillar and post
And he changes the pump
　　To a grim, silent ghost.
But this wonderful weaver
　　Grows weary at last,
And the shuttle lies idle
　　That once flew so fast;
Then the sun peeps abroad
　　On the work that is done;
And he smiles: "I'll unravel
　　It all just for fun!"

Students are to read the poem in their groups and arrive at a consensus as to what the poem means to them. Then they decide on how they will mime their interpretation. One person is selected to serve as the narrator and will read the poem aloud as the rest of the group mimes their interpretation. For the most part, props and lighting effects should be discouraged, but most groups will want to do a little practicing before their presentation. Care should be taken, however, to keep practice to a minimum so the presentation is as improvisational as possible.

When students are ready — twenty-five minutes is usually sufficient preparation time — each group can make its presentation to the class. Again, videotaping the presentations is helpful, since they may be shown and discussed in greater detail later if time becomes a factor. Emphasis should be placed on discussing the differences and similarities in interpretation which will arise from this approach, causing students once again to consider the importance of context and reader/viewer experience.

Adding the Voices

One of the most difficult elements in literature for many students to grasp is the concept of voice. Although students are accustomed to identifying speakers in short stories, novels, and plays, they may not be as alert to finding the significance of voice in poetry; this happens most often because the conventional signals of dialogue often do not appear in poems and not infrequently the speaker is providing an internal monologue or, as in Robert Browning's "My Last Duchess," a dramatic monologue.

Because of these voice difficulties, students can benefit from practice which, once again, engages them directly with a text and helps them identify roles to play. One method to dramatize the importance of voice is an activity called "Hearing Voices," adapted from William Strong (1981). Students receive the following handout.

Hearing Voices

Directions: Note that the following sentences are clustered in pairs. In the space beneath each cluster or beside it, combine the sentences into one; work for conciseness wherever possible. As you work through the clusters, you should detect an emerging pattern. Try to continue that pattern according to the directions which appear at the end of the last cluster.

1. I have two voices.
2. The voices are always with me.

3. One voice is always joking.
4. It is always looking for fun.

5. The other voice is somber.
6. It views life seriously.

7. One voice is for outside of class.
8. The other voice is for learning.

9. One voice is for finding escape.
10. The other voice is for finding a job.

11. One voice believes in living for the "now."
12. It believes in finding immediate pleasure.

13. The other voice has discipline.
14. It believes in working for future success.

15. The tension is real.
16. The tension is between these two voices.

Directions: Now that you have a sense of the two voices, identify a real situation in which these two voices might debate each other. Use the same pattern as emerged from the clusters to develop a dialogue between the two voices. Remember to keep the two voices "in character." Try to reach some kind of resolution or settlement between the two voices at the end of your dialogue. Hint: You could start your dialogue by establishing a context or setting for it, using a sentence such as "I often have a tough time making decisions. Just the other day, I got into an argument with myself about. ... I can still hear my two voices. ..."

Use the back of this sheet to develop your dialogue. When you finish your script of the dialogue, read your draft aloud to a partner; see if that person recognizes the difference between your two voices.

Students actually produce scripts as a result of this kind of activity and can pair off to practice with a partner and then take turns presenting their scripts. These readings can be taped and then used for later discussion as well. A very useful adjunct to this activity is to have students exchange scripts and read them back to each other; the

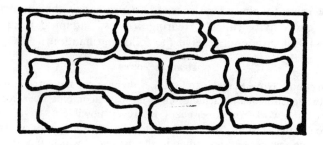

Stone Pattern for "Mending Wall" Sequence

authors then have an opportunity to determine how others are hearing their voices and how true their "reading" is in reflecting the tones the authors intended.

After students have had experiences such as have been outlined here, they should be ready to weave all of these elements into a full-fledged lesson which encompasses a number of dramatic elements to reinforce the meaning of a poem. Here is such a sequence based on Robert Frost's "Mending Wall," adapted from a similar one developed by Margaret Grant, an elementary teacher in Missoula, Montana.

For this sequence, at least two class periods probably will be necessary. Materials needed include copies of Frost's "Mending Wall" (easily found in most American literature anthologies), a roll of butcher paper, and individual 8½″ × 11″ sheets of paper with large stones drawn on them, something like in the figure shown.

After students enter the classroom and take their seats, stretch a long strip of butcher paper down the middle of the room, leaving students at their seats on both sides of the paper. Make no comments while doing this, simply unroll the paper and fasten it at either end to the wall or a nearby desk or bookcase. Let students study this new arrangement for a few minutes and then begin a discussion with them about how they feel having such a "divider" or wall in the classroom. Encourage them to begin to identify other walls they believe are in their lives or that they have experienced.

Once the discussion begins to flow, pass out one of the 8½″ × 11″ "stone wall" sheets to each student. Ask students to identify the different kinds of walls they think exist in their own lives as well as the lives of others. They are to place the name of each wall within a "stone" on their papers. Encourage students not only to name their walls but to add details about them and to fill as many of the stones on their papers as possible.

After students have responded in writing, encourage them to pair off and discuss each other's walls. Following this activity, ask students to return to their papers and select one stone and "free write" about the wall it represents. Students should simply write as quickly and as fully as possible about any memories, associations, details, etc., that their wall suggests to them. Allow about two or three minutes for this activity; go longer if students appear to be involved. Then have students share their thoughts in small groups or the whole class. Summarize with the class what they feel about the walls in their lives or in the lives of others and ask them to determine if some walls are positive factors while others are negative. How do we know the difference?

At this point, "Mending Wall" is read aloud to the class if time permits, and students are asked to identify what they think is happening in the poem. Why is the wall-mending an annual ritual? Whose voices are heard in the poem? This part of the sequence can be assigned as homework if time becomes a factor.

The next step in the sequence is to place students in groups of three. Invite each of them to become the speaker in the poem who is writing in his journal late at night after having mended the wall. What is the writer thinking about? What might he like to say to his neighbor? Provide about five minutes for students to write a journal entry that they believe the writer might have created. Then have students share their journal entries with each other within the groups. Some of these can then be shared with the whole class if sufficient interest exists.

Following the sharing of the journal entries, have one student read "Mending Wall" aloud. As the student reads, the rest of the class is to think about the walls they identified on their papers earlier and what connections, if any, they might make between their walls and the ones being reflected in the poem. Invite students after the reading of the poem to share their ideas moving back and forth between their own walls and those they find in the poem.

With students still in groups of three, pass out envelopes to each group. Each envelope contains three different role cards, one for each member of the group. Each student must draw a card from the envelope but not share it with anyone else. Students are to assume the roles described on their cards and write from that viewpoint in the form suggested on the card. They should make every effort to become the "voice" of their character. Here are a variety of roles which might be used:

1. You are John, the neighbor in "Mending Wall." You have just finished walking the fence with Bob, the narrator of the poem. The fence-mending in order, you go home. Over cups of coffee with your wife, Sarah, you share your experience of mending the wall.

2. You are the narrator in "Mending Wall." You've walked and rebuilt the fence with your neighbor John today. Throughout the rest of the day, the scene has replayed itself in your mind. It is now evening. Write a letter to one of your close relatives who knows John. Reflect upon your time with John today.

3. You are Jim, the son of Bob, the narrator of "Mending Wall." Both your father and neighbor John have passed away. You've returned to your father's farm after a long absence to take one last look before the farm is sold. You decide to visit the mending wall. While walking the wall, you meet John's son, Jarvis, and the two of you strike up a conversation. Recreate the conversation that takes place.

4. You are Jarvis, the son of John, the neighbor in "Mending Wall." Both your father and his neighbor Bob have passed away. You've returned to your father's farm after a long absence, trying to decide if you want to live there. You decide to visit the mending wall. While walking the wall, you meet Bob's son, Jim, and the two of you strike up a conversation; recreate the conversation that takes place.

5. You are the narrator in "Mending Wall." You've walked and rebuilt the fence with your neighbor John today. Throughout the rest of the day the scene has replayed itself in your mind. It is now evening and you're relaxing with your newspaper in the kitchen while your wife, Mary, does the dishes. You find yourself wanting to talk to her about your time with John. Share your thoughts with her.

6. You are Bob, the narrator of "Mending Wall." Almost one year has passed since you and John last walked the wall. This morning you received a call from Sarah, John's wife, informing you of John's death and asking you to present the eulogy at his funeral in two days. Write the eulogy.

7. You are John, the neighbor in "Mending Wall." Almost one year has passed since you and your neighbor Bob last walked the fence to replace the stones. This morning you received a call from Mary, Bob's wife, informing you that Bob has passed away. Disturbed by the news, you decide to take a walk out to the wall. Your grand-daughter (or grandson), who is visiting, asks to come along. Together the two of you walk the wall. The grandson/daughter is curious as to why you're spending time walking along a dilapidated stone wall. How do you explain your action?

8. You are Sarah, the wife of neighbor John in "Mending Wall." Your husband has just completed walking the wall with his neighbor Bob, the narrator in "Mending Wall." You are in the

local grocery store, getting the week's groceries, when you encounter Mary, Bob's wife. The two of you strike up a conversation about your husbands' annual ritual of walking the wall. Recreate the conversation.

At this point, students may want to begin the dialogues in class and then finish them for homework. When students return to class, they should get into their groups and share their dialogues, reacting and assisting each other in clarifying and making as consistent as possible the voices that have emerged. Students may do some further revision and then the dialogues or monologues can be shared in larger groups or with the entire class.

An excellent application of drama at this point is to develop actual dramatizations where the class is divided into two large groups and students, where appropriate, work in pairs to present their scripted dialogues as a kind of improvised drama or readers' theatre. These might well be taped for later discussion or use in other classes. Students may wish to combine scripts they hear and produce one overall script with a number of scenes, in this way creating a dramatic rendition of the poem itself plus interpretations of how the action of the poem represents only one element in the lives of the people involved.

Approaches such as this focus students' attention on and promote direct, dramatic engagement with a poem's text rather than leaving students to stay on the outside, looking only at the teacher's staged interpretation. Creative dramatics techniques provide a route into a poem's text as well as a means for extending that text into a larger world. The directness and highly focused imagery of poetry motivate students to produce dramatic response that is original, spontaneous, and highly imaginative. And because the sound and shape of poetry have as great an appeal as the content and mood, the joining of drama and poetry seems a natural for the literature classroom.

Works Cited

McCaslin, Nellie. Fall 1985. "The Values of Drama and Theatre for Children and Young People Today." *English Language Arts Bulletin*, pp. 4–7.

Sechrist, Elizabeth Hough, ed. 1946. *One Thousand Poems for Children*. New York: McCrae Smith Co.

Spolin, Viola. 1963. *Improvisation for the Theatre*. Evanston, IL: Northwestern University Press.

Strong, William. 1981. *Sentence Combining and Paragraph Building*. New York: Random House.

17

"Into her snowy-white bosom/ They plunged a fatal knife" Teaching the Ballad

Danny L. Miller

Some teachers may shy away from teaching the ballad, expecting students to react in much the same way as they do the first time they are exposed to Shakespeare's language. Yet few types of poetry are as immediately accessible as the ballad. A popular form of poetry—that is, interesting *to* the people as well as "of the people"—ballads have been sung for centuries, and continue in popularity today as a type of contemporary music. The Beatles' "Eleanor Rigby," Suzanne Vega's "Luka," Billy Joel's "Down Easter Alexa," and Jimmy Buffett's "Changing Channels" use the ballad form. Even in the medieval period the popular form of the ballad was contrasted with its "elitist" counterparts, such as the more esoteric and intricate works of the Pearl Poet, "Sir Gawain and the Green Knight" or "The Pearl."

The primary reason for the accessibility of ballads lies in both their content and form. The content of ballads, that is, the stories they tell, is the kind of things we might read about in the daily paper (or, more rightly perhaps, the "scandal sheets" like the *National Enquirer* in the checkout lanes at the supermarket) and be shocked or horrified by: murder, rape, patricide, poisoning, ghostly visitations. A classroom activity in this connection might be to have students bring in some of the "scandal sheet" papers, look at the attention-grabbing headlines, and try to compose a ballad based on one of the stories (something like "The Ballad of Bigfoot's Baby" or "The Ballad of Princess Di"). The stories ballads tell are shocking and unusual, but the feelings they evoke are familiar to all because ballads arouse in us universal emotions such as love, anger, jealousy, or stubbornness.

The content of ballads should appeal to young readers. Murder, for instance, is the subject of a good number of ballads. In "Lord Randal," the reader learns that the handsome young Lord Randal has been poisoned by his "true-love." "Edward" tells the story of a son who kills his father. "Pretty Polly" recounts Willie's murder of "Pretty Polly" as he "stabbed her to the heart and her heart's blood did flow." And "Bonny Barbara Allen," perhaps one of the most famous ballads, is the tale of a girl who poisons a boy who has slighted her at a dance. Barbara then seems to repent and prepares to commit suicide.

Several of the Appalachian mountain ballads (as well as some of the Scottish and English ballads) were based on actual murders— "Tom Dooley" (popularized in the 60s by the Kingston Trio), "Lula Viers," and "Pearl Bryant," for example. Usually these ballads tell the story of a man or men killing a woman; often the motive for the murders is that the woman is pregnant with the man's child. Very often, too, the women suffer horrible grisly deaths which are vividly depicted, as in the following stanza from "Pearl Bryant," based on a murder which occurred near Fort Thomas, Kentucky, in 1896:

> While the banners waved above her
> The shrill was a mournful sound
> A stranger came and found her
> Cold, headless on the ground.

Another example comes from the murder ballad "Knoxville Girl":

> I took her by her golden curls,
> I throwed her round and round;
> I throwed her into the river
> That flows through Knoxville town.

These exciting stories should find an eager audience in junior high and high school students, steeped as they are in eerie films of terror and murder such as "Halloween" or the series of "Friday the Thirteenth" movies.

"The Wife of Usher's Well" is a ghost story, which should also interest the junior high school audience. "The Wife of Usher's Well" is the story of an old woman whose three sons have drowned at sea, but who return to sit up with her one night:

> It fell about the Martinmass,
>   When nights are long and mirk,
> The carline wife's three sons came home,
>   And their hats were o the birk.

> It neither grew in syke nor ditch,
>   Nor yet in any sheugh;
> But at the gates o Paradise,
>   That birk grew fair eneugh.

The fact that the sons' hats are not made of any earthly material, but of something growing by the gates of heaven, indicates that the sons are ghostly visitors to their mother.

Some ballads have a bizarre twist or a macabre sense of humor. "The Twa Corbies," for instance, takes the interesting narrative approach of having the first person speaker ("as I walked all alone") give up his role as speaker to the two ravens he overhears (in a rather supernatural twist, the two ravens are speaking—a la Heckle and Jeckle) discussing their dinner. The dinner they are discussing, we soon find out, is the corpse of a slain knight. The knight has been killed by his lover, a fact which the reader deduces based on the knowledge that the knight's lady is the only one who knows where his dead body lies rotting. But this murder story seems an incidental sidelight in the ballad; the main focus is on "the twa corbies" as they gleefully discuss sitting on the corpse and picking the bones clean, plucking out his bonny blue eyes, and pulling out his golden hair to feather their nest.

The ballad "Get Up and Bar the Door" is one of the few humorous ballads. It is a description of a husband and wife who argue over who will bar the door. On a cold and windy night, the husband tells his wife to "go out and bar the door":

> It fell about the Martinmas time,
>   And a gay time it was then,
> When our goodwife got puddings to make
>   And she's boiled them in the pan.

> The wind sae cauld blew south and north
>   And blew into the floor;
> Quoth our goodman to our goodwife,
>   "Gae out and bar the door."

The goodwife refuses her husband's command, for she is busy cooking, and so they make a pact that the first one who speaks will have to bar the door. Around midnight two travelers come to their house, but the visitors cannot get either the goodman or his wife to answer them since neither one wants to be the first to speak. Finally, perhaps in an attempt to provoke them to speak:

> Then said the one [visitor] unto the other,
>   "Here, man, tak ye my knife;
> Do ye tak off the auld man's beard,
>   And I'll kiss the goodwife."

At this point, the old man speaks up angrily in defense of house and wife: "Will ye kiss my wife before my een [eyes],/And scad me wi pudding bree [scald me with hot pudding]?" The hilarious climax, of course, comes when the wife wins the bet despite (or in fact because of) her husband's gallant chivalry:

> Then up and started our goodwife,
>   Gied three skips on the floor:
> "Goodman, you've spoken the foremost word,
>   Get up and bar the door!"

Ballads are also appealing to young readers and writers of poetry because of their narrative and dramatic form. Ballads are immediately accessible because they are *narrative* poems, that is, they tell a story, usually in a straightforward chronological way. In addition, they usually describe, often through dialogue, one immediate dramatic action or episode: "Edward," for example, presents a mother's relentless questioning of her distraught and bloody son as to why he has come this way; "The Twa Corbies" portrays the humorous conversation between two ravens, leading up to a more serious revelation of murder; "Lord Randal" shows a slighted lover's revenge, again, as in "Edward," through a dialogue between mother and son. This compression and intensity of action produce a strong sense of immediacy and drama in ballads. "Pretty Polly," for example, conveys the dramatic intensity of Polly's murder:

Pretty Polly

> I courted Pretty Polly the live long night
> Then left her next morning before it was light.
>
> O Polly, pretty Polly come go away with me
> Before we get married, some pleasure to see.
>
> He led her over the fields and the valleys so wide
> Until pretty Polly, she fell by his side.
>
> Oh Willie, oh Willie, I'm afraid of your ways,
> I'm afraid you will lead my poor body astray.
>
> Polly, pretty Polly, you're guessin' just about right
> I dug on your grave the best part of last night.
>
> She threw her arms around him and trembled with fear
> How can you kill the poor girl that loves you so dear?
>
> There's no time to talk and there's no time to stand.
> Then he drew his knife all in his right hand.
>
> He stabbed her to the heart and her heart's blood did flow
> And into the grave pretty Polly did go.
>
> Then he threw a little dirt over her and started for home
> Leavin' no one behind but the wild birds to moan.

Eliciting the formal aspects as students look at a ballad can lead to
lively class discussions. Ballads are built around the very accessible
formal principle of repetition. First, there is the repetition of certain
formulaic phrases from poem to poem (such as "it fell about the
Martinmass time" or he rode "a milk-white steed"). The choral refrain
is also a characteristic of many ballads, as in the famous chorus of
"Tom Dooley":

> Hang your head, Tom Dooley,
> Hang your head and cry;
> Killed little Laura Foster,
> Poor boy, you're bound to die.

In addition, many of the ballads follow a pattern of repetition which
helps to create a mood of suspense. Teachers might ask students, for
example, to consider how the pattern of questions and answers between
mothers and sons in "Edward" and "Lord Randal" helps to create the
intensity and suspense of the two ballads: Why are the questions and
answers repeated? Are there any variations in the repetition of the
questions and answers? Do the answers become increasingly angrier or
more revealing?

Lord Randal

"O where hae ye been, Lord Randal, my son?
O where hae ye been, my handsome young man?"
"I hae been to the wild wood; mother, make my bed soon,
For I'm weary wi' hunting, and fain wald lie down."

"Where gat ye your dinner, Lord Randal, my son?
Where gat ye your dinner, my handsome young man?"
"I dined wi' my true-love; mother, make my bed soon,
For I'm weary wi' hunting, and fain wald lie down."

"What gat ye to your dinner, Lord Randal, my son?
What gat ye to your dinner, my handsome young man?"
"A gat eels boil'd in broo; mother, make my bed soon,
For I'm weary wi' hunting, and fain would lie down."

"What became of your bloodhounds, Lord Randal, my son?
What became of your bloodhounds, my handsome young man?"
"O they swell'd and they died; mother, make my bed soon,
For I'm weary wi' hunting, and fain wald lie down."

"O I fear ye are poison'd, Lord Randal, my son!
O I fear ye are poison'd, my handsome young man!"
"O yes! I am poison'd; mother, make my bed soon,
For I'm sick at the heart, and fain wald lie down."

It is easy to see that the final line of "Lord Randal" has greater emotional impact on the reader because it changes the pattern established by the rest of the stanzas of the poem.

Often, within a ballad itself there will be repeated phrases or lines that help to give unity and perhaps add to the song-like quality of the poem. "Shady Grove" is a good example:

Shady Grove

Cheeks as red as the blooming rose, Eyes the deepest brown,
You're the darlin' of my heart, stay till the sun goes down.

Shady Grove, my little love, Shady Grove, my dear,
Shady Grove, my little love, I'm goin' to leave you here.

Shady Grove, my little love, Standin' in the door,
Shoes 'n stockings in her hand, little bare feet on the floor

Wish I had a big, fine horse, Corn to feed him on,
Pretty little girl to stay at home, feed him when I'm gone.

Shady Grove, my little love, Shady Grove, I say,
Shady Grove, my little love, Don't wait till Judgment Day.

As well as providing exciting content and an examination of some formal aspects of poetry, a study of ballads is valuable in at least two other ways. First, the study of ballads could be used by the teacher as a means of beginning to discuss context, especially historical context, in literature, a poem's relationship to the particular time and place in which it was created. Reading poetry perceptively often depends on reading it in the context in which it was written. The majority of the English and Scottish ballads were written during the fourteenth and fifteenth centuries. In the Appalachian region of the United States, ballads were produced in the eighteenth and nineteenth centuries. Looking at the ballads produced during these periods is a good way to begin to discuss the historical and cultural context, such as the isolation of the Appalachian region, which resulted in the perpetuation of the old ballads into the twentieth century. However, it may also be a valuable lesson to young students to learn that feelings and emotions have remained pretty much the same for hundreds of years. The basic emotions of love, anger, pride, jealousy, stubbornness, gloating, etc., which ballads are based upon are remarkably unchanged even today.

Secondly, teachers can use a discussion of ballads to introduce a rudimentary exploration of different critical approaches which will be valuable in reading literature in general. It is not too early even in junior high school to begin to discuss different ways of looking at literature — the idea that there are no single "answers" in the exploration of poetry, but just different ways of seeking those answers. For instance, the historical approach noted above might be one way of examining the ballads, and an insight from this kind of exploration would be that the themes and subjects of the ballads — some sung as long ago as five to six hundred years — are very much the same as those of today.

Another critical approach might be attempting to explain the psychological motivations of the characters, such as "Edward" or "Bonny Barbara Allen." It might also be interesting to consider the motives behind the singing of the ballads. (Why were they so popular? What purposes did they serve?) Since the ballads are anonymous, a biographical approach would not be possible (but would help to show students the concept of biographical criticism). However, the teacher could discuss the fact that rather than having a single author, the ballads in fact were group productions, composed by the whole community which refined and perpetuated them. (See Suggested Classroom Activity "Writing a Ballad as a Group.")

There is some debate as to whether men or women were chiefly responsible for composing and passing the ballads from generation to generation, although it is generally agreed that it was mainly women. This suggests another critical approach, feminism. The ballads, in fact, have been analyzed by feminist critics who have seen in them an inordinate number of seduced and murdered women (the whole genre of murder ballads has this theme). But there are some women in the ballads who murder their lovers, and a ballad such as "Get Up and Bar the Door" could be seen as a statement of female triumph in the "battle of the sexes." By looking at the ballads from many different critical angles, students can become aware that there is not one single method of analyzing or writing poetry — and this should open many doors to them.

Some teachers might be a little reluctant to use ballads in junior high school classes because of their language, which may be a little difficult, or because of the somewhat "immoral" content in some of them. But the language, which may at first be perceived as a barrier (because of the unusual or different words and pronunciation) can in fact be used to spark an awareness of language differences and thus a focus on language itself.

I vividly remember my first introduction to ballads in high school. I remember especially how the title "The Twa Corbies" ("The Two Ravens") intrigued me. This is, in fact, one of my first real memories of being aware of language differences and thus of language itself. The peculiar Scottish words (or pronunciation) in this and other Scottish ballads caught my attention and led me to a fuller awareness of language in general — one of the major goals of any study of reading and writing poetry. That initial interest in language is perhaps what led me to a career in teaching English literature, and later an interest in Appalachian mountain literature and the Appalachian region where I am from and where many of the ballads continued to be sung well into the twentieth century. Certainly an awareness of language is one of the chief aims of a study of any genre of literature and the ballads served this function in my case.

Although telling stories of seduction, violence, and murder, ballads are traditionally ethical. Like most folklore/folktales, to which ballads are closely related, ballads traditionally affirm and reinforce the positive moral and ethical values of the common people — evil is punished. Tom Dooley hangs for his murder of Laura Foster; John Lewis rots in jail for the murder of Omie Wise, as does the murderer of the Knoxville Girl.

Overall, the potential value for younger readers and writers of poetry in studying ballads outweighs the disadvantages. The content of the ballads excites students' interest to the extent that they are willing to engage in a close reading of the texts. The narrative form helps as well, since it is one of the most familiar literary genres, and other formal features, such as repetition or formulaic phrases, are easily identified. And, finally, ballads are useful in discussing the historical contexts for literature and in introducing different critical approaches to a work.

Suggested Classroom Activities

Finding the Motive

One fun classroom activity related to the study of ballads might be "finding the motive." Ask students to search for clues as they read the ballads in order to fully understand what happens. In "Edward," for example, we have no ideas as to why Edward has murdered his father unless we closely examine his dialogue with his mother. Likewise, it is hard to tell why Bonny Barbara Allen has poisoned her lover, without a careful reading of the poem. The reader needs to determine the motives for the murders (or other actions), which are often only implied. Writing a one-paragraph explanation of the motives of the characters (such as "Why does Edward kill his father?") can lead to a lively class discussion as students compare answers.

Writing a Ballad as a Group

Since ballads were produced by the community at large and not by one single author, it would be useful to have the entire class work on writing (or "producing") a ballad. Students could take a newspaper account of a violent crime (most provocative, of course, would be the murder of a lover) and turn it into a ballad. Local folklore might provide the story idea for a ballad. In my community, there are many folk stories of ghostly hitchhikers or prom-night encounters with ghosts, for instance. The class could work on this in steps. First, they could develop a story line (the action). Next, the group could suggest first lines or work toward producing a refrain. Creating suspense and mystery could be a component of the group's production.

Acting Out or Dramatic Reading

Since many of the ballads are written in dialogue form, with one speaker asking questions and the other answering them, another classroom activity might be a dramatic reading by two class members, or even an acting out of the story.

Singing the Ballads in Class

Someone in class might play the guitar, or even perhaps the traditional mountain dulcimer, and might be prevailed upon to accompany her or himself or another student who would sing a ballad. Group singing of ballads, even without accompaniment, would be fun. A ballad like "Shady Grove" would be easy for this. Likewise, there are many recorded versions of the ballads which are available and interesting for the students to hear. (The names of several recordings which could be used are provided at the end of this essay.) In some areas, such as the Appalachian region or the Ozarks (and in other areas with visiting performers) traditional ballad singers might be invited to visit classes and sing the "old ballads."

Examining Modern Musical Ballads and Writing Songs

Another way of interesting students in the traditional ballad form and in poetry in general might be to discuss some of the modern musical ballads (any popular song that essentially tells a story). The Beatles' songs, like "Rocky Raccoon" or "Eleanor Rigby," are ideal for this purpose, and then there will always be popular new songs one can choose from (ask the students to name some). I have found that young people really like to write songs. I taught a group of fifteen- and sixteen-year-olds recently in an Upward Bound program. I asked them to keep a journal and told them that they could write whatever and however they wished. One young man, who was obviously experiencing a great deal of angst in love, wrote songs almost exclusively, especially about his painful love. If I had asked him to write "poetry" he would probably have thought I was crazy, but through the medium of his "songs" I was able to teach him about poetry.

Examining Modern Written Ballads

Several modern poets have written literary ballads which could be compared with the traditional forms. Charles Causey's "Ballad of the Faithless Wife" and William Stafford's "Traditional Ballad" are two of the best.

Recordings

One of the chief sources of records of ballads is Smithsonian/Folkways Records, which has over two thousand, many of them traditional Appalachian (and British and Scottish) ballads. Most of these recordings are available on cassette (not record) for $10.95 plus mailing. A catalog of the company's holding can be obtained from: **Smithsonian/Folkways Records, 955 L'Enfant Plaza, Suite 2600, Washington, DC 20506 (202-287-3251 or 202-287-3262).**

Three particular recordings of interest might be the following by Jean Ritchie, renowned ballad singer from Viper, Kentucky: *British Traditional Ballads in the Southern Mountains*, Volumes 1 and 2 (catalog numbers 23−01 and 23−02) and *The Ritchie Family of Kentucky* (catalog number 23−16). Jean Ritchie's own record label is: **Flying Fish, Inc., 1304 W. Schubert, Chicago, IL 60614.**

The Smithsonian Institution also will have available after July 1, 1991, a collection of folksongs, including several ballads (some sung by Jean Ritchie), entitled *Folk Song America: A Twentieth Century Revival* (6 LPs, 4 cassettes or CDs). This recording can be purchased by calling **1-800-336-5221.**

Betty Smith is another well-known singer of traditional ballads. On one album she sings a version of "Omie Wise." Smith's recordings can be obtained from: **Folk-Legacy Records, Inc., Sharon, Connecticut 06069.**

June-Appal Recordings, in connection with Appalshop of Whitesburg, Kentucky, has many recordings which contain traditional ballads. One can receive a catalog by writing: **June-Appal Recordings, Box 743, Whitesburg, Kentucky 41858.**

Lily May Ledford, one of the original Coon Creek Girls, sings "Pretty Polly" on the album *Kentucky Music Weekend*, distributed by: **Iroquois Amphitheater Association, Metro Parks and Recreation, P.O. Box 37280, Louisville, Kentucky 40233.**

The McLain Family Band also sings "Pretty Polly" on its first album and its album *In Concert at Carnegie Hall*. The McLain Family Band can be reached at: **The McLain Family Band, CPO 1322, Berea, Kentucky 40404, 606-986-8111.**

The Prairie Ramblers sing "Shady Grove" on the album *Kentucky Country*, distributed by: **Rounder Records, One Camp Street, Cambridge, Massachusetts 02140.**

Appendix: Three Appalachian Murder Ballads

This first ballad is based on the actual seduction, murder, and decapitation of Pearl Bryant near Fort Thomas, Kentucky, in 1896. Pearl's murderers, Walling and Jackson, two dental students from Louisville, were hanged for the crime.

Pearl Bryant

Down in a lonely valley
Where the fairest flowers bloom,
There's where poor Pearl Bryant
Lies mouldering in her tomb.

(chorus)
While the banners waved above her
The shrill was a mournful sound
A stranger came and found her
Cold, headless on the ground.

She died not broken-hearted
Nor by disease she fell,
But in a moment's parting
From the one she loved so well.

One night when the moon was shining
The stars were shining too.
Softly to her dwelling
Walling and Jackson drew.

They said, "Come, Pearl, let us wander
Down by these woods so gay;
Come, love, and let us ponder
Upon our wedding day."

The way seemed dark and dreary,
She was afraid to stay;
She says, "I am so weary
Let us retrace our way."

"Retrace our way? No, never,
Among these woods to roam;

You bid farewell forever
To parents, friends and home."

Down on her knees before them
She pleaded for her life;
Into her snowy-white bosom
They plunged a fatal knife.

"Dear Jackson, I'll forgive you,
Though this be my last breath;
You know I never deceived you,
Now close my eyes in death."

This next ballad is an Appalachian version with Knoxville as its setting
of an older English broadside entitled "The Berkshire Tragedy."

Knoxville Girl

I met a little girl in Knoxville,
A town you all know well,
And ever Sunday evening into her home I'd dwell,
I took her for an evening walk about a mile from town;
I picked a stick up offen the ground
And knocked that fair girl down.

She fell upon her bended knee,
"Oh, mercy," she did cry,
"Oh, Willie dear, don't kill me here,
I'm not prepared to die!"
She didn't speak another word,
I even beat her more,
Until the ground around us stood
And then her blood did pour.

I took her by her golden curls,
I throwed her round and round;
I throwed her into the river
That flows through Knoxville town.
Go there, Go there, you Knoxville girl,
This dark and lonely night;
Go there, Go there, little Knoxville girl,
You'll never be my wife.

I started back to Knoxville,
Got there about midnight;
My mother she was worried
And woke up with a fright.
"Oh, son, oh, son, what have you done
That bloodied your clothes so?"
I told my anxious mother
I was bleeding from my nose.

I called for a candle to light myself to bed
I called for a handkerchief to bind my aching head.
I rolled and tumbled the whole night through
And troubled there for me.
The flame of Hell around my bed
Before my eyes could see.

They took me down to Knoxville
And locked me in a cell;
And all my friends tried to get me out,
But none could go my bail.
And here I'm worrying my life away
In this dirty old jail,
Because I murdered that Knoxville girl,
The girl I loved so well.

On the Banks of the Ohio

"Come, my love, let's take a walk,
Just a little ways with me,
And as we walk along, we'll talk
About our golden wedding day."

"Only say that you'll be mine,
And in your arms no other shall twine,
Down beside where the waters flow,
Down on the banks of the Ohio."

He drew a knife across her throat.
And to his breast she gently pressed,
Say's "Please, oh please, don't murder me,
For I am unprepared to die."

He took her by the lily-white hand,
And led her down to the riverside,
And as he threw her in to drown,
He watched her as she floated down.

"Going home between twelve and one,
Thinkin' of the deed I done,
I murdered first the girl I love,
Because she would not marry me."

18

Teaching Meter to the Reader

R. L. Barth

Pray thee, take care, that tak'st my booke in hand,
To reade it well: that is, to understand
Ben Jonson

It has been my experience that very few teachers—on whatever educational level—teach poetry, or are capable of teaching poetry, as if it were poetry. This is no idle paradox: to such teachers, the poem is an organized group of words essentially indistinguishable from prose. They "discuss" the intellectual content of the poem, its symbols, metaphors, similes, images, and so on, with a kind of bucolic innocence, assuming they have done justice to the poem and the poet. In fact, they have not "discussed" the poem at all. While it is perhaps an obvious fact, I might nevertheless remind the reader that, however useful, metaphors, symbols, and other forms of figurative language are not essential to the poem. Indeed, some of the most moving poems in the English language—and I am thinking of various poems written in the plain style—largely dispense with them. A poem is a poem, and not prose, precisely because of its more tightly organized and controlled language, that is, its rhythm. In the case of formalist poetry, which is my concern here, that initially means meter. The poem is a species of metrical composition. Furthermore, rhythm carries much of the emotion of any given poem. If one has not attended to that rhythm, then, one can hardly say with truth that the poem has been either "discussed" or understood.

Before proceeding with my own methods of teaching meter, I wish to make clear that meter and rhythm are not synonymous terms, though they are occasionally used as such for convenience. Meter is the ideal of the line; rhythm is its actuality, the way in which the line is heard. Take the following hypothetical line:

Ĭ ám.Ĭ ám.Ĭ ám.Ĭ ám.Ĭ ám.

The meter is obviously iambic pentameter, and the line is as ideal as anyone could wish. Here, there is little, if any, divergence between meter and rhythm. Even supposing it were possible to duplicate this line a number of times and create a poem, the result would be stiff and, even, boring. Such an instrument could not provide an economic or subtle medium for thought. Of course, such an ideal poem could not really be composed (though perhaps any number of versifiers have come uncomfortably close). Rather, one must account for rhythm, which may be achieved in either or both of two main ways: *variation* and *substitution*. When accounting for rhythm, the most obvious fact is that in a line of, say, iambic pentameter, neither all of the accented nor unaccented syllables will be exact equivalents. Furthermore, since one *measures* syllables only in relation to other syllables within the foot, there will be times when the unaccented syllable of one foot might well receive a heavier degree of stress than the preceding accented syllable. Let me quote Jeffrey Akard's paired epigrams, "For the End of a Decade":[1]

I.
With practice we learn patience, Time endured,
The opposite of idle hope,
Extends into the future, is the word
By which despair expands its scope.
II.
Patience, the true humility,
Teaching me to let what will be, be.

In the first line, the accented syllable of the second foot ("we") receives less stress than the unaccented syllable of the third foot ("learn"). One has the effect of four degrees of stress rising to a culmination on the first syllable of "patience." This aspect of rhythm is achieved through *variation*. The second possibility, *substitution*, can be seen in the first line of the second epigram: "Patience, the true humility...." The first foot ("Patience") is a trochee opening an iambic poem. Finally, one should note that caesural placement and line endings also contribute to rhythm.

These opening comments are meant only to provide the merest sketch of the prosodic workings of a poem. Much more could — and perhaps should — be said, but space limitations militate against it. For I must come to my subject: How shall meter be taught? One thing

should now be obvious: Meter must be taught. It is basic to an understanding and perception of rhythm (in the traditional, formal poem, at
least, though it should be noted that good free verse poems, of which
there are not as many as a reading of contemporary journals and
anthologies might suggest, also have clearly perceptible rhythms).

My own teaching of meter — hence, rhythm — centers on three distinct though necessarily interrelated tools: Most important is audible
reading, then terminology, and finally, examples. First, students must
hear poems read aloud, frequently; and they must be encouraged to
read poems aloud themselves. Only later will they be able to hear
poems properly in their minds. If this approach sounds relatively easy,
there are real problems associated with it. Teachers must train themselves to read poems aloud and correctly in the first place. Generally
speaking, I confront three types of audible reading in the early stages
of a poetry class: reading poetry as if it were prose, not attending to
the rhythm at all; sing-songing (often taught by Miss Jones somewhere
along the educational lines as a stirring exercise in Longfellow); and
reading dramatically (that is, oral interpretation as an exercise in acting).
All are incorrect; the third method is the most dangerous, for it carries
the sanction of "feeling" and highly wrought emotion — in other words,
it is "poetic." In fact, the correct method is that elaborated by Yvor
Winters in his crucial essay "The Audible Reading of Poetry" (In *The
Function of Criticism: Problems and Exercises*, 1957, pp, 81–100;
Athens, OH: Swallow Press) as a reading somewhere between sing-
song and conversation. Winter's essay, as well as his various recordings,
should be required reading, and listening, for anyone who teaches
poetry.

Only by hearing poems read constantly will the students ever hope
to train their ears, as they must if they are to understand poetry.
Make no mistake: This is a skill, and it can be acquired only with hard
work. However, I have found numerous students amenable to the
discipline required. Furthermore, it suggests to them the various spiritual, intellectual, and moral struggles attendant on writing well. When
I taught high school, I also coached the baseball team. It was a fact
understood by all my players/students that a certain degree of skill
(and skill that could, to some extent, be achieved by hard work) was
necessary to make the team; an even greater degree of skill was
necessary to make the starting team. Surely, poetry is a more serious
discipline?

About my second tool, I shall have little to say. One must provide
the student with basic terminology. This is easily accomplished with a
few pages of terms and definitions. I have heard it argued that time
spent mastering this material is "deadening" for the student. If true,
that is too bad. One cannot talk about prosody or any other discipline

without the language. (To return to my earlier example: it was certainly assumed by my players/students that they had at some point mastered the terminology of baseball. They understood bunts, pitch-outs, stolen bases, and so on; and they would have been scandalized by anyone who did not.) What I find equally interesting about my colleagues who argue that prosodic terminology is "deadening" is that they do not scruple about having students learn, for instance, the terminology of figurative language. Enough said.

Third, and finally, I use extensive handouts containing individual lines and brief passages for illustrative purposes. These generally concern "special problems," and I find them extremely useful for discussing everything from substitution to the pronunciation key in the dictionary. For example, one particular page contains some thirty-five lines of iambic pentameter by various poets ranging in time from George Gascoigne to Thom Gunn, arranged in chronological order. In some line or other, this page provides an example of most of the special problems I might wish to address. On the one hand, it covers the working of prosody and related subjects on a small scale, providing, as it does, substitutions, alliterations, caesural placements and so forth. On the other hand, it is set up in such a way that it suggests and therefore allows me to talk about larger issues, such as the evolution of the iambic pentameter line. Naturally, the progress and ability of the students help determine when particular issues are introduced.

Let me give a few examples from this sample page, to suggest how I use it. My first example is from George Gascoigne's "The Passion of a Lover."

> I smile sometimes, although my grief be great. . . .

This is a representative line of early sixteenth century plain style composition. Minimally, it can be used to illustrate these tendencies: the relatively equal and obviously unstressed quality of the unaccented syllables, along with the relatively equal and obviously stressed quality of the accented syllables; the use of alliteration, frequently to underline accented syllables; the use of the caesura after the fourth (sometimes the sixth) syllable; the end-stopped character of the poem's lines.

Next, consider the following line from John Donne's "The Dream":

> So, if I dream I have you, I have you. . . .

Here, I might discuss the nature of the line's rhythmic movement, contrasting it with Gascoigne's line. Donne's caesuras are more varied (even falling within the foot), the quantity (or variation) of syllables is less heavy, more subtle. Equally important, the line usefully points up how rhetoric and meter/rhythm reinforce each other. For some reason, students want to read the last part of this line thus: "Ĭ háve yŏu, Ĭ háve yŏu." In fact, this is the correct reading: "Ĭ háve yŏu, Í hăve yóu." Similarly, this line may lead back to a discussion of the syllables of a foot only being considered in relation to the syllables of the foot itself. Here, the repeated phrase falls across three different feet, and the arrangement of syllables is different in each foot. Obviously, this is an example of Donne's artistry, not accident.

Finally, consider the following line from Wallace Stevens's "Sunday Morning":

> Complacencies of the peignor, and late ...

According to dictionary pronunciation, the word "peignor" can correctly be pronounced with the accent on either syllable. As this line (and poem) is written in iambic pentameter, it is much simpler to posit a pronunciation that does not disturb the rhythmic nature of the line. A substitution in the fourth foot here would be uncalled for, not to say inept. This line might be used as the starting point for a discussion of local pronunciations and idioms, along with their rhythmical effects on the poem. If the discussion lends itself to substitutions generally, one might point out that substitutions are not used only to point up something important in the poem; they might just as profitably be used for the sake of rhythmical variety.

These remarks have been brief. Still, I think my essential approach has been indicated. The subtleties and shadings that remain suggest themselves inevitably as the course progresses. I do not pretend the teaching of meter is easy; it is not. And yet, it is not a pedantic exercise, but an absolute requirement in any poetry course. And we might as well be honest with our students: reading poetry requires, demands, hard-won skills, though it can be enjoyed—if only, in the truest sense, when these skills have been developed. To turn it into a game is an exercise in intellectual dishonesty.

Notes

1. Reprinted from *The Epigrammatist*, I (April 1990), with the author's permission.

19

Some Applications of Literary Critical Theory to the Reading and Evaluation of Student Poetry Writing

Patrick Bizzaro

Methods of instruction in writing courses—especially now that we have come to see writing and reading as interrelated processes—often reflect a teacher's stated (or unstated) emphases and values as a reader and evaluator. In fact, pedagogy *seems* to be designed as a way of reinforcing the way a teacher determines meaning in a text. I am limited to saying "seems," however, because as a profession we have performed so little of what Sharon Crowley (1989) calls the "interrogation of the strategies used to teach reading and writing" (48).

This essay reports the findings of such an "interrogation." In it, I explore the ways literary critical theories—specifically, the New Criticism, Reader Response, and Deconstruction—can aid teachers as they read and evaluate student writing. I hope to show how critical theories can be consciously adapted for use in examining student texts in such a way as to make evident to students what the teacher values as meaning-making in discourse. What's more, since such methods enable us to read texts differently, by permitting varying amounts of intrusion in a student's writing process, literary critical theories may provide a much-needed panacea to teachers of poetry writing classes who often shy away from the hard task of evaluation or who simply read and evaluate student poetry on the basis of personal preferences often times left unexplored and just as often left unacknowledged even by the teachers themselves. By using literary critical theory here to evaluate student poetry writing, I intend to explore the notion that teachers in any writing course (e.g., composition, fiction writing, poetry writing) should not rely upon the same methods of reading and evaluation in analyzing the writing of experienced student-writers as they do with beginning student-writers. But why should literary-critical theory and composition theory come into play in evaluating student writing? And how can New Criticism, Reader-Response Criticism, and Deconstruction profitably provide teachers with models for offering insight into student poems?

The applications that follow are arranged so that the poem evaluated first is one written by the least experienced student (as measured by her background as a reader and writer of poetry), followed by one written by an intermediate writer, and finally by one written by the most experienced student-writer of this group. The methods I employ reflect adaptations of literary-critical theories, which enable me to intrude most in the process of the least experienced student-writer, and least in the process of the most experienced. In short, I believe literary theory has much to offer us as we learn how to comment on poems written by students with varying backgrounds and experiences as poets.

New Criticism and Primary Trait Scoring: A Reading of a Poem by Penney, A Beginning Adult Poet

I am not surprised to discover in my reading methods the habit of reading from a New Critical perspective. Perhaps because many in my generation of English teachers have backgrounds in literary analysis, the New Critical methodology persists in our methods of reading and evaluating student writing. What's more, to secure the privilege of reading through the New Critical lens, we have devised entire pedagogies, textbooks (including many texts designed for use in poetry writing courses), research projects, methods of mass testing, and strategies for evaluating such tests that make New Critical estimations possible. Support for this view is offered unknowingly by Willa Wolcott (1987), who quotes notes from a recent meeting of the National Testing Network in Writing, which state, "A large question ... is how in assessing writing do we build into writing prompts the stimuli that evoke what we desire from students?" (41). The clear intention underlying the development of writing prompts designed to test students is the production of writings that reflect what the testers value as readers and evaluators. And the reading valued is text-based, as the following comparison suggests.

It is interesting to juxtapose the language of current theories for evaluating student writing with language expressing the New Critical values and emphases. Take this brief excerpt from Charles Cooper's explanation for "Developing an Analytic Scale" (1977):

> Procedures to follow in developing an analytic scale are simple though time-consuming. Since the features that make up the scale must be derived inductively from pieces of writing in the mode for which the scale is being constructed, the first requirement is for large amounts of writing. .... (14)

Compare Cooper's explanation with the following excerpt from Rene Wellek's well-known "The Analysis of the Literary Work of Art" (1963):

> The real poem must be conceived as a structure of norms.... The norms we have in mind are implicit norms which have to be extracted from every individual experience of a work of art and together make up the genuine work of art as a whole. (257)

I don't imagine Cooper intended to echo so clearly Wellek's insistence that the measure of a text's value comes from norms that are implicit to the kind of text it is and extracted from all other texts of its kind. Still, such a close correspondence in theory between Cooper and Wellek shows that the attitudes, values, and emphases of the New Criticism are, as William E. Cain (1984) says in *The Crisis in Criticism*, "so deeply engrained in English studies ... that we do not even perceive them as the legacy of a particular movement" (105).

Methods of evaluation, such as the Analytic Scale (described above) and the derivative Primary Trait Scoring reflect the effort among composition theorists to establish clearly the reader's responsibility to the text and to set boundaries within which the reader/evaluator can legitimately function. Like other recent approaches to the evaluation of student writing, based on values so basic to our way of thinking about reading and evaluating that we do not perceive them as possessing any particular theoretical basis at all, the Analytic Scale and Primary Trait Scoring are products of a theory that perceives the reading and evaluating of student writing as text-based activities. More specifically, the activity of developing primary traits—"those features of a piece [of writing] which are relevant to the kind of discourse it is" (Cooper 1977, 11)—permits us to evaluate features that make a poem, for instance, a poem, thereby enabling teachers to state clearly to student-writers how a text will be read and what the student should do in revising the text.

Primary Trait Scoring, as I have argued elsewhere, when combined with interactive teaching strategies (e.g., conferences, interactive journals, workshops, etc.), satisfies the six criteria I believe to be essential to assessing student poetry writing (Bizzaro 1990): evaluation must encourage the teaching of the writing process; respect the essential integrity of the poem, as defined by the discourse community or in the developing relationship between writer (student), reader (instructor), and text; reward careful revision by providing an objective standard against which the revised version will be measured; encourage students to view writing as a process of discovery; provide students with tools that may be used in discussing the revision of a specific poem or of poems generally; and, provide instructors with tools to identify and help remedy specific problems in the writing of an individual beginning poet and, if possible, in the writing of beginning poets, generally (57–58). Moreover, Primary Trait Scoring echoes many of the concerns of the New Criticism by serving teachers best who must examine, read, and evaluate in-process poems by *beginning* poets, those whose experiences as readers and writers of poetry are limited.

Penney, whose early draft of "Chasm" appears below, is a high school English teacher and an MA candidate who wrote her poem as one of the writing requirements of the four-week Summer Institute of the Coastal Plains Writing Project (a site of the National Writing Project) at East Carolina University. I classify Penney as a beginning poet in spite of the fact that she teaches literature on the high school level and studies literature in advanced courses in graduate school because of her lack of experience as a writer of poetry and her relative unfamiliarity with contemporary poets, poetry and poetics. The amount of instruction in the Summer Institute concerning the *writing* of poetry amounted to roughly one hour, though I did encourage Penney to write poems once she expressed an interest in doing so, and I did confer with her at various times, at her request.

Here is the first draft that Penney permitted me to see of her poem, "Chasm":

Chasm

Faded photograph, 1944
The daughter is the mother, revisited.
One black and white image
Explains it all . . .

Tears spent in angry frustration —
Both desperately seeking her place
In the world,
A bridge across the pain.
No one listens
When both talk at once.
Too many feelings
Bleed
Into shades of gray.

The girl is caught
Between her present and her future;
The woman caught

Between her future and her past.
They clash with the violent
Force
Of pent-up sameness.
They scream into a black void
Of misunderstanding.

At last
The three-by-five impression
Sheds light into the darkness
Which lies between ...

In conference with Penney, I pointed out that this is a very good draft, especially for a first poem. I am not surprised, however, to see such a competent draft because Penney, who is an excellent student, has read a great deal of poetry, most notably the English Romantic poets, and is a strong writer of other kinds of texts. I pointed out that the best lines in her poem are those offering new perceptions or perceptions that are entirely hers: "No one listens/When both talk at once" and "They clash with the violent/Force/Of pent-up sameness."

Penney was to attend to the following list of primary traits in revising her poem. Since we did not have a common body of literature to which we might refer for examples, I found my comments on the first draft rather broad. As a result, I also marked up her poem to provide her more specific guidelines (see figure).

1. Remember: lines that are not clichés in normal conversation or, for that matter, even in other kinds of written discourse are sometimes cliché in poetic discourse. Naturally, only a considerable amount of reading will solve that problem. The underlinings in your draft indicate where I believe you will need to rethink how you have expressed yourself to avoid "poetic clichés."

2. An additional area you need to work on is your verbs. Verbs should make "unusual" connections with their nouns. Avoid "tired" verbs whenever you can. I've placed verbs most in need of revision in blocks in your draft.

3. I think your poem does a good job of "showing" what you mean rather than "telling," at least most of the time. But on occasion, I think an image would help you along. I've indicated where.

Through conferencing together and identifying three general kinds of changes that she might make in her poem, we were able to agree on how the poem would be read and evaluated once revised. The revision, however, indicates some new trouble areas, since Penney "hyper-corrected" in certain places, often drawing now on her background as a reader of poetry, albeit nineteenth-century writers.

Chasm

Faded photograph, 1944
The daughter is the mother, revisited.
One black and white image
Explains it all . . .   *stronger line*

Tears spent in angry frustration--
Both desperately seeking her place
In the world,
A bridge across the pain.
No one listens
When both talk at once.   *good - this is very strong + suggestive*
Too many feelings
Bleed
Into shades of gray.

The girl is caught
Between her present and her future;   *make an image*
The woman caught
Between her future and her past.
They clash with the violent
Force
Of pent-up sameness.   *interesting line*
They scream into a black void   *good*
Of misunderstanding.

At last,
The three-by-five impression
Sheds light into the darkness
Which lies between . . .

--Penney

Penney's first draft with my comments

Chasm (revised version)

Faded photograph, 1944
The daughter stands
In unfamiliar shoes on
Undeniable feet
Beneath unquestionable knees.
A solitary figure,
Reflected
In yellow black and white,
Transcends ambiguity.

Tears lost in angry frustration —
Femininity,
Innocence and experience
Both incomplete, unfulfilled —
Reading for truth
Grasping for light
Clawing for comfort.
No one listens

When both talk at once.
Too many feelings
Bleed
Into a moist gray fog.

The girl crouches
On the precipice of her future
As stones of her present
Give way
to uncertainty.
The woman waits,
Poised on the selfsame brink,
Her footing eroded
By the past.
They clash with the violent
Force
Of pent-up sameness.
They scream into a black void
Of misunderstanding.

At last,
The three-by-five impression
Warms the darkness
Which lies between ...

Penney has attempted to conscientiously attend to the three traits previously identified; let me examine her new version of the poem one trait at a time.

1. Clichés: Penney has done a great deal to rid her poem of clichés, and she should be commended for her efforts. However, remedying one problem has created another, making at least one more draft necessary. In attempting to be more specific about what she meant by "explains it all," Penney has introduced language more abstract than that of draft 1; "Transcends ambiguity" is a concept in need of development. While Penney has managed to solve the problem of "A bridge across pain," which bothered me in draft 1, her alternative description of that pain (lines 2–7 of the second stanza) is also vague.

    Penney has attended to the primary traits identified within her earlier draft but, in doing so, she has introduced new problems. In her next draft, I would have her focus on the invention of a scene which suggests the ideas she wants to convey. I might also ask her to attempt to go back to draft 1 and salvage by developing it further the line "The daughter is the mother revisited" as a way of solving the problem of abstraction in stanza 1.

2. Verbs: Of the three components of her poem in need of revision, Penney has done the most to improve the verbs in her poem. In

stanza 1, the decision to change the "to be" verb into an action verb leads to an image instead of the puzzling "The daughter is the mother, revisited," an interesting paradox which is not adequately developed in the earlier draft. The new verb, "stands," suggests to Penney a new image of the woman standing in a certain way. But Penney takes this image too far and ends up again in the unproductive abstract of "undeniable feet" and "unquestionable knees." Again, a solution might be to reintroduce the paradox of daughter as mother once more (and in this case, reading Carolyn Kizer's wonderful "The Blessing"), developing that particular image further by referring back to the photograph.

3. Imagery: The imagery is still the strongest element in the poem, but in stanza 1, yet another problem is introduced, one that might be listed in a taxonomy of difficulties beginning poets inevitably must confront, the tendency to explain the image (as students have been taught to do in composition classes), instead of permitting the image to suggest its meaning to the reader.

   In stanza 2, the original version is more concrete than the revised, where the author seems to draw from her experiences in reading William Blake, as though those abstract notions of "innocence" and "experience" can be shared with her readers. The stanza's last five lines are five of the stronger lines in her earlier draft. In the third stanza, Penney does a good job of staying visible, of permitting the image to do the work it should do.

In commenting on Penney's poem, I have attempted to offer an analysis specific to the poem written, commentary that would measure Penney's relative success with "Chasm" and permit me to move from observations about poetry in general to more specific observations about elements of her text. This in-process evaluation of Penney's poem helped me reach three tentative conclusions I had not reached before in employing Primary Trait Scoring to the evaluation of student poetry writing.

For one, teachers of poetry writing know quite well that they always run the risk, in commenting on the poems of beginning student-writers, that the revision will, in fact, make the poem less effective. In some ways, this is true in Penney's poem. But we should aim at something higher in using the New Criticism in commenting on poems by beginning writers: the writer's increased fluency with elements of poetic writing.

Second, we must expect that with beginning poets, revision of one set of problems often gives rise to a new set. As a result, I believe beginning poets should work hard on numerous drafts of a small number of poems. That the process is recursive, as it must seem to

Penney when she is asked to return to her first draft to find help in writing her third, simply reinforces what we already know to be true about writing in general. If the process were linear, everyone would be able to write a great poem. Unfortunately, the writing of poems, like the writing of other kinds of texts, involves some guesswork in offering solutions to the problems writers inevitably confront.

And, third, in using the New Criticism to respond to Penney's poem after not having employed such text-based methodology for several years, I felt that I had appropriated Penney's poem. This disappointed me since I made every effort not to. I hypothesize that one of two things happened. Either I appropriated her text unknowingly, on the one hand, through the methods I employed in commenting on her poem; or, perhaps because Penney's background as reader and writer limited the ways she might have conceived of her poem, she simply gave in to my requests about revision. Proof that something went awry can be found in the hypercorrections of her second draft. She has, it seems to me, interpreted my comments and applied them where they were not appropriate. In any event, from my limited experience in employing New Critical methodology in reading and evaluating a poem by a beginning adult poet, I believe we should expect to see poems hypercorrected as such students come to discover what a poem should achieve. I believe such hypercorrection in response to text-based commentary is as common as the hypercorrections in the language of other students learning a second language or a new dialect of their first language.

I would not, of course, grade either of these drafts. I would hope that Penney would continue to work on this poem, as well as others she has written, seeking further comments as the poem evolves. The final version of the poem, as chosen by Penney, would receive a grade reflecting how well I believe she has met the various primary traits we have identified as the poem has progressed from draft to draft.

Reader-Response Criticism and the Interactive Journal: A Reading of a Poem by Terri, An Intermediate Adult Poet

Among difficulties that arose in my reading and in-process evaluation of Penney's poem was text appropriation, an unwanted though mostly unavoidable by-product of attempts to provide Penney quickly with information she needed to write her poem. Such appropriation is unwanted since it takes the power of writing away from students, keeping them subordinate to the authority of the teacher. But, in the absence of adequate reading experiences, students are unable to generate the kinds of texts their teachers expect them to produce, especially in poetry writing classes where, unlike courses in the writing of compositions, students enter the course having received little prior instruction in appropriate reading and writing skills. And, though teachers should make every effort *not* to take over a student's text—since such appropriation often results in apprehensive hypercorrection of the kind Penney demonstrated—some learning can, in fact, result from the methodology of authoritative readership or "teacher modeling," especially for inexperienced student-writers in a poetry writing class who will learn chiefly by observing what their teachers do.

Observations about the drawbacks to the use of New Critical techniques of evaluation are well known. But the change from the product pedagogy to the process pedagogy was precipitated by an awareness that meaning arises not from the text alone, as the New Critics would have us believe, but from an interaction between reader, writer, and text. The various theories associated with this view of meaning-making have been called Reader-Response theories. My purpose here is simply to apply Reader-Response Criticism as it may be of use with an intermediate poet, such as Terri.

The New Critical methodology, as adapted for use in Primary Trait Scoring of the sort applied to Penney's poem, focuses on the text, in the belief that what makes meaning available can be found there. Certainly we are saying, as I implied by the *kinds* of comments I made on Penney's poem, "I, the teacher, am an exemplary reader. Your job is to please *me*. If I can't be moved by your text, you better take my advice on *how* to move me." The advantage of employing New Critical methods in reading and evaluating, in process, the poems of students is that they give teachers the opportunity with beginning poets (as a plumber might with an apprentice) to say, "Move over and let me show you how I would do it." Appropriation of the text (or the pipewrench), from this perspective, seems both useful and inevitable.

But the disadvantage of employing such teacher-centered methodology is that students are prevented from asserting authority over their texts. Still, an inexperienced writer will have no more luck writing something called a poem than, unfamiliar with the "rules" (if, indeed, there are any), they would have playing Australian Rules Football. As Cynthia Onore (1989) writes, "As long as judgments of what may be 'better' or 'worse'—that is, of what constitutes improvement in writing—remain the province of teachers alone, then the writer cannot fully and authentically engage in choice making and problem solving" (232). But the unsolved problem in employing Reader-Response Criticism in a poetry writing class is the determination of when and how a student will be able to "authentically engage in choice making and problem solving." Let's look at excerpts from my reading and evaluation of an interactive journal written by Terri to explore these matters further.

Terri was a student in my undergraduate Introduction to Poetry Writing class. But she was unusually experienced as a student entering such a class, having written poetry without instruction for some time and having nearly completed requirements for her master's degree in English. Given her past experiences as a reader and writer of poetry, I believe Terri qualifies as an intermediate writer (in any case, her experiences are more numerous than Penney's though fewer than those of Deb, my third example). While my comments on Penney's poem, using the New Criticism, focus chiefly on the text, since that is where the New Critics believe meaning exists, my comments on Terri's work, using Reader-Response, focus chiefly on her Interactive Journal where she and I negotiated over the course of a semester those characteristics of poetry writing that I would apply in examining (that is, in reading and evaluating) her poems.

Since I have already attempted elsewhere to answer the question, "Can reader-response critical tools be profitably employed in the evaluation of student poetry writing?" (Bizzaro 1990b, 256), I hope to demonstrate here how reader-response can be employed specifically to instruct intermediate students in the writing of poetry, while at the same time, offering a method for reading and evaluating a student's poem which places authority equally in the reader, the writer, and the text. To do this, I focused not only on the drafts of poems Terri wrote during the semester, but on changes she made each week to her answer to the question, "What kinds of things would you take into consideration in evaluating a poem?" Terri, and others in her class, were required to keep journals in which they "wrote drafts of poems, reactions to poems read for class discussion, and an answer once each week to the above question" (Bizzaro 1990b, 260). My job was to respond to the poem and to the answer to the question, attempting to influence Terri's response and negotiate with her a set of criteria for evaluating (and, in the end, grading) her poems. What follows are three of my interactions with Terri and one of her poems, evaluated in accord with the criteria she and I agreed upon as characteristic of poems she hoped to write.

Terri's Interactive Journal
(Terri's entries are first; my responses follow in italics.)

January 11

If a poem touches me in any way, such as, if it brings a similar event in my life to my mind, then I find it valuable. If I can identify with the author or situation in any way, then I usually find the poem important in some way. The only time I do not find a poem worthwhile is if it does not make any sense to me. After reading a poem, I want to feel impressed or touched in some way. I do not want to be left sitting there, thinking to myself, "What in the hell did that mean?"

How does a poet manipulate language in the making of imagery? Are some kinds of images more confusing to you than others?

February 15

My ideas have developed somewhat in the area of my biases in evaluating poetry. I now put more importance on using colorful verbs and very descriptive adjectives. I have become more concerned with avoiding the use of any "to be" verb forms or the word "so." Enjambment is vital because I like the breathy quality it evokes when reading an enjambed line aloud. A good example of this is May Swenson's "The Watch." Once again, I'm affected the most by poems that evoke a passionate response whether that emotion is happiness, sadness, anger, loneliness. Poetry for me should be introspective and have *feeling*. Poetry like Merwin's "A Door" does not interest me because I can't seem to find any meaning in it.

Let me ask a few questions. First, what, exactly, makes a verb colorful? Second, in terms of enjambment, how about the surprise it makes possible? And, third, was your reaction to Merwin the same even after our discussion in class? Why not explore for yourself the difference in language between a poem like Swenson's and one like Merwin's? Excellent exploration this time, Terri.

February 21

[Entitled: Response to your questions and comments from last week's answer to: "What do I look for in evaluating a poem?"]

You asked "what, exactly, makes a verb colorful?" Colorful verbs, to me, are lively, passionate and feeling words. Verbs that dance on your tongue. Verbs that stand out on a page. Sometimes the duller verbs can't be avoided, however.

I never thought about enjambment causing surprise in a poem but now I see what you mean.

Even after our discussion of Merwin's "A Door," I still couldn't find any meaning that I could identify with. It didn't create any mood or feeling for me.

One aspect that I've failed to mention in my area of biases: Structure is vital to me. I like poems that aren't traditionally structured—for example, any one of e.e. cumming's poems, William Carlos Williams' "This Is Just to Say," May Swenson's "Women Should be Pedestals" and Nikki Giovanni's "Dreams." I like the cummings and Swenson poems because of their structure and lower case usage. Thematic structure in "This Is Just to Say" is especially interesting but hard to do myself.

Thanks for responding to my earlier questions. As far as colorful verbs, you describe the way they sound and look; how about the way they mean? As for understanding—that is, that something occurs to you, as reader, piece by piece—in the way the author presents the

image? Certainly, Williams could have presented the picture in a different
word order. Also don't give up yet on Merwin or on surrealism!

Clearly, Terri's journal shows wonderful growth in her ability to
converse with me about her personal preferences in poems. Her first
journal entry (January 11) was brief and to the point, reflecting what
she had brought with her into the class, based upon her past experiences
as a reader and writer of poems. Admittedly, Terri prefers poems that
she is able to understand precisely because they concern experiences
similar, perhaps, to those she has had, poems that "make sense" to
her. This observation on her part gave rise to my concern over what
exactly happens in language that makes sense to Terri as opposed to
language that does not. In her entry of February 15, Terri is far more
specific, if not about what makes sense to her, about what does not:
"Poetry like Merwin's 'A Door.'" I can see, as well, that she has
benefitted from class discussions concerning verbs, enjambment, and
feeling in poetry. But I question her in my response because I want her
to take her personal preferences one step further, making them useful
in helping me understand what she values in her poems. In her third
journal, she does take us both a step further, incorporating her personal
biases and mine (since she conscientiously responds to my questioning
and class discussions) in the development of a growing sense of what I
will evaluate in examining one of Terri's poems.

In evaluating Terri's poems, I will keep in mind that a poem Terri
would like to have written must possess a surface simplicity. What's
more, I will pay close attention to the strength of her verbs in creating
an overall mood or feeling. Her poem should convey some passionate
feelings, which I construe to mean something she feels strongly about.
What's more, I will help her in my responses in the structuring of her
poems, including use of enjambment for effect.

Since I had already reported elsewhere that "when we teach
students to write poetry, we teach them to generate texts that represent
their understanding of what constitutes poetry" (Bizzaro 1990b, 265), I
was not surprised to receive in the poem that follows a draft which so
nearly fulfills Terri's expectations, as described in her journal, of what
a poem should accomplish.

> I remember
> never being able
> to understand
> your words
> for they were
> old and indistinguishable
> already.
> By the time I was able to be interested in you and your past
> You were 74 and I felt silly asking you to repeat
> yourself over and over.

I still sleep under the expertly-sewn quilts you made for me.
They warm me as your love once did.
The big black Bible,
which I remember always lying upon your coffee table,
now lies upon mine.
My father, your youngest son,
reminds me of you as he grows older
and his voice grows gruff
and his eyes grow weak.
You are one of the cornerstones in my childhood
and I only hope that I can become
half the woman you were.

This draft of Terri's poem accomplishes much of what she would want a poem to accomplish. It is a direct narrative of a subject for which she feels passionately. In fact, her imagery is clear and understandable, high priorities for Terri. Since this is but a draft, and since I am responding to it in terms of our mutually determined criteria, I would recommend that she look more closely at her verbs since, by consolidating her language a bit, some of the choppiness of the poem's rhythm might be remedied. Additionally, though the enjambment is often effective (it is clear that she has taken some care with line breaks), she might want to consider restructuring her piece once some of the language is consolidated.

Because this is but a draft, I will withhold a grade for the time being, hoping she will revise in the manner I have urged. When she submits her poem for final critique, I will use our mutually agreed-upon list of criteria as the basis for a grade, since those criteria reflect semester-long negotiations between a reader and a writer concerned with the development of a specific text.

Still, the benefits of Reader-Response techniques should be clear. The teacher is able to read and evaluate student poems while keeping the student involved in negotiations concerning what the *student's* poem should accomplish. Such a negotiation occurs not over the word choice, imagery, and word order of the text, but in the journal where meaningful interaction can occur between teacher and student and the text ultimately at issue. Most notably, the teacher is not apt to appropriate the student's text when using reader-response methodology. In short, authority is dispersed, and the meaning results from the interaction of reader, writer, and text.

Deconstruction and What Is Excluded: A Reading of a Poem by Deb, an Advanced Adult Poet

A New Critical-based methodology, such as the Primary Trait Scoring employed in reading and evaluating Penney's poem, places the authority where it has been all along, in the judgments of the teacher-reader, whose principal responsibility is to bring past experiences as a reader and writer of the kind of text in question to the reading and evaluating of the student text. The appropriation of the student text (or what we might call "teacher-modeling") is often the result of the teacher's efforts to introduce characteristics of a kind of text to a student fundamentally inexperienced as a reader and writer of that particular kind of text (e.g., poems). While discursive authority resides in such an analysis in the teacher's judgments about elements in the text, Reader-Response-based methodology enables teachers to disperse the authority for discourse. Reader-Response Criticism makes possible interactions in journals of the sort kept by Terri, and such interactions make the poem-as-text less the object of pedagogical concern than how the poem is read. As David Bleich theorizes, "The poem itself, as an object of specifically critical judgment, tends to disappear" (in Mailloux 1990, 43). As a result, my interaction with Terri focuses chiefly on her answers to the central question of the course: "What kinds of things would you take into consideration in evaluating a poem?"

While New Criticism and Reader-Response Criticism are geared by design toward the development of pedagogy, the use of Deconstruction as a method of reading and evaluating student poetry writing seems, I suppose, an inappropriate adaptation of the theory. Near the end of her remarkably succinct discussion of Deconstruction, Sharon Crowley (1989) concludes, "I am not sure that a deconstructive pedagogy can be realized—the term is itself an oxymoron" (45). But she usefully makes some guesses as to what a deconstructive pedagogy might attempt. First, it would reject the teacher as authority in matters pertaining to disseminating and judging knowledge. Second, the notion of the writing process would focus on "differentiation" (46)—how the writing process differs for each writing task. Third, if writing is a process of entertaining differences, so must a course in writing: "a syllabus for a writing class would always be in revision" since students would be actively involved in rewriting the teacher's syllabus (46–47).

Adapting Deconstruction to the purpose of reading and evaluating student writing is no small task. What it offers, however, is unique and thus far untried with student writing: commentary that clarifies for the advanced student-poet what one reader believes has been knowingly or unknowingly included and excluded from the text. This commentary is most appropriate for advanced writers because it carries the added benefit of making the writer the authority for the making of the text. But how might such a reading be made? Steven Lynn (1990) describes a deconstructive reading as a process of "teasing out" contradictory meanings, and offers three steps for doing so: "first, a deconstructive reading must note which member of an opposition in a text appears to be privileged or dominant ...; second, the reading shows how this hierarchy can be reversed within the text, how the apparent hierarchy is arbitrary or illusory; finally, a deconstructive reading places both structures in question, making the text ultimately ambiguous" (106).

I adapted Lynn's process in offering a reading of Deb's poem. An advanced writer of poetry, Deb was a student in my graduate-level course in Contemporary Poetry and a candidate for an M.A. with a creative writing emphasis. She had taken several poetry writing courses prior to entering my course, including an advanced poetry writing course for graduate students. Deb had read widely the works of a great many contemporary writers, had studied the aesthetics of contemporary poetry, and even knew something about Deconstruction. In fact, she seemed receptive to any effort on my part to comment on her poems in some novel way.

What follows is Deb's poem, "My Father's Solitude."

My Father's Solitude

Driving into the yard these last nights,
I have heard my father in the workshop,
drilling and sawing and staining
picture frames.
Like cobwebs they hang in every corner
dark, dusty, and deliberate.

Tonight, I wait in the drive,
motor running and radio off.
I remind myself that
today I have been a good wife.
Have ironed my husband's white shirts and
put the denims out to dry,
have eaten lunch and
(as he told me)
not thought about the size of my thighs,
or picture frames.

On the day of my mother's burying
my father gave me his solitude.
I did not ask for it.
He gave it in his faltering gaze,
his unsteady hand and slow pace.
Then we not speaking
rode back to the family loud house.

Tonight, I wait in the gravel drive
for the lights to go out,
my father to emerge in coveralls and
make his way to the house.
I pull out into the quiet.

What follows is my response to Deb, in the form of a letter.

Dear Deb,

Let me respond to "My Father's Solitude" by offering a reading of your poem intended to let you know what *I* see happening in it and what I do not see happening that might. What I'd like you to do is revise your poem, if you'd like, and/or write a brief note back to me responding to my comments.

Please approach what follows as one reader's response to what you have constructed. As I have read your poem, I have consciously approached your writing as an effort on your part (and on mine) to construct meaning. As in the construction of a room in a house, you have included certain things *inside* the room (and, with any luck, I have noticed them, though I confess to sometimes forgetting the color of my own dwelling when telling people how to find me!). But this approach assumes as well that there are other things, those outside the room, that you have excluded. Sometimes drafts of various kinds of writings give us windows to look through so that we can better see those things that have been excluded. Often these exclusions are notions in conflict with those in our texts that we have either overlooked entirely or consciously decided not to deal with.

What I want to do in my reading of your poem is bring what I see outside, through the windows, into view for you, without imposing too much on your writing process, but in such a way that you can consider whether you want these elements to contribute to the meaning of your poem by continuing to exclude them or if you want to bring them in.

Please read "you" in my comments below as a way of addressing the "I" in the poem. It's just easier this way.

"MY FATHER'S SOLITUDE" — WHAT I SEE IN THE ROOM YOU'VE CONSTRUCTED

This poem seems to take place at your father's house on "these last nights." I see several relationships that you have developed in this poem. The immediate one, and the one that I sense inspired you to write, is between you and your father. He is distant. You know his presence only because you can hear him "in the workshop" doing what, I suppose, are typical male things in the world of your poem, "drilling and sawing and staining," creating picture frames that he hangs "in every corner," suggesting to you the image of "cobwebs."

The next stanza locates us in "Tonight." And a second, more complex (because it gives rise to the first), relationship is developed. Now you are determining if you are a "good wife," by measuring your behavior against some standard. For if you are a good wife (though we're not yet sure what that *really* means, are we?) you can justify your relation with your father (that is, you can remain somewhat distant, observing from outside his workshop) because you have a new relationship with a second man (as this other man's wife) that you are trying to be good at — whatever "good" means in that context.

You do list specific things that a "good" wife must do: iron shirts for your husband, dry clothes, eat lunch, and not think about bodily imperfections ("as he told" you) or about picture frames. But I think, in truth, you are calling these criteria into question (more on this in the next section).

In stanza three, you give shape to "solitude" as though it is something that can be given to someone else, like a handkerchief. On the day of your mother's burial, this is what your father gives you—his tangible solitude for you to do something with—though you do not apparently want it. Then you describe *how* he gives it: in "his faltering gaze," "unsteady hand," and "slow pace." After that, two quiet people (your father and yourself) return to the "family loud house," establishing a kind of difference in your responsibility to your father and the responsibility to him of others in your family.

Back at "Tonight," you continue to wait for your father to leave before you leave. By making this stanza parallel with your second stanza, you seem to suggest that, in the end, nothing really has changed between your father and you. Rather than having his solitude in your hands, you continue to watch him from a distance. This seems a kind of resolution to the problem of who takes care of the old people when they are no longer independent. But the fact of your watching suggests as well that once he is no longer capable of taking care of himself, you will be there for him, like it or not.

This poem is written in an open form. There are, of course, repetitions of sounds, especially the -ing. You have relied heavily on imagery to depict various people in their various roles. Your line breaks are at the end of units of logic, usually after a strong word (rarely a conjunction and never a preposition).

WHAT I SEE OUTSIDE THE ROOM YOU HAVE CONSTRUCTED

I don't see much made of the other side of certain conflicts in the poem, and, perhaps, by my pointing them out you will care to do something with them (or care not to). Certainly, you may not have intended to do anything with the other concerns that I bring through the window below.

In stanza one, an interesting juxtaposition is created between the masculine and aggressive (at least, hardly fragile) activity of "drilling and sawing and staining," on the one hand, and hanging these frames "Like cobwebs," on the other. Ironically, these masculine productions hang "Like cobwebs," suggesting a kind of delicateness that seems almost contradictory. What's more, the cobwebs you describe are more like picture frames than cobwebs—"dark, dusty, and deliberate."

Another unexplored relationship (or one only superficially explored in this poem) seems to be between you and your mother. Have you inherited a sense of the wife's role that you cannot abide by? This is suggested in your poem, but not developed except in your rebuttal to guilt about your father being alone, that you "have been a good wife" today. Do you feel pressure to become for your father (especially given what you write in stanza 3) *his* "good" wife when he gives you his solitude? Before her death, had your mother carried this great burden of your father's solitude? In her absence, does this responsibility come to the daughter descendant?

Another relationship barely touched here seems to be between you and the rest of your family. Again, this is suggested without being quite developed. You are given your father's solitude. They are not. You are "not speaking," but the house you return to, where your family is (are they there or not?), is "the family loud house."

Finally, another interesting series of juxtapositions exists in your treatment of time. There are these demarcations indicating time: "these last nights," "Tonight," "On the day of my mother's burying." Missing here is a clear sense of what the relation is between these demarcations.

Let me add that the open form, while less restrictive in some ways, excludes from the poem the possibilities of restriction suggested by a closed form with a definite meter and rhyme scheme.

I hope this gives you a way of looking at your poem. Please show me any revision you make, or kindly write me a note responding to my commentary.

Thanks,
Pat Bizzaro

This kind of commentary is intentionally non-judgmental. In making these remarks to Deb, I assume that she knows what she wants her poem to do. My role is to reflect back to her what she has done (at least, in terms of my reading) and what she has not done, though perhaps might in revision. The value of using Deconstruction is that it places the authority for the poems of an advanced writer squarely with the writer. It also acknowledges that what is meaning-making in the poem is not only what the author intentionally includes in the poem, but also what she knowingly or unknowingly excludes.

Conclusion

The on-going responsibility for teachers of writing is to continue the interrogation of what they do when they teach reading and writing. This responsibility holds as well for teachers of poetry writing. Naturally, many poets who teach students to write do not want to demystify the process of making a poem. No doubt, the use of "methods" or "procedures" in helping students write poems might seem to many practicing poets to be contradictory at best and dishonest at worst. But I blame these very attitudes for preventing interested theorists from doing the same kind and amount of work with the teaching of poetry writing as they have with the teaching of composition. If the teaching going on were improved, we might have a larger audience for the poetry that is published and fewer contemporary poets who sound like their teachers.

On the other hand, poetry has always held a very special place among writers. More than one successful writer has echoed the belief that if a person can write a poem he or she can also write just about any other kind of text. Poetry arises from a mysterious source. And the hardest gift from nature to duplicate through any artificial means is talent.

Still, if poetry writing is being taught in the university, and if record numbers of students are enrolling in those courses, then we need to make certain that we are helping students become the best poets possible. But we can be certain that students will continue to enroll in Introductory Poetry Writing having read little, if any, poetry prior to entering that course. Such students need to be led, as far as is possible, into some recognition of what the writing of poetry entails. Some (a very few) of those students will continue into intermediate and advanced courses. Perhaps others who have survived the introductory course will become readers of poetry. In either case, introductory students will continue to learn best in the time available in a semester if the teacher employs strategies — perhaps, among others — inherited from the New Critics. Once these students advance to the intermediate and advanced courses, they should be able to take greater and greater control of their own texts, having by now had experiences (comparable to those we expect students in composition courses to have had prior to entering English 101) as readers and writers that will make it possible for them to develop whatever talent they might have. These students will benefit, as did Terri and Deb, from a teacher's ability to read differently. And pedagogical methods, as I have shown, will continue to be dictated by the way the teacher makes meaning in a text.

There are, of course, other ways to read texts. The three methods employed here were chosen to reflect not the range of reading styles, but the amount of intrusion in the student-writer's process each style demands. Clearly, the less experience the student has as a reader and writer, the greater the intrusion warranted. On the other hand, more experienced students, such as Deb, require less intrusion. More work needs to be done, of course, to determine the results of these kinds of readings and others that might be made as well as to determine what combinations of methods result in the best writing by individual students. Still, I hope these readings offer other theorists a point of departure.

Works Cited

Bizzaro, Patrick. 1990a. "Evaluating Student Poetry Writing: A Primary Trait Model." *Teaching English in the Two-Year College* 17: 54–61.

———. 1990b. "Interaction and Assessment: Some Applications of Reader-Response Criticism to the Evaluation of Student Writing in a Poetry

Writing Class." In *The Writing Teacher as Researcher: Essays in the Theory and Practice of Class-Based Research*. Donald Daiker and Max Morenberg, eds. Portsmouth, NH: Heinemann.

Cain, William. 1984. *Crisis in Criticism*. Baltimore: Johns Hopkins University Press.

Cooper, Charles, and Lee Odell, eds. 1977. *Evaluating Writing: Describing, Measuring, Judging*. Urbana, IL: NCTE.

Crowley, Sharon. 1989. *A Teacher's Introduction to Deconstruction*. Urbana, IL: NCTE.

Lynn, Steven. 1990. "A Passage into Critical Theory." In *Conversations: Contemporary Critical Theory and the Teaching of Literature*. Charles Moran and Elizabeth F. Penfield, eds. Urbana, IL: NCTE, 99–114.

Mailloux, Steven. 1990. "The Turns of Reader-Response Criticism." In *Conversations: Contemporary Critical Theory and the Teaching of Literature*. Charles Moran and Elizabeth Penfield, eds. Urbana, IL: NCTE, 38–54.

Onore, Cynthia. 1989. "The Student, the Teacher, and the Text: Negotiating Meanings through Response and Revision." In *Writing and Response: Theory, Practice, and Research*. Chris M. Anson, ed. Urbana, IL: NCTE, 231–60.

Wellek, Rene. 1963. "From the Analysis of the Literary Work of Art." In *Modern Criticism: Theory and Practice*. Walter Sutton and Richard Foster, eds. New York: Odyssey, 257–61.

Wolcott, Willa. 1987. "Writing Instruction and Assessment: The Need for Interplay Between Process and Product." *College Composition and Communication* XXXVIII: 40–46.

Resources

Introduction

The conventional resource for teaching poetry is the basic textbook, most often a literature anthology containing a representative selection of poetry from various periods and countries. Most of the selections in the traditional textbook do not even begin to hint at the rich potential which lies in poetry, both past and present. Many teachers, like students, are unfamiliar with where to look for new selections or how to go about the process of identifying possible selections or poets to supplement the regular fare.

One of the most exciting and certainly new resources to explore in the teaching of poetry is the computer. Although one might not be inclined to believe that there could be an effective linkage between machines and poetry, in truth, the computer age is even influencing the teaching of poetry in highly positive and innovative ways. Computer applications to the teaching of poetry are a well kept secret. In fact, it might seem that poets and poetry ought not to have anything to do with the computer revolution. Stephen Marcus provides an extensive review of what currently is available via the computer to assist students and teachers with poetry. While offering an analysis of where current computer applications may be most beneficial, Marcus also discusses the role which attitudes will play in whether or not the computer becomes an important element in extending students' writing and appreciation of poetry. He begins by assessing the role that word processing plays today in writing and then offers fascinating glimpses of what may lie beyond simple word processing into the realm of shaping poetic expression. While the typewriter may have served as a kind of "personal printing press" for poets such as e.e. cummings, T. S. Eliot, and Ezra Pound, what might the computer hold for future poets? Marcus also offers a review of current software packages which teachers might want to obtain for use in their classrooms to promote the writing and exploration of poetic text.

But why stop with computers? Why not look for other media which could enhance the teaching of poetry? Michael Cohen suggests that the joining of the visual, in this case art, and poetry can enrich students' experience while also broadening their perspective on the role of the arts in literature. Cohen provides a sequential approach that results in carefully prepared audiovisual presentations that can be created either by the teacher or by students. His sample script combines the art of Picasso with the poetry of Keats and Wallace Stevens, suggesting a model for replication with other art works and poets.

The traditional literature anthology tends not to provide much information or representation concerning ethnic poetry. Few teachers have had courses or done extensive reading in ethnic literature. As a result, important aspects of our literary heritage and culture often remain unknown to students. For teachers seeking to reach beyond the traditional anthology and locate poetry that acknowledges ethnic contributions, articles by Deirdre Raynor and Sally A. Jacobsen and Anna Lee Stensland provide up-to-date listings of Afro-American and Native American poetry. Suggestions of black poets include both historical and contemporary selections along with listings of appropriate recordings and an assessment of which black authors appear most frequently in school anthologies. Stensland offers a number of suggested readings which should do much to overcome the stereotypical selections which frequently are provided as representative of Native American writings and which also contribute to the stereotypes in the minds of many Americans.

Finally, for those teachers who want to find works which will appeal directly to adolescents, especially for those students who are reluctant readers, Charles R. Duke offers an annotated listing of inexpensive paperback poetry collections which a teacher might find useful as the basis of a classroom library from which selections can be taken to address a variety of issues and interests appropriate to students from junior high age up through college. Included along with the collections is a short listing of outstanding books focusing on teaching poetry which might also become part of any high school literature teacher's professional library.

20

Machinery for the Muse: Computers and Poetry

Stephen Marcus

[The] only people left out of this [computer] revolution are poets.

—BettyAnn Kevles

Any sufficiently advanced technology is indistinguishable from magic.

—Arthur C. Clarke

Introduction

The computer can provide students with new powers and incentives for studying and writing poetry. But it hardly seems to matter.

At the last two National Educational Computing conferences, tours of the exhibit areas revealed only two or three software programs designed specifically for studying and writing poetry. It was the same at the recent World Conference on Computers and Education (held only once every five years). Discussions with publishers at these events confirmed the predictable explanation: texts for teaching poetry itself are a "very hard sell." So it's not surprising that few companies are willing to risk investing in software development for an area that's not that profitable to begin with. The first quotation above (Kevles 1982), then, is still a common view for good reason. It may be somewhat less applicable in recent years, but it's certainly operative when it comes to educational computing.

It isn't just a case of merchandise and marketing, though. English teachers' attitudes about the proper relationship between the muse and

179

the machine are still strongly biased against *any* such connection. To use Ellen Nold's words (1975; see also, McCorduck 1979; Boden 1977) there is a long tradition of "fear and trembling" in English teachers' responses. Nold was one of the first to discuss this at length, noting that in a request for topics for a national meeting of the Conference on College Composition and Communication, the person making the request characterized the then current age as one in which "computers ... seem to control our thinking or to make us passive in our concerns about the human condition ...."

With particular regard to computers and poetry, things have changed very little since at least 1979, when a composition teacher/poet bristled at a colleague's mere mention of using computers to help write poetry. (This same published poet has since, however, made great efforts to transport a desktop computer to a writer's colony.) It shouldn't be surprising, then, that even ten years later, an ERIC bibliography on Poetry-Writing Instruction should include only three references to computer-based articles, two of which are from the same issue of a journal (ERIC/RCS, Fast Bib No. 13, February 1989).

It's the second sentiment quoted at the start of this chapter that represents the more uncommon perspective, in this case from science-fiction writer Arthur C. Clarke. It's an appropriate perspective to adopt when considering the use of computers in the teaching of poetry, and it's the attitude that more properly informs most of the present discussion. Due in part to limited space, the focus here will be on computers and more familiar kinds of software, with only a passing reference to the potential of other technologies for generating computer-based multimedia environments related to poetry writing and teaching. It's important to remember that even in writing instruction *per se* we have only barely begun to figure out how best to teach students the basic operation of word processors for *transcribing* their work, let alone for creating or revising it. It's perfectly fitting, therefore, to concentrate here on the more familiar applications of technology and merely to suggest what the future may hold. We really have only an inkling of the ways in which the magic of the machine will inspire and encourage students to express themselves and to fathom the expressions of others.

Overview

Within the general confines of this present discussion, then, the linking of computers, poets, and poetry occurs in at least five regards:

- poetry written with the aid of word processors
- poetry written on the subject of computers

- poetry redefined in terms of the technology used to produce it
- poetry generated by computers
- poetry written with interactive software guiding its form and content

Each of these areas will be considered below, at greater or lesser length. In addition, mention will be made of the use of data base software and multimedia technologies. Software and publications will be listed in the References and Software Resources section, which will also contain information about specific software mentioned in the discussion.

The more general question being addressed is how computers can be used in classrooms to help students write and study poetry. How the technological magic contributes to the artistic mystery is also of no small concern.

Poetry on Computers

The use of word processors provides some of the same advantages to poets as to prose writers. Material may easily be rearranged, deleted, expanded, and corrected. Cross-outs, erasures, and retypings are eliminated. For Peter McWilliams (1982), who described these advantages:

> This capability is especially valuable to poets striving for visual impact as well as verbal meaning. . . . Poets and other writers now have a tool that remembers and displays the best of what they have created. With it, experimental alterations can be made quickly, silently, and nearly effortlessly. . . . A tool such as this just might free the poet's mind of the mundane and allow true inspiration to flow unfettered.

In addition, many teachers now store assignments for writing and studying poetry as word processing files. As students work on their thinking and language skills, they are also learning and practicing word processing skills like search-and-replace, block moves, cursor placement, insert vs. typeover modes, etc. For example, fifth-grade teacher Sue Whisenand had for several years been having her students use the computer to write and store poems about the life-cycles of plants, but she had never taught them the search-and-replace capability of their word processor, which allows the writer to have the computer automatically replace every occurrence of a given word or phrase with another word or phrase. After attending a workshop that demonstrated various uses of this feature, she immediately applied it in class. She had her students try changing their poems from "third-person impersonal" to "first-person personal," to see if what they had to say about the life cycles of plants had any relevance to their own life cycles. This is the kind of experimenting with thought and language that is done much more easily with the computer than otherwise.

Another application of word processing is the use of writing prompts stored as text files. The students can retrieve a particular assignment, work on it, and save it using a different file name. The original assignment file remains unchanged, ready for the next student or group to use it. Here is an example of such an assignment, from *Writing Works*. It starts with some general instructions before the actual writing prompts. (In the example below, some technical instructions have been omitted and only a few sample prompts are illustrated).

> Poems are often like dreams that talk.
> They tell you interesting things in strange ways.
>
> There are 11 "strange" pairs of phrases below.
> The two phrases in each pair may not seem to go together,
> but they do — or will.
>
> The first phrase is the beginning of a poem.
> The second phrase will be the poem's ending.
> You get to create the poem that connects the phrases.
>
> [Samples]
>
> • Inside her head she heard
>
>   and day by day she found her way.
> • I've broken many promises,
>   and told many lies.
>
>   But you'll never catch me
>   trapping clouds in bottles.
> • There's not a lot of wildness
>
>   Can you tell who is inside the cage,
>   and who is not?
>
> Okay ... now it's time for you to do some writing.
>
> Choose a pair of phrases. Move the cursor between the phrases
> and write the first draft of the poem that connects them.
>
> If you enjoy challenges, see if you can finish your poem
> in one screen-page. That will give you a Screen Dream.
>
> Before you begin to write, take a moment to feel your pulse.
> If you have a pulse, there's poetry inside you.
> Poetry gives that pulse a voice.

Again, this example illustrates a familiar technique (first line/last line) that is given a few new twists by having it done with a computer. If the pairs of lines were provided on paper, the space between the first and last portions in each pair would remain static. On a computer screen, that space is dynamic. It expands to accommodate the writer's ideas. Students can also easily modify the pairs of lines, for example by changing the order of a given pair to see how that affects what they might write (or what they have already written).

A similar approach can be used for text files that contain questions designed to help students think and write about poetry they are studying. Examples of such files are contained in commercially available materials like *WriteOn!*, *The Writing Lab*, and *WritingWorks*. Prepared text files that can be worked on with the students' word processor have the advantage of being easily tailored by the teacher to suit the students' vocabulary level and the focus of instruction. There are also the usual advantages of allowing the writer to make quick revisions, quickly save early drafts while continuing to work on the current version, obtain neatly printed copies, etc. To the extent that students are refining their word processing skills in the course of doing this writing activity, they may be introduced to special features of their word processor that make their writing task easier, more efficient, and more fun.

One other technique that might be mentioned is "invisible writing with a computer" (Marcus, and Blau 1983; Marcus 1990). This involves turning the monitor screen dark during certain prewriting activities. The intent is to develop fluency and to deal with the compulsion many people feel to fix typos and misspellings as they are creating drafts of their work — even when such efforts interfere with the flow of thought. Students practicing invisible writing have reported that what they wrote came more from their "subconscious" and that they were, in fact, freed from the habit of interfering with their prewriting by premature editing. In addition, in studies done with non-computer-based invisible writing, individuals reported that they were able to produce particularly thoughtful pieces of poetry (Blau 1983). This particular technique shows promise for helping students learn more about their writing habits when using a word processor and, in particular, when trying to concentrate on a difficult writing task like composing poetry.

Thus, word processor-based writing activities are one common use of new technology to accomplish traditional goals, whether the material helps students create or study poems. A particular advantage to this approach is that teachers can prepare their own files for students to work on. There are, to be sure, certain design-criteria that should be attended to but are often ignored. These include issues like the personality of the "speaker" on the screen or the "host in the machine" (Marcus 1985), the use of wider margins, shorter paragraphs and lines, special typographic symbols, etc. These considerations derive from the fact that designing a readable and engaging "television" screen is different from designing a ditto. Nevertheless, because teachers can easily "computerize" assignments they have already developed, or purchase and adapt commercially prepared materials, this approach is one of the most flexible and familiar applications. It's one of the most accessible for those teachers who are just beginning to incorporate technology into their instruction.

And Poetry on Computers

Sleek, sensual in its robust, organized plastic,
  inviting to the finger
      (and hence to the nerves of the arm, the brain,
      the great outdoors)
etched in religious hues and mystical language
      (data ... terminal ... yes ... no)
the future reptile slinks happily
through our lives.

(Reprinted by permission of the author)

The positive view that began the preceding section differs markedly from that afforded by a reading of the few poems written on the subject of computers, like the somewhat ambivalent one above by Harold Schneider (1981). This is perhaps an unfair comparison, since most of these sentiments were expressed before word processors allowed more poets to use, rather than just react to, the technology. Predictably, and understandably, most of these poems display anger, indignation, or ironic melancholy at the ways in which computers have been used to distort and demean the quality of life (Salamon 1958; Vagabzade 1964; Brautigan 1968; Gilbert 1970; Liteky 1974; Bradbury 1976). These expressions seem to grow out of a "fascination with the abomination" (to apply Joseph Conrad's phrase). It is difficult to find the use of analogy or metaphor drawn from the computer world to enrich an understanding of some other area of experience. And it is difficult to find a celebration of computers *per se* — not surprising given the anti-technology bias that is so strong in our literary tradition (but see the poems written about computers in the discussion of *Compupoem*, below).

That there is such limited material should be seen as an opportunity rather than a problem. Class discussions can center around such questions as these: What is it about computers that leads to this state of affairs? They seem to evoke strong emotions, so why don't people use poetry to express these feelings? What is it about poetry and about computers that makes them seem so at odds with each other? If you consider computers "unpoetic," how does that help clarify your definition of "poetry"? (See also the discussion questions elicited by the use of *Compupoem*, below.)

You can also send students on a kind of "scavenger hunt." Ask them to bring to class examples of poetry that focus on people's attitudes toward computers and related technology or that make use of computer jargon. Have them bring in advertisements that picture computers in metaphorical or figurative ways (visual as well as verbal). Ask them to write their own poems about computers.

Such activities can help develop students' poetic literacy and vocabulary, their sense of diction, metaphor, and figurative language. Students can also come to understand the degree to which "suitable" topics for poetry change from century to century and from discourse community to discourse community.

Poetry Redefined

It's not just the topics of poetry that undergo transformation but the forms themselves. In addition, Michael Newman (1986) suggests, "the properties of a medium can have a decisive impact on the nature of what the medium conveys." This is also the theme that Diane Silverstein (1988) explores in her discussion of technologies like the typewriter and the computer on the printed word — and in particular on poetry.

Silverstein notes how the typewriter's "precise regularity" provided poets like cummings, Eliot, and Pound with a "personal printing press" that helped guide accents and oral stress, almost like a musical score. She also reminds us of Kenneth Patchen's breaking of "visual conventions by writing his poems up and down the sides of a page, and then over the border onto the sides of the next page."

Patchen's work perhaps illustrates attempts to deal with what Edmund Skellings (1983) has referred to as poets' "irritation in the eight-and-a-half-by-eleven, black-and-white cell of Gutenberg's prison." Skellings has developed *The Electric Poet*, with which the words of poems can "flash and spin, change color, move in time, rotate and disappear." This program has been used, for example, at schools for the deaf, where the students can now "see" sound patterns by using color and timed display of text. In another setting, teachers at primary and elementary schools have noted that color "enhances and reinforces a child's recall, both visually and auditorily. . . . *The Electric Poet* is very effective with learning disabled children because they have many subtle memory problems. The computer has teaching capabilities that cannot be gotten from a textbook."

Poet and programmer Jim Rosenberg provides another, more complex, example of how a computer makes possible new conceptions of what constitutes a poem. As described by Dick Barnes (1980) in his profile of Rosenberg's work, the poet initially devised (without computers) what he termed "word-nets," structures from which "a reader might generate any number of poems by the arbitrary choice of where in the net to begin and which way to go at the knots." Eventually, he began to produce diagrams that were themselves intended as poetic artifacts.

> The diagrams are a logical development from the word-nets; they
> became necessary when . . . using clusters instead of single words. The
> idea was to try to use word clusters as musicians use tone clusters,
> allowing the words to be free of traditional syntax as the notes are from
> traditional harmony. A difficulty that arose was that words themselves
> have syntactical implications, a kind of signal that is disrupted when
> words of different syntactical characteristics are juxtaposed. . . . [The]
> way out [of this problem] was to provide a different kind of "syntax"
> indicated by the notational device of the diagram.

These diagrams became themselves the poetic composition, being
based on the presentation in random order of words and phrases
Rosenberg had stored in a computer. He began using his terminal to
compose the diagrams, make changes in them, and, of course, to print
them. Their non-linear nature, however, required quite a different sort of
information processing on the part of the "reader":

> In these new poems, the parsing is done according to diagrams that
> give information about juxtaposition, subordination, and mediation
> between the clusters of words and between complex configurations of
> them. This information, provided visually, does not translate out
> verbally; the reader is obliged to grasp these relationships silently, as
> it were, according to the wordless shapes. Furthermore, the notational
> key provides rules for parsing that, while preserving indeterminacy,
> allow some but not all paths between configurations.

Dick Barnes, himself a published poet, has noted that reading
these diagrams "requires, not more intellectual effort than I am accustomed to make when reading a poem, but a different kind of effort."
Studying the diagrams, trying to grasp the nonverbal syntax of it all
directly, produces a kind of music that answers the movement, not of
the eye or the ear, but of the mind.

It's probably not coincidental that both Silverstein and Barnes
refer to the capability of technology to emphasize the musical dimensions
of poetry. In addition, if technology is in some respects indistinguishable
from magic, then the kind of computer-assisted redefinition of poetry
described above allows for the kind of sleight of mind that Barnes
experienced in his "reading" of Rosenberg's work. From a related
perspective, it has been suggested that not only "random association,
but the image of computer forms, the array, the nested loop, the
structure and even the punctuation of languages like LISP can suggest
new syntactical arrangements to the poet, can free the image or the
word from its dependence on previous expectable contexts" (William
Dickey, San Francisco State University, personal communication).

While the discussion above is perhaps far removed from the poetry
curricula of most classrooms, it does deal with one of the more challenging interactions between technology and poetic language. Skellings

(Edlin 1981) believes that the computer "is going to change the way we perceive" language and literature. If a change in message derives from a change in medium, then the kinds of technological aids described above (and below) may very well cause us to adjust our notions of what constitutes poetry, what forms it can take, and how it is to be "read." All suitable topics for English classes.

Poetry by Computers

Rosenberg's computer-based diagrams, particularly, invite debate on the question, "Is this really poetry?" For philosophers like C. L. Stevenson (1957) the question "what is a poem?" is, of course, a difficult and profound one, and ways to address it can only be hinted at in the course of the present discussion. For example, Louis T. Milic (1971a, 1971b) has suggested (1971a) that "one interesting result of my activity in computer poetry generation is a new definition of poetry." Milic's definition involves the violating of logical sequence and semantic distribution categories (two dimensions that certainly apply to Rosenberg's work).

As noted above, Rosenberg's diagrams derive, in part, from the computer's ability to rapidly generate random groupings of words and phrases. This procedure is a common one for producing what appear to be poetic "utterances" (Ahl 1978; Dwyer and Critchfield 1978; Danielson 1981; Stewart 1983). Hale Chatfield (1985), for example, using *LIFESONGS*, can rapidly generate examples of the over 268 million variants of four sonnets "composed so that each of their first through fourteenth lines are interchangeable."

More sophisticated heuristics can replace mere randomization, using instead rule-governed procedures derived from natural language. As an introductory example, Milic (1971a) provides a sentence structure formula such as this: Article + Noun(1) + Verb + Preposition + Article + Noun(2). Lists of words in each class are used as data variables in a program that reads and sums the variables. Sentences generated in this manner can seem quite poetical in their surprising juxtaposition of images or meanings.

Another method is to start with a "real" poem, to pick one part of speech — for example, all the nouns — and then to take them all out, alphabetize them, and re-insert them into the poem in the new order. The same procedure is used with the adjectives and the verbs. Using a more sophisticated set of procedures, Milic (1971b) has devised his *RETURNER* poetry program, which combines randomness, iteration, and various checking routines that "ensure grammatical agreement and concord." With a program like *The Poetry Generator* (Stewart 1983), a student can produce poems in the manner of writers like Shakespeare,

Dickinson, and Frost by using formats and vocabularies characteristic of the writer. The similarly titled *Poetry Generator*, developed by Rosemary West (Dewdney 1989), is also fully automated. Thomas Easton's *Thunder Thought* (Dewdney 1989) is designed for human collaboration, producing what Easton calls "raw poetic material for a human mind to refine." Michael Newman's Orpheus A-B-C: The *Poetry Processor* (Newman 1986) includes a feature that "lays out the lines of a given poetic form [and] allows a human being to fill in the lines according to whim and then to end them with the help of a rhyming dictionary" (see also, Dewdney 1989).

The use of poetry-generating software in instructional settings has been wonderfully illustrated by Alfred Kern and James Sheridan at Allegheny College (Kern 1983). They taught students about poetry, to write poetry, to program a computer to write poetry, and to use computer-produced poetry as early drafts for their own. The students agreed that they were "learning more about poetry within the constructs of the computer than they had learned in conventional classes." And "many students found their way to my office to say they did not begin to know enough about the English language."

For individuals like Milic (1971a), the utility of such computer applications to the writing of poetry is not necessarily "the usual poetic intention (prophecy, self-expression, aesthetic creation)." Rather, the concern is with "what the doer can learn about language, about poetry, and about poets from [these sorts] of simulation[s]." In addition, there's the perspective of Goldenberg and Feurzeig (1987), who have provided an extensive treatment of how to teach the computer to model language behavior. They suggest that it is "not 'cheating' to write the poem that the machine *almost* created but was too stupid to recognize." And Kern (1983) would add:

> If the computer now inspires students to know more about poetry, if the symbols of binary logic allow easier and readier learning, why not use it? One claims the teaching moment where and as one can.

There is, finally, a rather nontraditional question that must be added to the ones noted above. Since one of the implications of the work described above is "the demolition of the critical axiom that the poem is sufficient. ... [We] must now ask a new question before beginning an exegesis: Who or what wrote this poem?" (Milic 1971a).

Poetry with Computers

The last question above is basic to the work with interactive software for studying and writing poetry. Like some of the word processor-based text files described earlier, these programs usually combine some direct instruction on poetic topics with a series of prompted writing activities that produce drafts of poems. Theses programs differ significantly from the text files described above insofar as they are much less under the control of the teacher or student. They have their unique operating systems (just as different word processing programs do), and the material and writing procedures provided by a given program can be modified only to the degree that the program's operating system allows.

A program like *Introduction to Poetry* provides a tutorial on the basic concepts of meter and common stress patterns. *Poetry Palette* provides guidance for writing and learning about poetry, including poetry written in shapes, with echoes, with opposites, in free verse, and with traditional rhyme and meter. It also includes a graphics library and a 12,000-word rhyming dictionary. *The Poet's Pen* helps students write diamante, cinquain, and haiku. *Poetry Express* helps students create haiku, limericks, rhyme, diamante, and other forms. *The Poet's Journal* provides activities for analyzing, generalizing, brainstorming, and creating poems. *Writing Poetry* provides a "workbook" that includes extensive help screens and exercises for critiquing and writing poems. *Haikuku, Star Alpha, Poetry Workout* and *Poetry Tutor* provide a wide variety of writing and study aids. (For sources, see the Software References at the end of this chapter.) These programs attempt to replicate some of the familiar kinds of writing activities often used in English classes. Encountering them on a computer can also generate in both teachers and students a wide range of reactions concerning the suitability of using technology to inspire "creative" writing.

My own earlier efforts to explore the computer-assisted composing process for writing poetry included developing a computer program called *Compupoem*, which give students an opportunity to use a computer for all stages of the composing process (Marcus 1982a, 1982b, 1983, 1984). In addition, working with *Compupoem* has provided occasions for students to deal in a very personal way with the questions noted above concerning the definitions of poetry and poet.

The discussion below, while focusing on certain features of this particular program, addresses issues that to various degrees are relevant to all of the programs mentioned earlier in this section. While different programs may be more or less "feature-rich," they all attempt to create with a computer the kind of dialogue (limited though it may be) that occurs in one-to-one classroom tutorials.

In the case of *Compupoem*, we have a writing "game" that prompts the student for different parts of speech and formats the words into a haiku-like poetic structure. The student may then select from fourteen different Advice Options, which provide suggestions on such things as choosing adverbs, prepositional phrases, nouns, etc., on Zen and the art of computer use, and on other relevant topics (see below). Students may also see their poems instantly rewritten in different formats in order to examine the relationships between form and impact. Like the other programs mentioned at the start of this section, *Compupoem* is quite different from most of the programs that generate random sequences of poetic phrases. Instead, it elicits the student's knowledge and imagination and depends on active involvement in the writing.

The process is also different in important ways from "fill-in-the-blanks" activities like Mad-Libs, in which the user's words are inserted into a predetermined template. *Compupoem* requires that the student supply both the parts and the overall conception of the whole. In addition, while most language arts word games and drill-and-practice activities are "won" by the user's coming up with the correct responses, *Compupoem* explicitly encourages the attitude that "winning" results from the creation of interesting and satisfying responses.

Compupoem has been used with students (fourth grade through graduate school) and faculty (kindergarten through university) and with out-of-school adults from a variety of backgrounds (including engineers and professional poets). The authors of the poems below range from fourth grader to university professor.*

Paul's Poem
The riveter
brawny
sweatcaked at Miller Time
carefully slouches
Bethlehembound.

Cathi's Poem
The sonata for eyes
   magenta, secretive
     sidestepped through their
      dreams stealthily with
       sorrow.

Stephen's Poem
The wide, slow river,
Meandering,
Like the worst of schooling
(In one year and out the other)
Unknowingly
Cuts its ruts.

Harold's Poem
The reptilian brain

Sheridan's Poem
The words
   masterful, serving
for inspiration
   gently, insistently
solace.

Mary's Poem
The bellhop
   pink, quixotic
before the convention
   frequently, sorely
wishes.

Emily's Poem
The thief
   sneaky, stupid
Into the jail
   quietly, quickly
Breaks in.

Marla's Poem
The tree house
full of childhood memories

---

* All reprinted by permission of the authors.

sweet, juicy	suspended
in the nick of time's swamp	on the lonely oak tree
gracelessly	softly, in a whisper
beckons.	swaying.

In certain respects, *Compupoem* doesn't do anything that any classroom teacher doesn't do: it gives directions and advice. In other respects, however, its computer-assisted dimensions provide unique occasions for exploring each stage of the composing process.

To begin with, the prompts, which ask for different parts of speech, constitute a heuristic device for generating both the subject of the poem and the substance. The use of a computer encourages rapid and copious pre-writing of poems — and while quantity does not always engender quality, the ease with which "first drafts" can be produced proves to be a significant factor for those for whom writing does not come easily. (It was especially important for those who noted that they didn't have the *faintest* idea of how to begin writing a poem: for them, producing something even resembling a poem was a transforming experience.)

The prompts, appearing as they do in a somewhat alien context (i.e., on a computer screen), aid in pre-writing. The actual "writing" of the poem is accomplished in an instant. The students see a list of ideas suddenly transformed into a poetic whole. Whether or not this first draft is a satisfying or "correct" version of a student's overall idea and intent, it provides more refined raw material than does the list of ideas or qualities that the prompts initially elicit. Even with young writers, many of these first drafts deserve and reward attention. They invite the reader to focus on some specific image or event, to note its beauty, significance, or humor.

Before the students are presented with the Advice Option menu, they are encouraged to write their poems on paper before proceeding. Not having the computer simply store the first version derives from my attempt to encourage the students to take back "ownership" of their words and poems, to take responsibility for shaping the poems by revising in the course of recording. (It's also true that at the time this program was developed, there were very few printers in classrooms.) In this regard, it's interesting to note the responses students have given to the following evaluation question:

Who wrote your poem? (Circle a number.)
(you)   1   2   3   4   5 (the computer)

Students tended to circle higher numbers for early poems and lower numbers for later ones. The degree to which students felt that both the form and the content of their poems were of their own device was thus a rough measure of the nature of their composing process. (See also, the discussion of Zen advice, below.)

While there does exist an Advice Option that will rewrite the poem in different ways, I thought it important to retain and encourage the students' involvement in immediate decisions about revising their poems. They soon learn that one of the "rules of the game" is that if they do not value their work enough to write it down, it will soon disappear. They will lose the chance to reconsider their words. It thus provides a new kind of object-lesson in valuing themselves. It is also worth noting that Special Education teachers have reported that the Instant Rewrites option was far and away the most popular. Just a few keystrokes allowed them to accomplish a task that would normally have been exceedingly frustrating.

In the course of developing *Compupoem*, I encountered a few people whose reactions suggested that I should address the issues of computer anxiety, the nature of poetry, and the definition of a poet (1981, 1982a). Adapting some familiar advice, I included the following Advice Option, titled "Zen." Upon selecting that option, the students would see this text:

> Some people struggle with this game (i.e., the computer).
> They compete with it or feel themselves terribly constrained
> by its rules or by their own sense of what "poetry" is.
>
> Take a tip from some ancient Zen wisdom:
>
> > In the beginning, the computer is the master.
> > Then, the person is master of the computer.
> > In the end, neither needs to be master.
>
> If that doesn't inspire you, nothing will.
>
> Time to get back to work ...
>
> Want to write another poem?

Not many fourth graders get the two Zen puns in this advice, involving inspiration (and its relation to breathing) and "nothing" (or no-thing, the creative void available when the "noise" from inner anxieties has been quieted). It turns out they don't have to. They just go back and write more poems.

Some students have had fascinating and fruitful objections to *Compupoem*. The writing it produced, according to one student, could not be a poem because the machine did the writing, with the student merely producing "words in answer to the computer's questions." Such objections provided wonderful opportunities for raising such questions as, "What *is* a poem? What *is* a poet? Having used *Compupoem*, are you now a poet (not necessarily a good poet, but a poet)? How do you know? What does a set of words need, how does it need to have been produced, in order for it to be considered poetry?" These questions are part of the stock-in-trade of any English teacher. They were given new power in the context of students' personal involvement in creating "poems" that were challenged as such by their peers. Class evaluations suggest that such discussions were valuable in generating new and broader insights into the creative process.

Another interesting aspect of people's approach to *Compupoem* relates, I believe, to students' differing cognitive styles. Some individuals reported that they built up their poems part by part (literally, part of speech by part of speech), using inductive, detail-oriented, perhaps "left-brained" strategies. In the words of one student, she was "amazed at how the words that seemed so separate fit together so well." Other students began with an overall, intuitive, visual, perhaps "right-brained" sense of the whole of their conceptions and then filled in the missing parts (of speech): "I tried to visualize what the eventual outcome of the poem would be and to think of words or phrases that would make the poem more interesting." Or: "When I chose my words . . . , the thought was not particularly well-developed. It was just an image in my mind."

As students grew more accustomed to the technology, they more often than not let their own styles determine their approach. They were also able to revise more freely the form and content when they recorded their work.

In an effort to encourage students to use *Compupoem* for exploring diverse topics, I included as an Advice Option some standard guidance from Synectics creativity training: make the strange familiar and the familiar strange.

> Try writing a poem about a very unpoetic subject, like thermodynamics, math, or economics.
>
> A math teacher, for instance, wrote an intriguing poem using the word "asymptotic" — which is also a great way to describe some people you probably know.
>
> So . . . get the words and metaphors from unpoetic places, and put poems in strange surroundings.

Such advice has produced poems on subjects as diverse as the hyperbola, the epidermis, scientists, and, of course, computers. In light of the poems about computers referred to in an earlier section, it is interesting to note the sentiments that "compupoets" expressed on this topic. One such example has already been quoted above, a complex image involving the sensuous and the mystical, characterizing the computer as a strange creature that, while healthy and vigorous, may yet be contributing to its own insouciant demise. A simpler (and more familiar) view is this one:

Stephen's Poem

The machines
    patient, forgiving
all around you
    quietly, softly
conspire.

On the other hand, much younger students characteristically expressed more upbeat attitudes. The following were written by two fifth graders:

Lisa's Poem	*Sho's Poem*
The computer	The computer
smart, exciting	fantastic, super
in a classroom	in the lab
quickly, intelligently	intelligently, joyfully
educates.	computing.

Students have reported that *Compupoem* elicited concerns for planning ahead, unity, and coherence. Many enjoyed being "quizzed" on parts of speech in a nonjudgmental, puzzle-like setting. One of the most significant assessments in this regard — and in perhaps a more significant context — came from Earl B. Oremus (1984), an eleventh-grade teacher. He describes how, after a very short session with the program

> Sheri, my most disaffected, dyslexic, anti-establishment, and anti-school (especially English) student approached me and requested some instruction on prepositional phrases. I almost fell over. I can think of absolutely no circumstances under which any approach I might have made to her on the same subject would have been greeted with anything but boredom and scorn. She listened eagerly to my words of wisdom on prepositions for a few minutes, cut me short with "Okay, okay, I got it," and rushed back to her computer. At the end of the period, she handed me a sheet of paper on which the following poems were erratically scrawled.

The forest,	The teacher
windy, dark	harsh, stearn
with eyes of emerald grace	in the classroom of darkness
descreatly, unpleasantly	students sit, almost scared
blinking.	wondering
	what is to be
	learned

> Needless to say, both Sheri and I are very anxious to get *Compupoem* back in business in our classroom. In fact, Sheri is the student who wanted to take a copy home for the evening so she could write some more poems. [Reprinted by permission of the author.]

That so much positive response can derive from such a simple activity bodes well for further development of computer-assisted language arts instruction that taps poetic sensibilities. Particularly for people who approach the computer with trepidation (teachers originally formed the bulk of this group), programs like *Compupoem* allow them to operate in a somewhat familiar arena, albeit with unfamiliar tools. This helps demystify the unaccountable "magic" of the technology as it helps advance their own and their students' computer literacy. And it helps put technology in its place—in this case, to enrich and enliven the study of poetry.

Data Bases, Multimedia, and Hypermedia

There are other computer-based applications available for helping students study and write poetry. The brief descriptions provided below don't begin to do them justice, but they should suggest the range and depth of resources available to teachers interested in incorporating technology into instruction.

To begin with, there are traditional data base applications, generally defined as software that allows you to organize, store and retrieve information in a sort of mix-and-match way. For example, the *Poetry and Mythology Data Bases* collection allows students to store samples of their favorite poems by title, author, theme, kind, etc., and to develop question-asking and research skills derived from inquiry-based models of learning. Michael Newman's *The Poetry Processor: Orpheus A-B-C* is actually a collection of tools, including a text editor, a data base, and a kind of "spread sheet" application. Among other things, it will scan poems for meter. A different kind of program, Louie Crew's *Muses*, keeps track of what poems have been submitted for publication, where they've been sent, what their current status is, etc.

The development of "hypermedia" applications, which allow different kinds of material (audio as well as visual) to be linked together, has opened up a great many paths for both the study and writing of poetry. Brown University's Intermedia system (Yankelovich, et al. 1986) has been used in English classes to create a data base of pictorial, biographical, and critical material on the poet Browning. The system is used by students for study and research, and they can make their own contributions to the ever-growing corpus, for use by future students.

From a poet's point of view, there are models like Thomas Tafuto's *The RoughNeck*. This "interactive anthology" of the author's work allows the reader to use the computer's pointing device (a "mouse") to point at an important word in one poem displayed on the screen and be taken immediately to other poems that deal with the same theme. Readers can also use a similar procedure to open up "windows" on the

screen to read the author's comments about what lies "behind" a
particular poem, to see images that reinforce the mood or theme of a
poem, or to see what others have written in response to the poem.
Readers can add their own comments, which will be retained in the
copy of the anthology when it is passed along to other readers.

Multimedia environment can include sound, graphics, video, text,
and animation. Hypermedia technology allows the integrating of these
media in ways not available before. The following scenario is hypothetical, but realistic. All the technology mentioned currently exists in
relatively inexpensive forms, even if it hasn't been combined in the
manner described below.

First, imagine students' seeing the text of a poem on the computer
screen. They could use an inexpensive voice digitizer to record their
voices reading the poem (perhaps two male and two female readers).
They could even use a video camera to show themselves reading and
have the video recorded by the computer and shown on a small
window displayed on the computer's screen. They could compare these
readings with those of other students who had stored their renditions
on the computer. They could also capture just a single video "still
picture" of one of their group and use some software to animate the
mouth and lips, giving the appearance of someone's reading the poem.
They could also have the computer "read" the poem out loud using its
voice synthesizer (and store this version). They could then open a
small video window on the screen in which they could see and hear the
poet, from a laser disc recording, reading the poem and perhaps talking
about the process of its creation. The students could work together to
formulate their own views on the poet, the poem, and the relationships
between all of this and a similar experience they had with a different
poet the week before. If there wasn't much material on this particular
poem already stored, they could use a scanner to add text, pictures,
and other images that related to the poem, and they could create their
own links between these components and the words that evoked them.
They could check the contributions of students who had studied this
poem the previous year and add their own contributions to the stored
file for the class. They could also prepare a multimedia presentation
for the class in which they followed a "path" they had chosen through
all the material available to them. Students could also use these various
media to help themselves create their own poems, so illustrate them,
and to provide a variety of audio and visual effects.

Conclusion

But why bother? What's the matter with just having a poem, some
chairs, and some people — a focused discussion in which everyone asks

questions and helps each other answer them? And why not give an aspiring student-poet a pad of paper, a No. 2 pencil, and a little peace and quiet?

These are appropriate questions to ask, and it's appropriate to assess whether attempts to create a techno-pedagogy constitute a retreat from what is usually considered at the heart of authentic attempts to study and write poetry, and whether such attempts really do interfere with — if not actually demean — the whole enterprise. Of course, it's also appropriate to assess the extent to which typical, and non-technological, pedagogy produces these same unintended and unfortunate outcomes.

The issue is, in part, whether the machinery will master the muse, the muse the machinery, or whether neither needs to be master. The future of computers and poetry depends to a certain extent on the companies that create the tools. It depends even more on the individuals who create, *using* the tools. New and increasingly rich technologies are both enhancing and transforming students' abilities, but the vitality of computers in poetry classes depends most on talented teachers who are inspired by an informed exuberance. As usual, they will be the major force in helping their students make the most of what the technology offers.

Software Resources

PLEASE NOTE:
The working rule for a list of software sources is: If it's printed in a book, it's out of date. It's impossible to predict whether, by the time this list is published, the programs noted below will still be available and, if they are, for what machines. Interested readers should attempt to contact the sources indicated and hope for the best. (The author welcomes information on additional titles and sources.)

COMPUPOEM, Stephen Marcus, SCWriP, Graduate School of Education, University of California, Santa Barbara, CA 93106.

ELECTRIC POET. Control Color Corporation, through local IBM Personal Computer Retail Dealer. (Ref. "Software Announcements," September 1984, SA-88 Program 6024172).

INTERMEDIA. Institute for Research in Information and Scholarship (IRIS), Brown University, Box 1946, Providence, RI 02912.

INTRODUCTION TO POETRY. Management Science America, Inc. 3445 Peachtree Rd., N.E., 8th Floor, Atlanta, GA 30326.

LIFESONGS, HAIKUKU, and CATALYST. Hale Chatfield, Hiram Poetry Review, P.O. Box 162, Hiram, OH 44234.

MARK V. SHANEY. Rob Pike, AT&T Bell Laboratories, 600 Mountain Ave., Murray Hill, NJ 07974.

MICROZINE (various titles). Scholastic, Inc., 2931 East McCarty St., P.O. Box 7502, Jefferson City, NJ 65102, 800−541−5513.

MUSES. Louie Crew, Drawer 30, Newark, NJ 07101.

ORPHEUS A-B-C: THE POETRY PROCESSOR. Michael Newman, 12 West 68th St., #2C, New York, NY 10023.

POETRY AND MYTHOLOGY DATA BASES FOR SCHOLASTIC'S PFS:FILE. Scholastic, Inc., 2931 East McCarty St., P.O. Box 7502, Jefferson City, NJ 65102, 800−541−5513.

POETRY EXPRESS. Mindscape, Inc., Educational Division, 3444 Dundee Rd., Northbrook, IL 60062, 800−999−2242.

POETRY PALETTE. Mind*Play*, Department C4, Unit 350, P.O. Box 36491, Tucson, AZ 85740, 800−221−7911.

THE POET'S JOURNAL. Hartley Courseware, Inc., P.O. Box 419, Dimondale, MI 48821, 800−247−1380, 517−646−6458 (in Michigan).

THE POET'S PEN. J. Weston Walch, Publisher, 321 Valley Street, P.O. Box 658, Portland, Maine 04104, 800−341−6094.

THE ROUGHNECK. Thomas Tafuto, Kabisa Computer Creations, 914 President St., Brooklyn, NY 11215, 800−857−8020.

THE WRITING LAB. Scholastic, Inc., 2931 East McCarty St., P.O. Box 7502, Jefferson City, NJ 65102, 800−541−5513.

WRITING POETRY. Intellectual Software, Queue, Inc., 338 Commerce Drive, Fairfield, CT 06430, 800−232−2224, 203−355−0906 (in Connecticut).

WRITINGWORKS. Scholastic, Inc., 2931 East McCarty St., P.O. Box 7502, Jefferson City, NJ 65102, 800−541−5513.

WRITEON! (various titles). Humanities Software. P.O. Box 950, 408 Columbia, Suite #209, Hood River, OR 97031, 800−245−6737.

Works Cited

The references below include citations in the text along with additional related readings.

Ahl, D. H. 1978. *BASIC Computer Games* (ed.) New York: Workman Publishing.

Barnes, D. 1980. Poetry by Design, Pomona Profile of Jim Rosenberg. *Pomona Today*, Winter, pp. 34−35.

Blau, S. 1983. Invisible Writing: Investigating Cognitive Processes in Composition. *College Composition and Communication*, 34, 3, October, pp. 297−312.

Boden, M. 1977. *Artificial Intelligence and Natural Man*. New York: Basic Books.

Bradbury, R. 1976. The Machines Beyond Shylock. *Computer Magazine* (formerly *Computer Group News*). Reprinted in Dennie Van Tassel (Ed.), *The Compleat Computer*, Palo Alto, CA: Science Research Associates, Inc., 1976, p. 29.

Brautigan, R. 1968. All Watched Over by Machines of Loving Grace. *The Pill Versus the Springhill Mine Disaster*. New York: Delacorte Press. Reprinted in Dennie Van Tassel (Ed.), *The Compleat Computer*, Palo Alto, CA: Science Research Associates, Inc., 1976, p. 5.

Chatfield, H. 1985. Computers and Poetry. *Newsletter* of the Association for Computers and the Humanities, 7, 2, Summer, 1–2. Reprinted from the *Hiram Poetry Review*, #37, Fall-Winter 1984.

Danielson, W. 1981. The Creative Computer? *Discovery*, University of Texas, Austin, Spring, 5(3), pp. 8–10.

Dewdney, A. K. 1989. Computer Recreations. *Scientific American*, June, pp. 122–25.

Dwyer, T., & M. Critchfield. 1978. *BASIC and the Personal Computer*. Menlo Park, CA: Addison-Wesley Publishing Company.

Edlin, J. 1981. A Visit with a Poet of Science. *INFOWORLD*, 3, 16 August 17, 44ff.

Gilbert, C. 1970. The Data Bankers. *The Atlantic Monthly*, May. Reprinted in Dennie Van Tassel (Ed.), *The Compleat Computer*, Palo Alto, CA: Science Research Associates, Inc., 1976, p. 155.

Goldenberg, P. E., & W. Feurzeig. 1987. A Grammar of Simple Poetry. In *Exploring Language with Logo*. Cambridge, MA: MIT Press, pp. 29–44.

Kern, A. 1983. GOTO Poetry. *Perspectives in Computing*, 3(3) October, pp. 44–52.

Kevles, B. 1985. Two Cultures: It Doesn't Compute. *Los Angeles Times*, Scientific View Column, Part V, 9, February 25.

Liteky, J. P. 1974. Traces. *SUNDAZ!*, August 30. Reprinted in Dennie Van Tassel (Ed.), *The Compleat Computer*, Palo Alto, CA: Science Research Associates, Inc., 1976, p. 170.

Marcus, S. 1981. *Teacher's Guide* for *Compupoem*. SCWriP, University of California, Santa Barbara.

———. 1982a. *Compupoem*: A Computer-Assisted Writing Activity. *English Journal*, February, pp. 96–99.

———. 1982b. *Compupoem*: CAI for Studying and Writing Poetry. *The Computing Teacher*, March, 9(7), pp. 28–33.

———. 1983. The Muse and the Machine: A Computers and Poetry Project. *Handbook for Establishing an Effective Writing Program* (rev.), California State Department of Education, 59–62). Reprinted from *Classroom Computer News*, November 1982, p. 28ff.

———. 1984. GOSUB:POET:RETURN Computers and the Poetic Muse. *Educational Technology*, August, pp. 15–20.

———. 1985. The Host in the Machine: Decorum in Computers Who Speak. *IEEE Transactions on Professional Communication*, PC-28, 2, June, pp. 29–32.

———. 1989. The State of the Art and the Art of the State. *California Technology Project Quarterly*, 1, 1, p. 16ff.

———. 1990. Invisible Writing with a Computer: New Sources and Resources. *Computers and Composition* 8(1) November, pp. 41–48.

Marcus, S., & S. Blau. 1983. Not Seeing is Relieving: Invisible Writing with a Computer. *Educational Technology*, April, pp. 12–15.

McCorduck, P. 1979. *Machines Who Think*. San Francisco: W. H. Freeman and Company.

McKean, K. 1982. Computers, Fiction, and Poetry. *BYTE*, July, 50–53.

McWilliams, P. 1982. Writing Poetry on a Word Processor. *Popular Computing*, February, pp. 38–40.

Milic, L. T. 1971a. The Possible Usefulness of Poetry Generation. In R. A. Wisbey (Ed.), *The Computer in Literary and Linguistic Research*. Cambridge: Cambridge University Press.

———. 1971b. The 'RETURNER' Poetry Program. *IAL* (Institute of Applied Linguistics), 11, pp. 1–23.

Newman, M. 1986. Poetry Processing. *BYTE*, February, 221–28.

Nold, E. W. 1985. Fear and Trembling: The Humanist Approaches the Computer. *College Composition and Communication*, October, pp. 101–105.

Pedersen, E. L. 1986. Computers and the Poetry Portfolio. Paper presented at the 76th Annual Meeting of the National Council of Teachers of English (ERIC, ED 277 012).

Salomon, L. B. 1958. UNIVAC to UNIVAC (sotto voice). *Harper's Magazine*, March. Reprinted in Dennie Van Tassel (Ed.), *The Compleat Computer*, Palo Alto, CA: Science Research Associates, Inc., 1976, pp. 90–91.

Schneider, H. 1981. Harold's Apple in Eden. First printed in Marcus (1982a), *op cit.*

Sheridan, J. 1982. The Computation of the Muse. Unpublished paper. Allegheny College, Meadville, PA 16335.

Silverstein, D. 1988. The Electric Poem. *College Literature*, XV, 1, 25–34.

Skellings, E. 1979. Color Graphics Poetry: A Vision of Information. Address to the National Educational Computing Conference, Iowa City, June pp. 25–27.

———. 1983. "The Electric Poet," *Perspectives in Computing*, 3, 4, December, 12–19.

Stevenson, C. L. 1957. On "What Is a Poem?" *Philosophical Review*, 66, pp. 329–62.

Stewart, G. 1983. Roll Over, Robert Frost. *Popular Computing*, February, pp. 28–41. Reprinted in revised form as "Poetry Generator," *The Apple Program Factory*, George Stewart. Berkeley, CA: Osborne. McGraw-Hill, 1984, pp. 219–31.

Vagabzade, B. 1964. Kibernetika. *The Washington Post*, 1964. Reprinted in Dennie Van Tassel (Ed.), *The Compleat Computer*, Palo Alto, CA: Science Research Associates, Inc., 1976, p. 188.

Watt, P. 1984. The Macintosh as Poet. *InfoWorld*, October 29, p. 25.

Yankelovich, N. 1986. Creating Hypermedia Materials for English Literature Students. IRIS, Brown University, October 8, pp. 1–8.

Zimmerman, J. 1985. The Racter Factor. *PacificSun*, March 1–7, pp. 3ff.

21

Keats, Stevens, and Picasso: Designing Audiovisual Poetry Presentations

Michael Cohen

Audiovisual displays using poetry and other art forms can be useful in poetry courses and general humanities courses, for they help to show the ways in which poems connect with the rest of experience. Since such displays are intended for out-of-class use, they do not need to be stringently tied to unit objectives, and they can have rather modest aims. They are also surprisingly easy to design. The two scripts below are offered as models for such displays, and they show the variation that is possible in poem selection, treatment, and goals. One display uses a poem from the traditional canon of favorites, Keats's "Ode on a Grecian Urn," while the other's subject is a more modern poem some might consider less accessible, Wallace Stevens's "The Man with the Blue Guitar." The Keats selection is treated in a fairly basic exposition approaching a complete gloss of the poem, while the Stevens' exhibit uses a freer, more heuristic and interdisciplinary approach. The Keats display asks the students to write a statement of the poem's theme once they have finished viewing; the Stevens asks for a statement connecting the display with the themes of the course. These are only two of many ways of eliciting student response, and more specific testing questions could be used with either kind of display.

Each presentation requires a small display area for printed materials (approximately 2½ by 2 feet), a recorded audio cassette, and several 35 mm slides (a descriptive list follows each script below). Prominently marked directions are needed to tell the students what to do first; after the tape player is switched on, recorded directions can tell them what to do next. Slides and cassettes can be conveniently handled together in carousel-type projectors, but any small cassette player and separate magnifying slide viewer will serve instead. The printed display materials for these scripts include the complete text of Keats's "Ode on a Grecian Urn," but only six representative cantos from Stevens's "The Man with the Blue Guitar." After the students have read the materials, switched on the tape and listened to the script, and simultaneously viewed the slides, they are asked to write a response in notebooks provided within the display area.

Script for an Audiovisual Display of Keats's "Ode on a Grecian Urn"

TURN ON THE SLIDE VIEWER AND LOOK AT THE FIRST SLIDE FOR A MINUTE OR TWO. THEN TURN ON THE TAPE PLAYER. [These directions must be displayed prominently, along with the complete text of "Ode on a Grecian Urn."]

The vase you are looking at is a Greek design and is called an **urn**. The poet John Keats was so impressed with the sculptured figures on such an urn that he wrote the following poem. In it he speaks directly **to** the urn and later in the poem, to some of the figures carved upon it.

[READING OF "ODE ON A GRECIAN URN"]

Some of the vocabulary of the poem may be unfamiliar to you. Look at the printed poem and notice its line numbers on the right side. Keats calls the urn a **sylvan** historian in line 3; sylvan means forest or woods. He talks about the scene being in **Tempe** or the **dales of Arcady** in line 7—these are rural places in Greece considered to be ideal for their beauty. The pipes and timbrels at the end of the first stanza (line 10) are small wind instruments like flutes and small percussion instruments like tambourines. In the second stanza, in line 13, Keats tells the pipes to play on, not to the **sensual** ear—that is, the physical ear—but to pipe to the spirit, and to play "ditties of no tone": (line 14)—that is, simple songs which, since they are only depicted on the silent vase and not real, are soundless, with no tone. In the third stanza, near the end, the word **cloyed** appears in line 29, when Keats says that ordinary human passion leaves the heart cloyed, or oversatisfied, having had too much. And finally, in the last stanza, Keats calls the urn an **Attic** shape in line 41; this means a shape from Attica, or Athens, where the style of objects like this was very simple and graceful. He also says in lines 41 and 42 that the urn is "with **brede** of marble men and maidens **overwrought**," or, in other words, worked over with a pattern or design of marble men and maidens.

It has long been common practice for poets to write about a work of art that has impressed them. Keats might have seen this vase in books of engravings which were available at the time he wrote the poem, but, whether he saw it or not, it is a typical and elaborate example of the type. There are leaf decorations along the top, a figure with pipes and another with a timbrel, and in the center of the part of the vase you can see a "bold lover" and a "maiden loth," that is unwilling or reluctant.

ADVANCE THE NEXT SLIDE [pause for at least 5 seconds]

We know of Keats's interest in Greek urns not only from this poem, but also from a drawing he made of another vase in the Louvre museum (and again, one that had been depicted in engravings for sale in England). The Sosibios vase is also "leaf-fringed," and almost out of the picture to one side is a young man with pipes. The Sosibios vase seems to depict some sort of religious procession, but it is nothing like that described by Keats in his fourth stanza.

ADVANCE THE NEXT SLIDE [pause for at least 5 seconds]

There are urns which have scenes of sacrifice on them, and an example is this vase which was in Holland House in London and also depicted in books of engravings. This vase shows a group of people preparing for a traditional sacrifice of a pig, a sheep, and a bull. [pause 5 seconds]

Although Keats may have had a specific urn in mind when he wrote the poem, it is more likely that what impressed him was what the urn accomplished in recording such scenes. For this reason, you should pay special attention not only to Keats's descriptions of scenes in stanzas one and four, but to what he says about art and time in stanzas two, three, and five.

Turn off the tape recorder and follow the instructions printed below the poem.

You may listen to the tape and look at the slides more than once if you wish.

BEFORE YOU LEAVE:

Find the notebook for your section and after signing your name:

1. In a paragraph state what you think is the main point of Keats's poem. Don't just copy the last two lines; think about the whole poem.

2. If you have already seen the other poetry display, tell which one you prefer and why.

Approximate time: 9 Minutes.
Slides:

1. A photograph of the Borghese Vase (Louvre).

2. A line drawing of the Sosibios Vase (Louvre) attributed to Keats.

3. A Piranesi engraving of the Holland House Urn.

Script for an Audio-Visual Display of Stevens's "The Man with the Blue Guitar"[1]

TURN ON THE SLIDE VIEWER AND LOOK AT THE FIRST SLIDE FOR A FEW MINUTES. THEN TURN ON THE TAPE PLAYER. [These directions must be displayed prominently, along with an open copy of *The Collected Poems of Wallace Stevens*, Alfred A. Knopf, Inc., 1954, in which cantos 1, 2, 5, 6, 15, and 25 of "The Man with the Blue Guitar" have been marked.]

The painting you are looking at is Picasso's *The Old Guitarist*, painted in 1903. It was part of an exhibition Wallace Stevens attended the year before he wrote the poem in front of you, "The Man with the Blue Guitar." The poem is a long one; in fact, it has thirty-three of these numbered stanzas, which are called **cantos**. We've only included six of these cantos here. Turn off the tape player and read through Canto One slowly and carefully. Then turn the player back on. [pause for 10 seconds]

Wallace Stevens begins his poem with a line that indicates he might be describing the painting: "The man bent over his guitar." But then things get complicated. He says the guitar player is a **shearsman**, and he also says that the day was **green**. Let's come back to these statements after we look at the rest of the canto.

People talk to the guitarist and ask him to play a tune of things exactly as they are. They also say he has a blue guitar and doesn't play things as they are. This may be puzzling at first, because we don't ordinarily ask a **musician** to describe the world for us—to play things as they are—though we may very well make such a request or demand of a photographer, a painter, a story writer ... or a poet: "Show us the world as it is." At the same time, we seem to want a little more from our artists: we want "things as they are," but we also want some inspiration, some view of things we hadn't seen before or things as they might be with a bit of imagination. Stevens's way of saying all this is, "we want a tune" (he might have said a picture or a poem) "beyond us, yet ourselves."

And now we can come back to the line describing the guitarist as a shearsman and the day as green. We can't understand these lines if they are just talking about a man with a guitar. But Stevens is talking about other kinds of art too—especially painting and poetry. Days aren't ordinarily green, or guitars blue, for that matter. But **pictures** have colored backgrounds, occasionally even green backgrounds so that in a picture it might make sense to say the day was green. But what if we tried to photograph such a picture with a camera which had a blue lens? Wouldn't it come out blue? Wouldn't things be changed on the blue camera? In Picasso's picture, everything **is blue**, except for the guitar. Everything has been made blue by the artist's vision—except for the guitar itself. Both Picasso and Stevens use musical instruments to represent the way artists look at the world.

But what does Stevens mean when he says the guitarist is a shearsman? Well, shears or scissors cut ... they cut away the unnecessary, and they also cut to refashion things into other shapes, as a tailor does. Stevens talks about "patching" things in the next canto, and in one of his letters he says that a tailor was what he had in mind when he used this word.

Let's stop for a moment to consider a question which might have occurred to you during the previous discussion — namely, "Why would an artist want to look at things through something so distorting as a blue lens?" Why, to put it another way, doesn't Picasso show us things and people as we ordinarily see them, instead of in strange shapes and colors?

First it might be a good idea to point out that Picasso does not paint the pictures he does because he isn't able to draw well; as the next slide shows, he is very capable of giving us the kind of art we may be more used to.

ADVANCE THE NEXT SLIDE [pause for 5 seconds]

But many of his paintings are even odder than **The Blue Guitarist**. Look, for example, at the next slide, which is a picture of Picasso's daughter with a doll.

ADVANCE THE NEXT SLIDE [pause for 5 seconds]

It is a disturbing picture, certainly not showing us "things as they are" in any usual sense. The face is especially strange; it is as if we saw the face through a prism, or from several different views at once, and there is a very unlifelike green cast to it as well. Why did Picasso paint this picture this way?

Picasso said that at a certain point in his life he realized "that painting had an intrinsic value, detached from any actual portrayal of objects. I asked myself," he said, "if one shouldn't rather portray things as one knows them than as one sees them." The difference between these two — things as one knows them and things as one sees them — may not be clear to you right away, but perhaps a child's drawing will help to make the difference clearer.

ADVANCE THE NEXT SLIDE [pause for 5 seconds]

What the child has done in his drawing is to show us both ends of the house at once. We know that we cannot see both ends at once, but the child **knows both ends are there** and has drawn them. He has also drawn the fence all the way around the house, even though we could not see part of that fence if we had the view of the front of the house which he shows us. He has drawn, not what he **sees** in one view of the house, but what **he knows about it**. To go back to Picasso's picture of his daughter, we know if we can't see both eyes of a face at the same time we are looking at a profile of it. But we also know that both views of the face are **there**. We even know that they are both necessary; that we can't really see what a person is like unless we have both views. That's what's behind the police photos of wanted criminals.

ADVANCE THE NEXT SLIDE [pause for 5 seconds]

One photo can't give us both views at once; we need two. Picasso is merely saying, "Why can't I give you both at once? After all, this isn't a photograph. It's my painting, and I can show you what I know about the subject, even if it's not what you would see standing in one spot." Another modern painter has expressed this idea: when a lady visiting his studio said, "But surely, the arm of this woman is much too long," the artist replied, "Madam, you are mistaken. This is not a woman; this is a picture."

In fact, people ask for more from their pictures, poems, songs, and other works of art than merely showing things "as they are." Stevens shows us this in cantos five and six. Turn off the tape player and read through these cantos slowly. Then turn the player back on.

Once again in these cantos we have the people speaking to the guitarist, although now Stevens does not conceal that he is talking about poetry as well as song, music, tunes. They say first that they don't wish to hear about the greatness of poetry, and then they describe their own world—there are no shadows, day is desire and night is sleep, the earth is flat and bare. Poetry, they say, must take the place of empty heaven and its hymns. Their world is plain and uninteresting; they want more, "A tune beyond us, yet ourselves," as they said in the first canto, but here things are more specific about what is wanted "beyond us."

> Ourselves in the tune as if in space,
> Yet nothing changed, except the place
>
> Of things as they are and only the place
> As you play them on the blue guitar,
>
> Placed so, beyond the compass of change. . . .

These are difficult lines, but the last one is a little clearer than the others. The speakers want things in the poem or tune "beyond the compass of change"—one of the things that's wrong with their world is its **change**. Nothing lasts, people die too soon, nothing stays the same. It would be nice to have things a little more stable, and that's one of the things art does—it can create a world where things seem final and unchangeable:

> Placed so, beyond the compass of change.
> Perceived in a final atmosphere;
>
> For a moment final, in the way
> The thinking of art seems final when
>
> The thinking of god is smoky dew.

Art at least seems to be something more permanent than the world and people—that is, the thinking, or creation, of god. More than one poet or philosopher has said that life is short but art is long.

Perhaps we can summarize some of the things that have been said and hinted at in as much of the poem as we have read. What is "The Man with the Blue Guitar" about? Well, it's about poetry: "Poetry is the subject of the poem," Stevens says in Canto 22. But it's also about music and painting. It's about art.

It's about the world depicted by art — what the people talking to the guitarist call "things as they are." It's about what art *must* do — that is, change "things as they are" a little or a lot in order to depict them. And it's also about what art ought to be able to do, according to those who speak to the guitarist — depict a world which is somehow more interesting, different but not too different, and perhaps unchanging — they ask quite a lot from the guitarist.

Since we can't possibly include all of the poem's 33 cantos, it may be best to finish with one which shows something else about art — namely, that it's play. After all, we've been taking the rest of the poem horribly seriously. So this is Canto 25, where Stevens's guitarist becomes a kind of circus juggler, twirling the whole world like a ball on his nose. And while this is going on, what do the inhabitants of this world think about it? Nothing. They don't even know it's going on. The cats move in the grass, and have other cats, and the grass turns gray, and the guitarist plays his song:

> He held the world upon his nose
> And this-a-way he gave a fling.
>
> His robes and symbols, ai-yi-yi —
> And that-a-way he twirled the thing.
>
> Sombre as fir-trees, liquid cats
> Moved in the grass without a sound.
>
> They did not know the grass went round.
> The cats had cats and the grass turned gray
>
> And the world had worlds, ai, this-a-way:
> The grass turned green and the grass turned gray.
>
> And the nose is eternal, that-a-way.
> Things as they were, things as they are,
>
> Things as they will be by and by . . .
> A fat thumb beats out ai-yi-yi.

Turn off the tape recorder now and follow the directions outlined in front of you.

You may listen to the presentation more than once.

BEFORE YOU LEAVE:

Find the notebook for your class section and after signing your name:

1. Explain in a paragraph what you think this display has to do with the themes for this course which were outlined on the syllabus.

2. If you have already seen the other poetry display, tell which one
    you liked better and why.

Approximate time: 13 minutes.
Slides:

1. Picasso, *The Old Guitarist* (1903), Art Institute of Chicago.
2. Picasso, *The Lovers*, (neo-classical period), National Gallery of
    Art, Washington.
3. Picasso, *Maia* [the artist's daughter] *with Sailor Doll* (1938), col-
    lection of the artist.
4. A child's drawing showing three sides of a house, after plate 10
    in Miriam Lindstrom, *Children's Art* (Berkeley, Los Angeles,
    and London: University of California Press, 1957).
5. An FBI "Wanted" poster with full-face and profile photographs.

When these scripts were tested in an interdisciplinary humanities
course, the students showed a slight preference for the Stevens display.
They also demonstrated that even so brief an exposure to the poems
enabled them to write a competent short statement of theme. A typical
example: "In Keats's poem, "Ode on a Grecian Urn," he explains the
everlasting impression on a Grecian Urn. In one passage two lovers
are about to kiss. They are caught in time, never aging, never changing,
beauty in its perfection. The main topic of the poem is that of everlasting
beauty and truth." There were also perceptive comments which went
beyond a simple statement of theme, as in the following: "Art defines
eternal truth more precisely than science or religion. Stevens is trying
to make a point about there being no absolute truth, and art is the
most effective means for defining truth. Truth depends upon where
you are at and what time it is. Without art we survive, with art we
live."

The value of such audiovisual demonstrations depends on students,
who need encouragement to use them thoughtfully and to repeat the
presentations as often as necessary until they understand them. The
presentations themselves need to be carefully planned so that they
address the objectives of the course and unit. These models are presented in the hope they will prove adaptable to different courses and
purposes.

Notes

1. Excerpts from Canto IV and Canto XXV are reprinted by permission
of Alfred A. Knopf, Inc., from *The Collected Poems of Wallace Stevens.*
Copyright © 1936 by Wallace Stevens, and renewed 1964 by Holly Stevens.

22

Teaching Afro-American Poetry:
Resources

Sally A. Jacobsen
Deirdre J. Raynor

"I let poems bend my life like a mobius strip/ ... I get high on poetry," writes Seattle poet Colleen McElroy. In "Reasons for Poetry" (*Winters Without Snow*, Berkeley, CA: Reed Books, 1979), McElroy describes the power of a poem in shaping one's world view. Afro-American poetry is a part of every American student's cultural heritage, but without the help of a teacher using additional resources, students will not expand their world views to include multiple cultural viewpoints. Twenty-five years ago, one would not have found any real representation of Afro-American literature in the typical literature anthology, especially not poetry. If there was a token Afro-American piece, it was included primarily as an expression of Afro-American community values.

Although more recently Black poets are receiving recognition for their individual distinction as poets, much remains to be done before the richness of the Afro-American contribution is fully recognized. For example, although Afro-American women are writing some of the richest poetry today, they are still not receiving the acknowledgment they deserve. One place to draw students' attention to the works of Afro-American poets, male and female alike, is the American literature classroom. Poems by Afro-American poets should be included in the regular literature curriculum, since not all students will take a "Black Literature" elective. Many teachers, unfortunately, remain unaware of the resources available to them for incorporating Afro-American poetry in the general curriculum.

Of first consideration for us, then, are general literature textbooks that integrate Afro-American poetry into the mainstream, and resources for poems and poets too recent to be included in standard textbooks. Black literature anthologies and secondary sources follow, with a note on recordings and film resources. These are valuable aids to teachers in planning and presenting their coursework, but they could also be used by students whose curiosity has been sparked in the classroom. Many of the resources described here would also be useful in a specialized course in Afro-American literature. Finally, books and articles are described that are primarily useful as resources for teachers.

Textbooks

Current editions of nearly all standard textbooks include five or more pieces by Afro-American poets. Even series that are under way — those, for example, published by Prentice-Hall and McDougal, Littell — show a dramatic increase in the amount of attention paid to Afro-American literature. However, many textbooks still emphasize only a particular moment in Afro-American history or identify a particular literary movement, such as the Harlem Renaissance. The ideal textbook would enable a reader to survey both male and female Afro-American poets from the past to the present.

McGraw-Hill's "Themes in Literature" series (revised, 1985) is impressive, with poems by Langston Hughes, Lucille Clifton, Margaret Walker, Richard Wright, June Jordan, Nikki Giovanni, and Gordon Parks being included in the ninth-grade *Insights* volume alone. Harcourt, Brace, Jovanovich's Pegasus Edition of the "Adventure in Literature" series (1989) and Ginn's Literature Series (Ginn & Company, 1986) follow close behind, with Ginn outdoing McGraw-Hill in its basic sequence for the middle school, particularly in *Responding: One* for seventh grade, edited by Robert S. Johnson and James N. Britton.

Elements of Literature: Fourth Course by Holt, Rinehart and Winston (1989) deserves mention because it includes modern poems by Langston Hughes, Robert Hayden, Lucille Clifton, Gwendolyn Brooks, and Ishmael Reed. Both "Theme for English B" and "Mother to Son" by Hughes appear in this text. "Theme for English B" is a good poem to use for discussing how we are shaped both by our distinct ethnic culture and by everything that constructs American culture in general. "Mother to Son" emphasizes that anything is possible, despite obstacles that may arise. Hayden's "The Whipping" is a powerful poem in which the poet juxtaposes past and present. "Miss Rosie," by Clifton, is full of vivid description, and students could imitate Clifton's use of description in their own poems. They too could create word portraits of street people, a relative or friend who stands out from the crowd, or a unique teacher. Gwendolyn Brooks's "The Bean Eaters" in this textbook, the title poem of one of her most famous volumes, also uses subtle details to paint a portrait, the more moving in its understatement. Finally, students will be intrigued by Ishmael Reed's ".05" because it invites the reader to think about the value of having someone to love and the pain of being rejected.

The Scribner Literature Series (1989) includes fewer Afro-American poems, although it must be said that the few that do appear have an immediate appeal to students. Scribner's *Introducing Literature* text has only Gwendolyn Brooks's "Life for My Child Is Simple and Good" and a haiku by Richard Wright, "A Balmy Spring Wind." Scribner's *Enjoying Literature* (1989) also includes only two poems by Afro-Americans, Langston Hughes's "The Dream Keeper" and Alice Walker's "For My Sister Molly Who in the Fifties."

As examples of how publishers are handling Afro-American representation, we will look at the eleventh-grade American Literature volumes published by Harcourt, Brace, Jovanovich (1989), Scribner/MacMillan (1987), Ginn and Company (1986), and Scott, Foresman (1985).

Harcourt, Brace, Jovanovich's *Adventures in American Literature Pegasus Edition* (1989) goes back as far as Phyllis Wheatley in the Revolutionary period, 1760–1790. In the Post-post-Civil-War period, several poems by Paul Laurence Dunbar appear, and this textbook includes two written in "standard" English, "Douglass" and "Life Tragedy." Students are thus given a chance to compare Dunbar's formal style with his poems in Black dialect, which receive more critical acclaim. "Life Tragedy" is a perfect poem to open up a discussion about what happens in a materialistic society in which people do not appreciate what they have. A teacher may want to get students to argue for or against the claim that the younger generation is self-centered, after discussing what "Life Tragedy" says about not having our values in perspective.

A section on the Harlem Renaissance is now standard in eleventh grade textbooks, and the one in *Adventures in American Literature* is large, with poems by Claude McKay, Jean Toomer, Langston Hughes, and Countee Cullen. Cullen's "Any Human to Another" serves as a good lead into a discussion of the similarities and differences between the various cultures making up American society. Since classrooms today are culturally diverse, discussions of diversity are essential in taking steps to embrace and understand difference, at best, and, at worst, to tolerate it. Darkness is a key metaphor in the poems by Hughes and Cullen in this Harcourt, Brace, Jovanovich textbook. Inherent in the metaphor of darkness is a sense of pride in Afro-American heritage. The poem which best illustrates Black pride is

Hughes's "The Negro Speaks of Rivers," in which Hughes takes the reader on a journey through the Afro-American experience of moving from the homeland to a new home in the United States. Hughes also alludes to the individual and group strength of Afro-American people which enabled them to survive despite the horrendous sufferings they have endured. McKay's "The Tropics of New York" and Hughes's "As I Grew Older" deal with memories and dreams, and in both poems the speakers long for a dream which is inextricably linked to being Afro-American.

Robert Hayden's "The Diver" and Gwendolyn Brooks's "In Honor of David Anderson Brooks My Father" are the final selections by Afro-Americans in *Adventures in American Literature*. While the Harcourt Brace Jovanovich volume contains more poems by Afro-Americans than other eleventh grade textbooks, its weakness is that no contemporary poets are included. The Black poets who appeal most vividly to students tend to be recent writers, and other publishers do a better job of nourishing that taste.

Harcourt Brace Jovanovich does, however, like several other publishers, include a section on Afro-American spirituals, reproducing "Go Down, Moses" and "Swing Low, Sweet Chariot." The spirituals reflect the importance of oral forms of art in the Afro-American community.

Scribner/Macmillan's *American Literature* volume (1989) begins its Afro-American representation in poetry with Phillis Wheatley and spirituals such as "Follow the Drinking Gourd," Margaret Walker with "Lineage" and Gwendolyn Brooks with "Strong Men, Riding Horses" represent the period 1930–1960. For contemporary African-American writers, Robert Hayden and Rita Dove are included; both poets' work should strike a responsive chord in students. No student, for example, who has wrestled with solving a theorem will remain untouched by Dove's "Geometry," and the picture of fatherly love in Hayden's "Those Winter Sundays" ought to stir powerful memories.

Ginn and Company, like Harcourt Brace Jovanovich, begins its representation with Phillis Wheatley in the Revolutionary Era in its *American Literature* survey (1986),and, although it does not match the number of poems by Afro-American poets in *Adventures in American Literature*, it surpasses that volume by including lively contemporary poets—Amiri Baraka/Leroi Jones, Mari Evans, and Alice Walker. Claude McKay represents the Harlem Renaissance.

Scott, Foresman's *The United States in Literature: America Reads* (Seventh Edition, 1985) is notable for offering W. E. B. DuBois's commentary on the spirituals it includes. This textbook publishes five Harlem Renaissance writers, and, of more recent poets, Robert Hayden, Gwendolyn Brooks, and Mari Evans.

Recent Individual Poets

Poets of the 1920s through 1950s — Langston Hughes, Arna Bontemps, Countee Cullen, Margaret Walker, Claude McKay, Robert Hayden, Gwendolyn Brooks, and Richard Wright; more recent poets Lucille Clifton, Mari Evans, Ishmael Reed, June Jordan, and Alice Walker; and even revolutionary poets Amiri Baraka and Nikki Giovanni — are represented in the literature textbooks being published today. But several contemporary Black poets whose vibrant language would unfailingly hook students on poetry are yet to be represented in the standard textbooks: Don L. Lee, Sonia Sanchez, Ntozake Shange, Rita Dove, Colleen McElroy, Maya Angelou, and Michael Harper are poets to whom teachers will have to draw students' attention.

Our favorites by Don L. Lee (Haki Madhubuti), born in 1942, are "But He Was Cool/ or: he even stopped for green lights" and "The Self-Hatred of Don L. Lee." More experimental in form than these, "A Poem to Complement Other Poems" rings an insistence on "change" through social outrages that Afro-Americans endure, culminating in a powerful rage wrought through word combinations — and a surprise ending. These poems are found in *The Black Poets* a paperback anthology edited by Dudley Randall (New York: Bantam, revised 1985), as are other poems mentioned below, unless otherwise noted.

A contemporary poet whose experimental forms students might want to try for themselves is Sonia Sanchez (born 1935). Her work is not found in textbooks because of her frank, powerful language, which is nevertheless very effective in conveying her agony for friends who have become hooked on heroin, or her indignation when an acquaintance's actions are not consistent with Black Power values. Like Nikki Giovanni and Ntozake Shange, Sanchez is superb at capturing the flavor, the vividness, of jive talk. "Nigger" and "Black Magic" in *The Black Poets* could be presented in class, while students could seek out and enjoy others on their own. Three poems by Sanchez are included in *Black Sister: Poetry by Black American Women 1746–1980*, edited by Erlene Stetson (Bloomington: Indiana University Press, 1981). The adventuresome might want to try Sanchez's poetry and prose collection, *homegirls & handgrenades* (New York: Thunder's Mouth Press, 1984).

Ntozake Shange is a poet whose works are too new to be found in textbooks and too good not to mention. Students will delight in Shange's rebellious disregard for spelling and punctuation. (Her jaunty tone and vivid images are conveyed effectively without it). Shange's most recent work is a collection of prose and poetry entitled *Ridin' the Moon in Texas Word Paintings* (New York: St. Martin's Press, 1987). This collection, like her 1982 novel, *Sassafrass, Cypress, and Indigo* (St. Martin's), grows out of Shange's interest in connections between visual art (i.e., paintings, tapestries, sculptures) and language. *Ridin' the Moon* incorporates reproductions of works of art with Shange's poetry and prose. In her work poetry pervades even prose forms. *Nappy Edges* (Bantam, 1980) contains not only marvelous poems like "what do you believe a poem shd do?" (in an interview with herself), but also verse essays, like her argument that the styles of Black poets are as distinctive as those of jazz musicians, in "takin a solo/ a poetic possibility/ a poetic imperative." This argument is also expressed in a poem, "Gardenias on the Borderline," in *Ridin' the Moon in Texas Word Paintings*. Another novel by Shange, *Betsey Brown* (St. Martin's, 1985) would especially appeal to adolescent readers. Students will find humor in *Betsey Brown* and will be able to empathize with the protagonist. They would also enjoy listening to selections from Shange's masterpiece, the choreopoem, *for colored girls who have considered suicide/when the rainbow is enuf*, like "graduation nite" or "toussaint" (recording available from Better Duck Productions, Box 3092, Berkeley, CA 94703). *Colored girls* is kept in print in an inexpensive Bantam edition. The choreopoem enjoyed a long theatrical run in New York, like her more recent poetic drama, *Spell #7* (in *three pieces*, St. Martin's, 1981).

Students will also enjoy reading the poetry of Rita Dove, who won the Pulitzer Prize in 1986 for *Thomas and Beaulah* (Pittsburgh: Carnegie-Mellon Press). Chronicling the lives of Thomas and Beaulah as both individuals and a married couple, the poems in this book explore various moments in American history, such as the Great Depression and the sixties March on Washington. All of the historical events are described in terms of their impact on Thomas, Beaulah, and their children. *Grace Notes* (New York: W. W. Norton and Company, 1989) is Dove's most recent collection of poems. Students may be especially interested in reading "Fifth Grade Autobiography," "Flash Cards," "Fantasy and Science Fiction," and "Sisters." In these poems Dove uses marvelous details and imagery to describe family and community bonds. These poems also exemplify the connections between past memories and present conditions. One of our favorite poems in *Grace Notes* is "Canary," dedicated to Michael Harper. "Canary" is about the great jazz singer Billie Holiday, and students can do some interesting analysis by comparing Dove's description with Shange's portrait of Holiday in "Gardenias on the Borderline."

Colleen McElroy is a master at using vivid images and eloquent language to express a broad range of emotion. Students may be especially intrigued by "Defining It for Vanessa" from *Winters Without Snow* (Berkeley, CA: Reed Books, 1979). This poem addresses the complexity of growing up and defining oneself as an individual. "Ruth" from *Queen of the Ebony Isles* (Middletown, CT: Wesleyan University Press, 1984) is an insightful poem dealing with conflict and love between mothers and daughters. McElroy's "Putting My Son On Board the

Columbia" (*Bone Flames*, Wesleyan, 1987) illustrates the complexity of a mother-and-son relationship and what happens when a young man leaves home and returns. These three poems by McElroy are useful for getting students to think about and examine the dynamics of their relationships with parents and guardians. They may also be found in a single volume by McElroy, *What Madness Brought Me Here: New and Selected Poems, 1968–1988* (Wesleyan, 1990). Her poet's perspective may be found in "Perspectives," above.

Students should also read poetry by Maya Angelou, better known for her autobiographical *I Know Why The Cage Bird Sings* (1969), detailing her molestation, recovery, and flowering in childhood and adolescence, and its sequels, *Gather Together in My Name* (1974) and *Singin' and Swingin' and Gettin' Merry Like Christmas* (1976 — all Random House). Angelou's latest book of poetry, *I Shall Not Be Moved* (Random House, 1990) is full of rich poems about love, the survival of Afro-Americans, self pride and cultural pride. Some of our favorites include "Our Grandmother," "Human Family," and the title poem, "I Shall Not Be Moved," very popular with audiences at Angelou's dramatic readings of her works.

Michael Harper (born in 1938) has two moving poems about tragic deaths of young Afro-Americans at White hands in *The Black Poets*: "American History," about the Alabama church explosion in the mid-sixties which killed four children, and "A Mother Speaks: The Algier Motel Incident, Detroit." Students would also be fascinated with Harper's later poems, in many of which he explores Black versus White identity with imagery from photography, identifying with the "negative" image. Some of these, along with Robert Stepto's excellent article discussing the poems and Harper's literary antecedent in poet Robert Hayden, may be found in *Chant of Saints* (1979 — see "Black Literature Anthologies," below). Students should also read poems from Harper's *Healing Song for the Inner Ear* (Urbana: University of Illinois Press, 1985). Some of the most interesting poems in this collection invite discussion of famous Black writers, musicians, and political figures such as John Coltrane, Paul Robeson, W. E .B. DuBois, and Martin Luther King, Jr.

Although Ishmael Reed and June Jordan, unlike the poets just discussed, have poems in some of the standard textbooks, their poems in which students might delight the most are not yet included. Berkeley, California, poet Reed (born 1938), also a fiction writer, believes that poetry "should be accessible to all people of all ages, without footnotes" (University of Cincinnati Fiction Festival, April 1, 1980). Reed produces wild juxtapositions of myth, film, Black identity, and childhood games and nursery rhymes in some of his best poems. "I Am a Cowboy in the Boat of Ra" is widely anthologized (e.g., in *The New Black Poets*, edited by Clarence Major, New York: International Publishers, 1969).

Reed's whimsical "black power poem" and "Beware: Do Not Read This Poem" appear in *The Black Poets*. Reed's ".05" is described above, in the discussion of Holt, Rinehart, and Winston's textbook, *Elements of Literature: Fourth Course* (1989).

June Jordan's latest books of poetry, *Living Room* (1985) and *Naming Our Destiny* (1989, both New York: Thunder's Mouth Press) are great sources for addressing current and historical events. "From Sea to Shining Sea" is one of the most powerful poems in *Living Room*. In it Jordan draws attention to the fact that racism, sexism, and classism are still prevalent problems in the United States and throughout the world. *Naming our Destiny* includes poems from other volumes of poetry by Jordan. In this collection we find poems, from those in remembrance of Martin Luther King, Jr., Fannie Lou Hamer, and Sojourner Truth, to ones about police violence and the sufferings of Nelson Mandela and other Blacks in South Africa.

For a brief description of Amiri Baraka's *Selected Poems*, (William Morrow, 1979), see the "Black Literature Anthologies" section below.

Black Literature Anthologies

If a school is not yet ready to replace a pre-1985 textbook series, the best alternative is to purchase a classroom set of a paperback anthology to be passed from room to room. Few anthologies exclusively of Afro-American writing have been published in the 1980s, but a number of comprehensive Afro-American literature anthologies appeared in the sixties and seventies, and some are still in print. For grades nine through twelve, *The Black Poets*, edited by Dudley Randall (Bantam, revised 1985) and covering the period from slavery to the 1980s, is a good choice, since it includes six or seven poems by each poet with whom students should be familiar. The fatter *Black Voices: An Anthology of Afro-American Literature* (New York: Mentor/New American Library, 1968), still in print, would also be a good choice, since it includes fiction, autobiography, and criticism, as well as poetry. Both have first rate introductions to help teachers and students alike to get their bearings. Arnold Adoff's award-winning *I Am the Darker Brother* (New York: Macmillan, 1968), containing just modern poems, would be a good alternative.

Chant of Saints: A Gathering of Afro-American Literature, Art, and Scholarship, edited by Michael S. Harper and Robert B. Stepto (Champaign, IL: University of Illnois, 1979), is still in print. It is an exciting contemporary anthology interweaving stories and poems of consummate craft with photographs of paintings and sculpture by Black artists, interviews, and critical essays — sometimes by creative writers, for example, Sherley Anne Williams's "The Blues Roots of Contemporary Afro-American Poetry." *Chant of Saints* is a "must" for the school library because of the literary and cultural roots it establishes for some of today's most accomplished Black writers; it is fascinating reading.

The New Black Poetry, edited by Clarence Major (New York: International Publishers, 1969), contains contemporary poetry since the forties, but few poets are represented by more than one poem. It is a good paperback to supplement other books that include poems appropriate for high school students. *The New Black Poets* prints Elton Hill/Abu Ishak's "Theme Brown Girl," capturing an element of Black identity in each of six places — Dakar, the Congo, Haiti, Harlem, Watts, and Detroit; Michael Nicholas's "Today: The Idea Market" on a school theme; and Quincy Troupe's accessible juxtaposition of rioting scenes with White indifference in "White Weekend."

One of our favorite anthologies focuses exclusively on the work of Black women poets. *Black Sister*, edited by Erlene Stetson (Bloomington: Indiana University Press, 1981), surveys the work of Afro-American women poets from 1746 through 1980. This book is a great source for teachers because it covers a wide variety of women writers through three centuries. By selecting poems from *Black Sister*, teachers can introduce students to poetry by Lucy Terry, Phyllis Wheatley, Georgia Douglas Johnson, Margaret Walker, Margaret Danner, Mari Evans, Carolyn Rodgers, Audre Lorde, Alice Walker, and Sherley Anne Williams, to name just a few. Because it ends with the Harlem Renaissance, Ann Allen-Shockley's collection, *Afro-American Women Writers 1746−1933* (New American Library/Penguin, 1988) is able to include some recently-recovered women writers for whom there is not space in *Black Sister*, since the latter embraces the prolific nineteen sixties and seventies. *Afro-American Women Writers 1746−1933* reprints poems by Lucy Terry, Phyllis Wheatley, Anne Plato, Alice Dunbar-Nelson, and many other earlier Black women writers.

Talk That Talk: An Anthology of African-American Storytelling, edited by Linda Goss and Marian E. Barnes (Simon and Schuster, 1989) is full of short stories and sermons as well as rhymes by Afro-Americans. In completing a unit on Black poetry, students and teachers will have fun studying and writing imitations of some of the works in Section Seven, entitled "Ah-La-Dee-Da-Dee-Bop-De-Bop: Raps, Rhythms, and Rhymes in the Storytelling Tradition." This section includes rhymes by Paul Laurence Dunbar, Maya Angelou, and Sterling Brown.

Two anthologies published in 1968 and now unfortunately out of print are worthy of mention here because of their unique contents. Teachers could tell students writing papers on relevant subjects of their existence, so that they could search them out in libraries or request them by interlibrary loan. *Dark Symphony: Negro Literature in America*, edited by James A. Emanuel and Theodore L. Gross (New York: Free Press, 1968) has an "Early Literature" section containing handy selections from Frederick Douglass and W. E. B. DuBois. Its "Contemporary Literature" section concludes with four articles on recent literature that help students place writers in the mainstream American literary tradition. *Black Fire: An Anthology of Afro-American Writing*, edited by Leroi Jones (Amiri Baraka) and Larry Neal (New York: William Morrow, 1968) is an "alternative" anthology containing many more writers of the Black Power movement of the sixties than other volumes mentioned above. *Black Fire* has a huge poetry section, as well as fiction, drama, and essays, including "African Responses to Malcolm X" and activist perspectives — one by Stokely Carmichael, for example. It is a useful reference for students who want to learn about Black militancy.

The work of many of the poets mentioned in the two sections above is available in single-author paperback editions. Just by browsing through some of these, one can find poems that a class would enjoy. To be convinced of Amiri Baraka's full power and range, for example, one needs to leaf through *The Selected Poetry of Amiri Baraka/Leroi Jones* (New York: William Morrow, 1979), perhaps finding a poem like "Look for You Yesterday/Here You Come Today" — the Lone Ranger poem: "My silver bullets all gone/ . . . & Tonto way off in the hills/Moaning like Bessie Smith" (pp. 10–13). One could capitalize on students' enthusiasm for poets in their textbooks by sending them to the library to see if single-author volumes by their favorites are in the school collection. If they are not, teams could take on the project of delving into public and college library collections to find poetry volumes to recommend adding to the school library, and perhaps even involve their parents and the business community in their enthusiasm by publicizing the library's need.

Secondary Sources

Heroism in the New Black Poetry: Introductions and Interviews, edited by D. H. Melhelm (University Press of Kentucky, 1990) focuses on the works of six contemporary poets, some of whose poems appear in the textbooks and anthologies mentioned earlier. *Heroism* includes interviews with Gwendolyn Brooks, Jayne Cortez, Haki Madhubuti, Dudley Randall, and Sonia Sanchez.

Interviews with Black Writers, edited by John O'Brien (New York: Liveright, 1973), contains interviews with Arna Bontemps, Owen Dodson, Michael Harper, Clarence Major, Ann Petry, Ishmael Reed, and Al Young, as well as with numerous novelists. Each interview is preceded by a photograph of the subject. For more interviews with women poets, see the book edited by Claudia Tate, *Black Women Writers at Work* (New York: Continuum, 1983).

Backgrounds to Blackamerican Literature, edited by Ruth Miller (New York: Chandler, 1971, paperback) is divided into two large sections: (1) "Historical Backgrounds" contains accounts of the slave ships, Negro insurrections, classes in the South, the Ku Klux Klan (by W. E. B. DuBois), the Black Muslims, and the Black Panthers. (2) "Literary Backgrounds" contains critical articles by and about Black writers, including Arna Bontemps on "The Negro Renaissance" and Arthur P. Davis on Gwendolyn Brooks. The chronology of significant events in Black American history and literature, 1501–1968, is a useful reference.

Teachers who want to focus on Black women poets and students who want to research them will find Gloria Hull's *Color, Sex and Poetry: Three Women Writers of the Harlem Renaissance* (Bloomington: Indiana University Press, 1987) a valuable book. (Notice that women poets are entirely omitted from the Harlem Renaissance sections in the school textbooks surveyed above.) In *Color, Sex, and Poetry*, the poetry of Alice Dunbar-Nelson, Angelina Weld Grimké, and Georgia Douglass Johnson is discussed in detail, and in addition, Hull describes how women such as Zora Neal Hurston, Jessie Fauset, and Nella Larsen were an essential part of one of the most exciting Black American literary movements. More recent writers are discussed in *But Some of Us Are Brave: Black Women's Studies*, edited by Gloria T. Hull, et al. (Old Westbury, NY: Feminist Press, 1982).

C. W. E. Bigsby in *The Second Renaissance: Essays in Black Literature* (Westport, CT: Greenwood Press, 1980; "Contributions in Afro-American and African Studies," No. 50) devotes two of his nine critical-historical chapters to Black poetry and thus provides an excellent guide to contemporary writers. Mari Evans has edited *Black Women Writers, 1950–1980* (Garden City, NY: Doubleday, 1984), a comprehensive anthology of criticism with essays on many more women poets than are covered in *The Second Renaissance*.

Recordings and Film Resources

Barbara Stanford and Karima Amin's *Black Literature for High School Students* (Urbana, IL: National Council of Teachers of English, 1978) and Randall's *The Black Poets* offer ample lists of phonograph records of both collections of Black poetry and single poets' work. *The Black Poets* also lists tape recordings, videotapes, and films—for example, Gwendolyn Brooks, 16 mm, 30 minutes, showing scenes in Brooks's Chicago neighborhood as she reads her poems (produced by WTTW, Chicago; order from Indiana University Audio-Visual Center, Bloomington, IN 47401; rental, $12.15 plus shipping and handling).

Holt, Rinehart, and Winston's "Impact" series of recordings is appropriate for specific mention here, since the records embody the principle of integrating Black poetry with White. The *Cities* album contains the most Black poetry of any in this series, including Langston Hughes's "A Dream Deferred" and "The City," Bontemps's "A Note of Humility," and a spiritual, "Go Tell It On the Mountain," but the *I've Got a Name, Search for America,* and *Conflict* albums carry two poems each by Black poets.

The American Audio Prose Library produces a variety of audio visual materials by contemporary authors. "Shange, Ntozake: Interview" is a taped interview in which Shange discusses what influences her as a writer. She also talks about how Afro-American culture is an inherent part of her work (48 min. price $12.95, The American Audio Prose Library, Inc., P.O. Box 842, Columbia, MO 65205).

"Angelou, Maya" can also be ordered from The American Audio Prose Library for $12.95. Angelou discusses *I Know Why the Caged Bird Sings,* and she reads some of her poetry.

Resources for Teachers

Probably the single most important secondary resource that teachers should have available to them is *Black Literature for High School Students* (also containing information explicitly for the middle school), by Barbara D. Stanford and Karima Amin (Urbana, IL: National Council of Teachers of English, 1978, paper). This immensely useful book includes a historical survey of Black writers, a chapter on adolescent literature, and comprehensive bibliographies. The second half of the volume is devoted to Black literature units appropriate for several secondary grade and ability levels and a wealth of stimulating supplemental activities—games, for example. The book opens with a frank discussion of problems which might confront the unsuspecting teacher teaching Black works for the first time and how to forestall them.

For teachers wishing to design units containing Black poetry along thematic lines, Jean Dubois's "An Introduction to Black American Poetry" would be useful (*English Journal*, May 1973, 718–723). The article prints a sample poem each for the themes of slavery (Hayden's "Runagate, Runagate"); acquiescence; integration (Naomi Long Madgett's "Alabama Centennial"); separatism (Dudley Randall's "The Melting Pot"); and militancy (Hughes's "Epiloque" and Margaret Walker's "For My People").

One's teaching style, however, may be to select poems so good one cannot resist presenting them to students, rather than selecting according to themes and movements in Afro-American literature. Also, the poets mentioned above are of such worth that the use of their poems should not be restricted to units on Black literature. A Gwendolyn Brooks sonnet, for example, can allow students to discover for themselves the connection between the sonnet form and the content or the outcome of the situation presented, rather than being forced to learn the form first.

In fact, Afro-American poetry (or any poetry) should not be limited to "literature units" in the classroom. Poetry is a very effective stimulus for students' writing. The "dream" poems by Langston Hughes found in several school textbooks and Black literature anthologies mentioned earlier could be used to prompt journal writing about students' own dreams, leading to class discussion of the writing and, in turn, to more polished writing. The poems by teenage writers, some of them Afro-American students, published by Millicent Lenz in "The Poetry of Today's Teenage Feminists, or How to Survive as Young, Gifted, and Female" (*Arizona English Bulletin*, February 1979, pp. 41–49) suggest other subjects besides dreams one might use to spark students' writing. (For this journal-to-publication method, see Tom Liner's article in the "Applications" section of this book.)

Students may also be interested in comparing and contrasting teenagers from the 1970s with those of today, given what the poems in the Lenz article say about teens of that decade. For an Afro-American poet's perspective richly evocative of the permanent value of poetry throughout life, one should read Naomi Long Madgett's "By Fools Like Me" in *Goal Making for English Teaching*, edited by Henry B. Maloney (Urbana, IL: National Council of Teachers of English, 1973), 99–104. After students read some of the rich poetry by Afro-American men and women, they may well experience the truth of Colleen McElroy's observation, that poetry has the power to "bend" one's life "like a mobius strip."

23

Resources for Teaching the Traditional Poetry of the Native American

Anna Lee Stensland

"If you would seek to know a people, look to their poetry." So wrote Thomas Sanders and Walter Peek, two modern American Indian collectors of the works of American Indian authors (1973, 103). The serious teacher of poetry to junior and senior high school students who wants to help them understand traditional Native American verse must first try to understand the place and the uses of poetry in American Indian life and then try to help students understand it. Natalie Curtis, who recorded American Indian music around the beginning of this century, when it was against the law for American Indians to sing their native songs in government schools, wrote, "Indian thought presents material absolutely unique . . . ." (1968).

Few examples of traditional American Indian poetry exist which were not originally songs, many of them religious. Such songs were neither entertainment nor the innermost expression of individual feelings, and they were not valued for their aesthetic qualities. The words of poetry were first and foremost the Native American's desire for power, the need to tap the supernatural forces in every phase of Indian life. Medicine men used the songs for healing, and other Indians used them to help with the hunt, with planting, in war, at the birth of a child, or at the death of an elderly person. Anything an Indian did might call on supernatural power, and this was tapped through song. The following, for example, is a Zuni invocation to the dawn, in which the singer calls upon the supernatural to make his crops grow (Bunzel 1930, 635):

Now this day.
My sun father.
Now that you have come out standing to your sacred place,
That from which we draw the water of life.
Prayer meal,
Here I give to you.
Your long life,
Your old age,
Your waters,
Your seeds,
Your riches,
Your power,
Your strong spirit,
All these to me may you grant.

Songs were usually accompanied by gestures and sometimes by dances. The music and gestures expressed meaning as much as the words did. One type of poem, which was inspired by visions and accompanied by dancing, was the Ghost Dance poem. A whole series of these songs and dances, begun at the time of the vision of Wovoka, a Paiute medicine man, in 1889, was ended with the tragic massacre of Chief Big Foot's band at Wounded Knee Creek in South Dakota in December, 1890. The Indians, following Wovoka's advice, wore a particular kind of shirt, which was believed to be bulletproof, and they danced and sang for days. Nowhere is there more powerful evidence of the belief in the power of the word, music, and dance. If the people followed the ritual, it was believed, the buffalo herds would return, people who had died would return to earth, and together, with those who danced, they would drive out the hated White Man. As the following example demonstrates, what the words said was not so important as the repetition of the words as a ritual which was to accomplish the miracle (Mooney 1896, 1054):

The whirlwind! The whirlwind!
The whirlwind! The whirlwind!
The snowy earth comes gliding,
The snowy earth comes gliding,
The snowy earth comes gliding,
The snowy earth comes gliding.

Every Native American male could create his own song. To do so was not the province only of especially talented individuals in the tribe. Each individual sang in order to bring himself into harmony with the tribe, Nature, and the Supernatural. The singer usually did not consider himself the author, but rather the messenger from the Great Spirit, who was the author. Most cherished of an individual's songs were those the male member of the tribe received when vision-seeking.

After preparing himself ceremoniously, the young Indian went out, often to the mountain top, where for days he would fast until he received a vision or dream which would determine his future. Some of these songs could not be shared lest their power be lost, so they could never be recorded. One song which was recorded is from the Teton Sioux (Densmore 1918, 1860):

> Where the wind is blowing
> The wind is roaring
> I stand.
>
> Westward the wind is blowing
> The wind is roaring
> I stand.

Some of the most lyric, and perhaps most understandable, songs for modern students are the love lyrics, which were believed to act as charms to bring back the loved one. Such a lyric was recorded from the Chippewa by Francis Densmore (1910b, 150−151):

> A loon
> I thought it was
> But it was
> My love's splashing oar.
>
> To Sault Ste Marie
> He has departed
> My love
>
> Has gone on before me
> Never again
> Can I see him.

Native American songs are usually very short, free verse forms, filled with strong sense imagery. Meter and rhyme are usually absent, except that syllables are added in order to complete the Indian drum beat. Some of the very short translations are as fine as some of the best imagist poetry (Densmore 1913, 254):

> As my eyes search the prairie
> I feel the summer in the spring.

Other poems are short because a simple image represents an entire myth which the tribe shares. A Papago woman once told anthropologist Ruth Underhill "The song is very short because we understand so much" (1936, 11). The Navajo "Song of the Rain Chant" is an example (Curtis 1968, 356):

> Far as man can see
> Comes the rain,
> Comes the rain with me.

The non-Indian reader needs to understand that the poem is talking about the Rain-Youth, a Navajo deity who comes from the Rain Mountain with the rain and sings as he journeys. A storm with thunder and lightning is the Male-Rain and the gentler shower is the Female-Rain. The two rendezvous and from this union comes all vegetation.

Traditional Indian poetry might best be understood by junior and senior high school students if it is taught in connection with mythology rather than with other poetry. Out of the study of myth must come some understanding of Indian life and values. Much Indian art of the past and present grows out of the myths of the tribes. Jamake High-water's history of Indian art, *Song from the Earth: American Indian Painting* (1976), contains both black and white and color illustrations of the works of artists from 1870 to modern times. Many of the works show tribal members in ceremonials as well as at everyday tasks where they are dancing, singing, or praying. Other publications of beautiful Indian art and photographs, which are available in school and public libraries, will also bring Indian life of the past to modern students.

Perhaps most important for students to understand is the power of the word in Indian poetry. N. Scott Momaday writes, "A word has power in and of itself. It comes from nothing into sound and meaning; it gives origin to all things. By means of words can a man deal with the world on equal terms. The word is sacred" (1969, 42). Modern young people might be reminded of word magic in their lives. For example, it is almost compulsive for many of us to, when someone sneezes, respond with, "God bless you," "Gesundheit," "Salud," or some other such expression. Somehow that is supposed to keep away a cold or other illness. Even quite young children learn that when two people walk, one on each side of a post, the friendship can be saved only by saying "bread and butter." When two people say exactly the same words in answer to a question in a conversation, the two must hook their little fingers in order to avoid bad luck. Many will remember how necessary it was to repeat, after stepping on a sidewalk crack, "Step on a crack; break your mother's back" in order to avoid its happening. Students and teachers can come up with even more serious, and less superstition-related, examples. Some may even remember, "In the beginning was the Word, and the Word was with God and the Word was God."

To complicate the teaching, teachers and students need to recognize that there are two types of Indian verse in translation: (1) that which has been translated directly from Indian originals, usually by ethnol-ogists—poetry which may not impress modern readers of poetry as great verse; and (2) that which employs Indian subjects and rhythms drawn from Native life and song to make interpretations of the spirit of Indian poetry. The latter may impress the teacher as better poetry, but she or he must also recognize that such poetry may be less truly

Indian. Two collections which are appropriate for the classroom are still in print:

> Bierhorst, John. *In the Trail of the Wind: American Indian Poems and Ritual Orations*. New York: Farrar, Straus, and Giroux, 1972. The arrangement here is thematic rather than geographical. Translations are chosen from well-known American Indian specialists, using mainly literal translations. The beauty of the book is enhanced by carefully chosen engravings.

> Day, Arthur Grove, ed. *The Sky Clears: Poetry of the American Indians*. Des Plaines, Ill.: Greenwood Press, 1983. This book is about American Indian poetry more than an anthology of poems, but it does contain more than 200 poems from approximately 40 Indian tribes as examples of points the author is making. The book is organized geographically by tribes. It is a useful reference book for teachers to have.

Traditional American Indian poetry is difficult, because it is so unlike poetry we know. The personal ownership of it, the oral tradition with its background in nature, and the singing and body movements which went with the verse are all missing for the modern reader. Poetry in print was alien to the traditional Indian. But any effort the teacher makes to help students understand will give them a different perspective on their own lives and help correct erroneous ideas about the First Americans.

Works Cited

Bunzel, Ruth L. 1930. "Zuni Ritual Poetry," in *Forty Seventh Annual Report*, Bureau of American Ethnology, Part 2. Washington, D.C.: Government Printing Office.

Curtis, Natalie. 1968. *The Indians' Book*. New York: Dover.

Densmore, Francis. 1913. Chippewa Music II Bureau of American Ethnology, Bulletin 53. Washington, D.C.: Government Printing Office.

———. 1918. *Teton Sioux Music*. Bureau of American Ethnology, Bulletin 61. Washington, D.C.: Government Printing Office.

Highwater, Jamake. 1976. *Song from the Earth: American Indian Painting*. Boston: New York Graphic Society.

Momaday, N. Scott. 1969. *The Way to Rainy Mountain*. New York: Ballantine.

Mooney, James. 1896. "The Ghost Dance Religion," in *Fourteenth Annual Report*, Bureau of American Ethnology, Part 2. Washington, D.C.: Government Printing Office.

Sanders, Thomas E., and Walter W. Peek. 1973. *Literature of the American Indian*. Beverly Hills, CA: Glencoe Press.

Underhill, Ruth. 1936. *The Autobiography of a Papago Woman*. Menasha, WI: American Anthropological Association.

Bibliography

Astrov, Margot. 1962. *American Indian Prose and Poetry: An Anthology*. New York: Capricorn.

Bevis, William. 1974. "American Indian Verse Translations." *College English (35)* p. 693–703.

Day, A. Grove. 1964. *The Sky Clears: Poetry of the American Indians*. Lincoln, NE: University of Nebraska Press.

Howard, Helen Addison. 1979. *American Indian Poetry*. Boston: Twayne.

Rothenburg, Jerome. 1972. *Shaking the Pumpkin: Traditional Poetry of the North Americas*. Garden City, NY: Doubleday.

24

Poetry Selection and Resources

Charles R. Duke

Time and again, when asked about what literary form they find most difficult to teach, English teachers usually identify poetry. The reasons for this may vary: lack of appropriate training on the part of teachers, student misconceptions about poetry, or, often as not, the inappropriateness of the selections used to introduce students to poetry.

Faced with the problem of finding appropriate poetry for young people, busy teachers typically turn to the most immediate resource: the literature textbook. Here, teachers reason, one should find all the material necessary to spark students' interest. Several selections later, combined with several class periods of muffled and not-so-muffled groans, sighs, and outright hostility, chastened teachers throw up their hands and come to the conclusion that nothing works. Here endeth the poetry unit.

Such experiences need not be the case. If we want to make any gains in helping students develop an appreciation and liking for poetry, we will need to expend much more effort in locating poems which students can respond to and find meaningful. To accomplish this, the teacher will need to spend a good deal of time becoming familiar with what is available in poetry—and that is no easy task, since poems appear in many places besides the traditional literary textbook: magazines, newspapers, gravestones, advertisements, television, songs, student writing, computers, and even bathroom walls.

Many of the previously mentioned sources can be used only if the teacher remains alert to their existence and diligently collects samples as appropriate works appear. A number of teachers maintain file folders into which they slip poems as they find them; periodically these files can be reviewed and selections used with various classes to test their effectiveness; those that work get collected into an informal anthology; others get discarded. On the other hand, familiarity with a wide number of collections also can give the teacher a substantial body of poetry to draw upon and then supplement with selections from other sources. In making selections from any source, however, the collector needs to keep several principles in mind.

1. **Select poems which deal with experiences that student can relate to**. Such selection does not mean that one must always choose contemporary works — although a good number of poems should come from modern times — but that the experience of the poem should be one accessible to students, either through their own experiences of a similar nature or through interest in a particular theme or concept.

2. **Select poems which can be grasped for their basic meaning in one reading**. Probably no greater damage has been done to the appreciation of poetry from students' perspective than forcing them to read poems which teachers wrestled with in undergraduate and graduate courses where line-by-line analysis and glossing were the principal activities, not the reader's response. Naturally, at some time in the students' experiences with poetry, they should encounter poems which stretch the mind and require considerable intellectual discipline in order to achieve understanding, but a steady diet of such works is the quickest route to apathy or outright hostility whenever poetry is mentioned. Selection should also mean that vocabulary is within reach of the student; an occasional unknown word is fine, but the student should not have to spend considerable time looking up unfamiliar words or consulting footnotes in order to achieve appreciation of the poem; the same may be said for images and symbols. The poem should not be overly long; shorter poems mean that more reading, oral and silent, can take place in one class period and a poem can be heard several times for several different reasons.

3. **Select poems which represent a variety of forms and language**. Traditionally, students seem to favor poems that rhyme and are somewhat humorous. Ann Terry (1974) in *Children's Poetry Preferences: A National Survey of Upper Elementary Grades* (National Council of Teachers of English) discovered that the 25 most popular poems among upper elementary students contained definite rhyming patterns. A review of collections of children's literature most frequently used in the early grades reveals that the majority of selections do, indeed, contain distinct rhyming patterns. Conditioned to believe this is the norm, students faced with unrhymed verse often reject it

as not being "poetry." While acknowledging the existence of rhyme in poetry, teachers may want to introduce gradually poems which further the recognition of cadence and sounds and of the differences between prose and poetic utterance.

4. **Select only those poems for which the teacher can develop an enthusiasm.** This advice may, at first glance, seem contradictory, since many teachers have been selecting works for which they have great interest and enthusiasm. However, it is primarily a case of using what you are most familiar with; for example, in the Terry study, of 41 poems most frequently read by teachers to students, only four were written after 1928. Such information suggests that teachers need to become familiar with more contemporary works for which they may also engender some enthusiasm because it is the "older" poems which so many students seem to reject. These contemporary poems can be found anywhere: magazines, poetry readings at local universities, and even creative writing classes should not be overlooked.

5. **Select poems that have been identified by students as favorites, or poems that they willingly want to read, study, and discuss, for use with future classes.** Many teachers have found that their best lessons on poetry occur when the students themselves are allowed to select the works to be studied. Providing students with collections of poetry and encouraging them to consult some of the sources mentioned earlier, teachers will inevitably find poetry becoming a more natural part of classroom activity. This free selection is not without surprises for the teacher used to dealing with the "old favorites." Rock lyrics, graffiti, and greeting card verse may all surface as student selections; but if teachers want to have equal time with their choices, then the same courtesy ought to be extended to students and their selections. Often such a mix produces a deeper appreciation for the strengths and weaknesses in all poetry.

Although placing grade level designations on types of poetry is not the most reliable means for arriving at a selection process — because it may suggest a growth pattern that may not always reflect the true reading and interest levels of a class — the following general summaries may prove somewhat helpful:

Grades 5-8: Students at this level tend to like story poems, folk ballads, humorous selections, and poems about animals and heroes; very short lyric poems and selections with strong rhyme schemes and a definite meter seem to work well. Students at this level, however, should also have some introduction to poems without the strong rhyme.

Grades 9−10: Students at this level can appreciate haiku and popular song lyrics as poetry; however, the liking for haiku may not be as widespread as once believed. Students find it difficult to grasp the "frozen moment" of the traditional Japanese haiku although the simplicity of the form appeals to them. Concrete poetry for some students may stir strong interest; short lyric poems, dramatic poems, and free verse poems about modern life, adolescence, and nature meet with favorable response.

Grades 11−12: Many students at this age can handle longer lyric poems, blank verse, and some of the traditional poetic forms such as the sonnet, literary ballad, and dramatic monologue. Poems exploring contemporary problems of love, death, human frailty, protest, and identity remain popular with students.

The primary source for finding such poetry remains the anthology. Although volumes of verse by single authors can be helpful, a steady diet of one poet's views tends not to excite much interest among students. Instead, an anthology of poetry becomes a quick and easy reference tool, simple to dip into for those few moments at the end of the class period when one wants to read a piece out loud just for the ideas or for the mood; or the anthology can be the source for sustained study, suggesting a series of poems which focus on a particular subject, time period, writing style, or mood. And the anthology becomes an ideal source for selecting one or two poems to complement the study of a short story, a novel, or a series of essays.

But simply having an anthology available does not solve the selection problem. Many poems which appear in anthologies do not work well when it comes to stimulating student interest. Therefore a teacher must be quite familiar with the contents of many collections and select only those poems which will be appropriate for particular students. For the same reason a particular anthology should not be kept too long as a prime resource.

The use of contemporary poetry with young people should be encouraged because many modern poets use allusions and images which are closer to the experience of young readers than those in poems from a different age. Selections from contemporary poets should yield interesting discussions and convince students that poetry is as much alive today as it was one hundred years ago. The poetry scene is constantly shifting and new collections appear frequently. Unfortunately, the teacher may have to dig to find new poetry because typically it does not appear in mainstream publications. However, a quick review of *Paperbound Books in Print* or *Books in Print* under the heading of "poetry" will provide an ample listing as well as addresses of small presses which specialize in contemporary poetry. Teachers might want to check to determine how many of the following contemporary poets' works they have read or used in class:

Maya Angelou	Denise Levertov
Amiri Baraka	Philip Levine
Marvin Bell	Colleen McElroy
John Berryman	Marianne Moore
Lucha Corpi	Robert Morgan
James Dickey	Joyce Carol Oates
Nikki Giovanni	Linda Pastan
Donald Hall	Marge Piercy
Michael Harper	Adrienne Rich
Judith Hemschemeyer	Carolyn Rodgers
Ted Hughes	Sonia Sanchez
Randall Jarrell	Anne Sexton
June Jordan	Ntozake Shange
Donald Justice	Gary Soto
X. J. Kennedy	May Swenson
Ted Koozer	John Updike
Maxine Kumin	Diane Wakoski
Joan LaBombard	Alice Walker
Don L. Lee	Richard Wilbur

The following list of anthologies, all available in paperback, only begins to suggest the richness of the field. No attempt has been made to deal with the myriad volumes of individual authors' works; the teacher seeking information on such materials should consult *Granger's Index to Poetry* or the *Index to Children's Poetry*, both of which are standard library reference works. Instead, an attempt has been made to offer a representative listing so that teachers may see what is available and start to compile a listing for themselves. In most cases, emphasis has been placed upon identifying collections of contemporary writers.

Representative Poetry Anthologies

Bierhorst, John, ed. 1987. *In the Trail of the Wind: American Indian Poems and Ritual Orations*. New York: Farrar, Straus & Giroux, Inc.
    Native American literature is still not as universally recognized as it should be but this collection provides a good introduction to an overlooked segment of our literary heritage. Students will be intrigued by the subject matter and the attitudes reflected in these poems.

Drake, William, ed. 1988. *The First Wave: Women Poets in America*. New York: Macmillan.

This unique collection takes a biographical approach to such poets as Amy Lowell, Sara Teasdale, Marianne Moore, and Edna St. Vincent Millay as well as a number of lesser known poets and examines how their poetry reflects their relationships with family, friends, husbands as well as how these relationships affected their creativity as writers.

Halpern, Daniel, ed. 1976. *The American Poetry Anthology*. New York: Avon.

This anthology presents poets whose work has been published since 1968. An excellent resource for becoming familiar with poets of the 1960s and 1970s.

Janeczko, Paul B., ed. 1985. *Pocket Poems: Selected for a Journey*. New York: Bradbury Press.

One of the most prolific of anthologists for adolescents, Janeczko provides here 120 short poems by poets such as Maya Angelou, William Stafford, Ted Kooser, William Carlos Williams, and Paul Zimmer. These short — no poem has more than sixteen lines — works are grouped by subjects such as love, goodbyes, pets, and the seasons. Other excellent Janeczko anthologies include *Going Over to Your Place: Poems for Each Other*, Bradbury Press 1987; and *Strings: A Gathering of Family Poems*, Bradbury Press, 1984. *Poetspeak: In Their Work, About Their Work*, Bradbury Press, 1983, is an outstanding collection of 148 poems by 62 contemporary poets; a number of the poets comment on how they came to create their works; this element will do much to demystify how poems come into being.

Larrick, Nancy, compiler. 1989. *Room for Me and a Mountain Lion: Poetry of Open Spaces*. New York: M. Evans.

An excellent anthologist, Larrick provides poems in this collection which celebrate the sense of freedom and identity which comes with being in nature. Other excellent Larrick anthologies include *Piping Down the Valleys Wild*, Dell, 1982; and *Bring Me All Your Dreams*, M. Evans, 1988.

Lewis, Richard, ed. 1966. *Miracles: Poems by Children of the English-Speaking World*. New York: The Touchstone Center for Children, Inc.

The value of this collection lies in its diversity; here are nearly 200 poems written by children around the world, their ages ranging from four to thirteen. The collection can be a valuable stimulus for getting students to write their own poetry.

Livingston, Myra Cohn. 1985. *Celebrations*. New York: Holiday House.

The celebration of holidays — sixteen of them — provides the theme for this collection; included in the celebration are the traditional Christmas, Halloween, New Year's, Passover, and the more contemporary Martin Luther King Day. Other interesting collections by Livingston, all of which have illustrations, include *Earth Songs*, 1986, and *Easter Poems*, 1985, which includes poems translated from Russian and German.

Lourie, Dick, and Mark Pawlak. 1988. *Smart Like Me: High School Age Writing from the Sixties to Now*. Hanging Loose Press (distributed by Teachers and Writers Collaborative).

Authentic voices — spanning twenty years, these poems written by teenagers should prove popular with today's adolescents; few of the poems have any dated references; the themes and concerns are as relevant now as they were twenty years ago.

Merriam, Eve. 1983. *If Only I Could Tell You: Poems for Young Lovers and Dreamers*. New York: Knopf.

Expressing emotions and establishing meaningful relationships rank high as problems faced by adolescents; this collection offers a variety of poetry addressing both issues. Merriam's other anthologies, *Jamboree*, Dell, 1984; and *A Sky Full of Poems*, Dell, 1986, will also speak to adolescents.

Peck, Richard, ed. 1990. *Sounds and Silences*. New York: Dell.

A well known writer of young adult novels, Peck in this collection offers selections which speak to concerns of adolescents: family, childhood, isolation, identity, realities, illusion, dissent, communication, love, war, pain, and recollections. This is an extremely useful thematic collection which, teamed with another Peck anthology, *Mindscapes*, Dell, 1990, should prove popular with young adults.

Peseroff, Joyce, ed. 1987. *The Ploughshares Poetry Reader*. New York: New American Library.

Ploughshares, a creative writing magazine, has attracted a number of contemporary poets; this collection highlights the work of over forty poets such as Robert Bly, Mona Van Duyn, W. D. Snodgrass, Maxine Kumin, Seamus Heaney, and Jane Shore. An excellent introduction to modern American poets.

Randall, Dudley, ed. 1985. *The Black Poets*. New York: Bantam.

This anthology covers Black American poetry from the slave songs through the 1960s. Photographs and critical biographies of the poets are included. The range of selections is sufficient so that the teacher should find a number suitable for a variety of audiences.

Raffel, Burton. 1984. *How to Read a Poem*. New York: New American Library.

This anthology is designed to be used as a text but can also provide the reader with over 200 selections and 100 poets; the selection is eclectic but the representation of both old and new poets is good and the accompanying discussions of selected poems should prove interesting.

Strand, Mark, ed. 1971. *The Contemporary American Poets*. New York: New American Library.

A contemporary poet of some achievement himself, Strand offers a collection of poets who have written since 1940; included are works from Robert Lowell, John Berryman, Theodore Roethke, Elizabeth Bishop, Richard Wilbur, and Alan Dugan; probably not appropriate as a classroom text, nevertheless, it will serve as a useful reference and resource.

Williams, Oscar, and Edwin Honig, eds. 1962. *The Mentor Book of Major American Poets*. New York: New American Library.

A handy resource to be kept on the desk, this collection provides a sampling of works by Taylor, Emerson, Longfellow, Poe, Whitman, and other early American poets along with the works from more contemporary writers such as cummings, MacLeish, and Auden. Williams also has edited *The Mentor Book of Major British Poets* (1985) which provides a sampling of Blake, Wordsworth, Coleridge, Hardy, Hopkins, Yeats, Lawrence, Graves, and Thomas. A good companion to the American collection.

Representative Professional Resources

Numerous articles about the teaching of poetry can be found in a variety of publications including *English Journal, College English, College Composition and Communication, Teaching English in the Two Year College* — all publications of the National Council of Teachers of English; other journals such as *The Journal of Reading, Exercise Exchange, Teachers and Writers' Magazine*, and a number of regional journals regularly carry articles which offer teaching suggestions related to poetry. The following titles suggest a sampling of the books available to the teacher who might wish to pursue in more depth different aspects of the teaching of poetry.

Bishop, Wendy. 1990. *Released Into Language: Options for Teaching Creative Writing*. Urbana, IL: National Council of Teachers of English.
Bishop, both a poet and a teacher of creative writing, has put together a highly practical guide to teaching poetry and fiction. Her suggestions for classroom activities and ways of stimulating student imagination are clearly presented and should prove useful to teachers at any level.

Collom, Jack. 1985. *Moving Windows: Evaluating Poetry Children Write*. New York: Teachers and Writers Collaborative.
Most teachers try to avoid evaluating student-written poetry for fear of stifling students' creativity. Collom provides sensible advice and abundant examples of how evaluation can be carried out which is both supportive yet challenging.

Dias, Patrick X. 1987. *Making Sense of Poetry: Patterns in the Process*. Portsmouth, NH: Boynton/Cook.
What really happens when students read a poem and how can a teacher capitalize on that experience to assist students in developing an appreciation for poetry? This book is not a discussion of methods for teaching poetry, but a thoughtful exploration of the gap we often find between how teachers and students read a text.

Dunning, Stephen, Joe M. Eaton and Malcolm Glass. n.d. *For Poets*. New York: Blanchard (distributed by Teachers and Writers Collaborative).
Originally part of a Scholastic literature series, this small volume offers a complete one month poetry teaching unit suitable for use with 8th–12th graders. Students have the opportunity to read and write poems in a connected way. An excellent teaching model.

Hardt, Ulrich, ed. 1989. *Oregon English Theme: Poetry*. Urbana IL: National Council of Teachers of English.

This theme issue of *Oregon English*, a publication of the Oregon Council of Teachers of English/Language Arts, provides a potpourri of useful classroom approaches to reading and writing poetry; the articles are by classroom teachers and frequently include samples of their own poetry.

Higginson, William J. and Penney Harter. 1985. *The Haiku Handbook: How to Write, Share and Teach Haiku*. New York: McGraw Hill.
Haiku has proven to be one of the poetic forms which students seem to accept naturally. This handbook includes a history of haiku, samples of traditional haiku, and numerous practical suggestions for using haiku in a variety of teaching situations.

Johnson, David M. 1990. *Word Weaving: A Creative Approach to Teaching and Writing Poetry*. Urbana, IL: National Council of Teachers of English.
Johnson explores the role of the poet in creating and using language; he includes many student examples along with those from published poets; much of the book focuses on writing related to themes such as personal origins, food, family, love, work, nature, dreams and death.

Koch, Kenneth. 1980. *Wishes, Lies and Dreams*. New York: Vintage.
Probably more teachers are familiar with Kenneth Koch's work than that of any other poet/teacher. This book has to rank with some of the best literature on the teaching of poetry. Koch's approach guides students into poetic texts and encourages them to try their own versions. Few students can resist. Other outstanding Koch books include *Rose, Where Did You Get That Red?* (Random 1984), which combines an anthology of classic poems with ten demonstration lessons, each using a "great" poem and showing how students responded. *Sleeping on the Wing: An Anthology of Modern Poetry with Essays on Reading and Writing* (written with Kate Farrell, Random 1982), discusses modern poetry and offers samples of twenty-three modern American and European poets' works and suggestions for using them in the classroom.

Mee, Susan. *Stories of the Poets*. n.d. New York: Scholastic (distributed by Teachers and Writers Collaborative).
Although most literature anthologies include biographical notes about authors, the notes are frequently sterile. This collection of twenty-two poets, including Blake, Whitman, Wordsworth, Dickinson, Yeats, Langston Hughes, Neruda, and Ginsberg, would be a good reference to have in the classroom. Students can easily handle the text and will appreciate the concise yet informal presentation of each poet's life.

Padgett, Ron, ed. 1987. *The Teachers and Writers Handbook of Poetic Forms*. New York: Teachers and Writers Collaborative.
This handbook provides seventy-four entries on traditional and modern poetic forms; all of the entries are written by teaching poets. Each form is defined, a brief history of its development is provided, and examples, old and new, are offered. Among the more unusual forms defined are eclogue, epithalamium, ghazal, renga, and senryu. A highly useful reference source which may also stimulate some teaching ideas.

Rosenblatt, Louise M. 1978. *The Reader, The Text, The Poem*. Carbondale, IL: Southern Illinois University Press (distributed by National Council of Teachers of English).

No teacher of poetry should be unfamiliar with Rosenblatt's work. The pioneer of reader response to literature, Rosenblatt provides a powerful argument for the importance of engaging the reader with text and acknowledging the reader's experience with that text.

Contributors

R. L. Barth has been a visiting poet at the University of California, Santa Barbara, and Emory University. His collections of poems include *Looking for Peace* (Abbattoir Editions 1985); *A Soldier's Time* (John Daniel and Company 1988); and *Simonides in Vietnam and Other Epigrams* (John Daniel and Company 1990). He is also the editor of *The Epigrammatist*.

Marvin Bell is Flannery O'Connor Professor of Letters at the University of Iowa, where since 1965 he has taught for the Writers' Workshop. His latest book of poems is *Iris of Creation*, released by Copper Canyon Press in 1990. He has also published seven books of poetry with Atheneum: *A Probable Volume of Dreams* (1969), *The Escape into You* (1971), *Residue of Song* (1974), *Stars Which See, Stars Which Do Not See* (1977), *These Green-Going-to-Yellow* (1981), *Drawn by Stones, by Earth, by Things that Have Been in the Fire* (1984), and *New and Selected Poems* (1987); a collection of poems co-authored with William Stafford: *Segues: A Correspondence in Poetry* (David R. Godine 1983); and a book of prose: *Old Snow Just Melting: Essays and Interviews* (University of Michigan Press 1983). His literary honors include The Lamont Award for his first book of poetry, Guggenheim and National Endowment for the Arts Fellowships, and Senior Fulbright Appointments to Yugoslavia and Australia. In 1990, he resumed in the pages of *The American Poetry Review* the column, "Homage to the Runner," which first ran in the 1970s. He lives in Iowa City, Iowa and Port Townsend, Washington.

Philip Billings teaches modern literature, composition, and creative writing at Lebanon Valley College, Annville, Pennsylvania. His poems have appeared in the magazines *Stone Country* and *The Windless Orchard*, in the bibliography *Literature and Medicine* by Joanne Trautman and Carol Pollard (Society for Health and Human Values 1975), and in *Porches* and *Porches, Volume 2*, self-published collections of verbal portraits of Annville's older citizens. He also enjoys visiting the Annville, Pennsylvania public schools to teach poetry writing.

Patrick Bizzaro teaches writing at East Carolina University, Greenville, North Carolina. He is the author of six chapbooks of poetry, most recently *Undressing the Mannequin* (Third Lung Press), and has won awards for his poetry from

239

NYQ and *Four Quarters*. He has just finished editing *The World between the Eyes: On the Poetry of Fred Chappell* for Ford-Brown's American Poets in Profile Series and is writing *Evaluating Student Poems* for NCTE. He is co-author of *Writing with Confidence* (D. C. Heath) with James Kirkland and Collett Dilworth. His articles on composition and rhetoric have appeared in a wide range of journals, including *CCC*, *Language Arts*, and *Teaching English in the Two-Year College*.

Michael Cohen is professor of English at Murray State University, Murray, Kentucky. He is author of *Hamlet in My Mind's Eye* (University of Georgia Press 1989); *Engaging English Art: Entering the Work in Two Centuries of English Painting and Poetry, 1680–1880* (University of Alabama Press 1987), and with Robert E. Bourdette, Jr., *The Poem in Question* (Harcourt Brace Jovanovich 1983).

Charles R. Duke is Dean, College of Education and Human Services, at Clarion University of Pennsylvania, Clarion, Pennsylvania. Formerly a high school English teacher and department chair, he has taught undergraduate and graduate English methods courses in writing, and in adolescent literature. He is the author of *Creative Dramatics and English Teaching* (NCTE 1973); *Teaching Fundamental English Today* (J. Weston Walch 1976); *Teaching Literature Today* (J. Weston Walch 1979); *Writing Through Sequence: A Process Approach* (Little, Brown 1983); and co-author of *Strategies for Teaching Basic Language Skills* (J. Weston Walch 1987), as well as over one hundred articles on the teaching of literature and writing. He has worked closely with student poets in schools, has edited collections of student poetry, is an active supporter of poet-in-the-schools programs, and conducts inservice workshops for teachers on the teaching of poetry. In addition, he has served as director of National Writing Project affiliates in Kentucky and Utah and is currently co-director of the NWP affiliate, the Penn Rivers Writing Project in Pennsylvania.

Nancy Eimers is an assistant professor of Creative Writing at Western Michigan University. She was a 1987 *Nation* Discovery Award Winner and received a National Endowment for the Arts Creative Writing Fellowship in 1989. Her poems have been published in various magazines, including *The Nation*, *North American Review*, and *The Antioch Review*. Wesleyan University Press has published a collection of her poetry, *Destroying Angel* (1991).

Tess Gallagher is a poet, short story writer and essayist, who writes and lives in Port Angeles, Washington. Her books of poetry include *Instructions to the Double* (1976); *Under Stars* (1978); *Willingly* (1984) and *Amplitude: New and Selected Poems* (1987), all published by Graywolf. *Portable Kisses* (1992) is her most recent book of poems published by Capra Press. Her short stories in *The Lover of Horses* have been reissued by Graywolf Press (1992) and are well known through broadcast on National Public Radio. Her essays are collected in *A Concert of Tenses* (University of Washington Press 1986). Gallagher co-authored two screenplays with her late husband, Raymond Carver: *Dostoevsky* and *Purple Lake*. She has been the recipient of three grants from the National Endowment for the Arts and a Guggenheim Fellowship. In 1989 and 1990, she held the Lois Mackey Chair in Poetry and Fiction at Beloit College.

Jim Heynen has a collection of short stories forthcoming from Knopf, Spring, 1993. His published books include the nonfiction *One Hundred Over 100* (1990); short stories, *You Know What Is Right* (1985); poetry, *A Suitable Church* (1981); short stories, *The Man Who Kept Cigars in His Cap* (1979). He twice has received a National Endowment for the Arts Fellowship, once for poetry, and once for fiction.

Sally A. Jacobsen is associate professor of English at Northern Kentucky University, Highland Heights, Kentucky, where she teaches poetry by American women and by British poets of the nineteenth and twentieth centuries. She has taught at the University of Massachusetts at Boston, M.I.T., and the University of Wisconsin at Platteville, and in the public schools in Monon, Indiana, and Beaverton, Oregon. Her poetry reviews appeared in the Corvallis, Oregon, *Gazette-Times* (1971–1973). She has published articles in *Insofarforth: Functions of Discourse in Science and Literature* (Michigan State University Honors College 1979), *Women's Studies International*, and the *Margaret Atwood Newsletter*. She currently is writing a book about portrayals of technology and values in American novels of the sixties, seventies, and eighties.

X. J. Kennedy is the author of the widely used text-anthologies *Literature, An Introduction to Fiction*, and *An Introduction to Poetry* (HarperCollins). With his wife Dorothy M. Kennedy he is co-author of *The Bedford Guide for College Writers* (Bedford Books). Collections of his own poems include *Cross Ties: Selected Poems* (University of Georgia Press, 1985), which won a Los Angeles Times Book Award. For children, he has written eight collections of verse, including *The Forgetful Wishing Well*, *Brats*, and *Fresh Brats*; and a novel, *The Owlstone Crown* (all Margaret K. McElderry Books).

Philip Levine, winner of the 1991 National Book Award for his poetry collection *What Work Is*, has also won the National Book Critics' Circle award and the American Book Award for *7 Years from Somewhere* and *Ashes: Poems Old and New* (both Atheneum 1979). His book of poems, *A Walk with Tom Jefferson* (Atheneum 1988) won the Bay Area Book Reviewer's Award. Recent volumes of poetry include *Sweet Will* (1985), *Selected Poems* (1984), and *One for the Rose* (1982), all from Atheneum. A book of interviews is *Don't Ask* (University of Michigan Press 1981). Levine teaches at California State University at Fresno and has taught at Columbia University and Tufts University. He spent 1965–1966 and 1968–1969 writing in Spain and produced *Not This Pig* (Wesleyan University 1968) and *The Names of the Lost* (Windhover 1976), both of which contain Spanish Civil War themes. *They Feed They Lion* (Atheneum 1972) portrays his solidarity with the oppressed.

Tom Liner is a poet, teacher, and administrator with twenty-five years experience in public schools. He is the co-author with Dan Kirby of *Inside Out* (Boynton/Cook 1988), and is the Language Arts Supervisor of the Dougherty County Schools in Albany, Georgia.

Stephen Marcus is associate director of SCWriP, a National Writing Project affiliate in the Graduate School of Education, University of California, Santa Barbara, where he also coordinates the alliance between the California Writing

Project and the California Technology Project. He is known internationally for his lectures and workshops on computers and the teaching of English, including his work to develop guidelines for computers in British language arts classrooms. He is the author of eleven software packages, including *Compupoem*, which was named in a national survey of teachers' favorite software (*Electronic Learning* 1984). He has published widely on the use of technology in English education, including *Computers and Literacy* (Taylor and Francis 1985), co-edited with Daniel Chandler. He is a member of the Commission on Media for the National Council of Teachers of English and is on the Board of Directors for the NCTE's Assembly on Computers and English.

Danny L. Miller, assistant professor of English at Northern Kentucky University, Highland Heights, Kentucky, is a native Appalachian and received the B.A. at Berea College, Berea, Kentucky. His article "The Mountain Woman in Fact and Fiction of the Early Twentieth Century" (*Appalachian Heritage*) was one of the first to examine images of Appalachian women in literature. He has been assistant editor of *MELUS*, the journal of the Society for the Study of Multi-Ethnic Literature of the United States; was assistant editor of *Minorities in America: The Annual Bibliography* (Penn State Press); and is currently editor of *The Journal of Kentucky Studies*.

Colleen J. McElroy lives in Seattle, Washington, where she is a professor of English and creative writing at the University of Washington. Winner of the Before Columbus American Book Award for *Queen of the Ebony Isles*, and the Washington State Governor's Award for *Bone Flames* and *Jesus and Fat Tuesday*, McElroy has published six books of poetry in addition to a textbook on speech and language development, and two collections of short stories. Her two latest publications are *Driving Under the Cardboard Pines* (short fiction), and *What Madness Brought Me Here: New and Selected Poems, 1968–88*. She also is poetry editor for *The Seattle Review*, writes for stage, screen, and television, and has received two creative writing fellowships from the National Endowment for the Arts, a senior Fulbright Fellowship in creative writing to Yugoslavia, and most recently, a Rockefeller residency for the Bellagio Center in Italy, and a Jesse Ball duPont residency for Hollins College, Virginia. Her work has been translated into Italian, Russian, German, Malay, and Serbo-Croatian.

James S. Mullican is a professor of English at Indiana State University, Terre Haute, Indiana. He taught high school English for nine years and has been a university supervisor of student teachers for twenty-two years. He is a former editor of *Indiana English* and is the author of more than seventy-five reviews and articles, including essays on poetry and the teaching of poetry.

Marie Wilson Nelson is a faculty member at the University of South Florida; prior to that appointment she taught writing and directed a writing program at George Mason University. A poet and writing researcher, she loves canoeing, Zen architecture, and studying how people learn. Her published works include poetry, articles on writing, research studies on gender and communication, and a book, *At the Point of Need: Teaching Basic and ESL Writers*. A new book on growth-based evaluation of writers and their writing is forthcoming from Boynton/Cook.

William Olsen was a 1982 *Nation* Discovery Award winner and a Merilmykjan Fellow at Bread Loaf in 1990. His book of poetry, *The Hand of God and a Few Bright Flowers* (University of Illinois Press 1988), won the National Poetry Series Competition and was awarded the Soeurrette Diehl Frazer/Natalie Ornish Award by the Texas Institute of Letters in 1989. His poetry has appeared in anthologies and has been published widely in magazines. He is an assistant professor of Creative Writing at Western Michigan University, Kalamazoo, Michigan.

Marge Piercy is the author of eleven novels, the most recent *He, She and It* (Knopf 1991). Her previous novels include *Small Changes, Woman on the Edge of Time, Braided Lives, Gone to Soldiers*, and *Summer People*. She has published eleven volumes of poetry, including *The Moon Is Always Female, Circles on the Water, My Mother's Body*, and *Available Light*, and in March 1992 *Mars and Her Children*. She edited an anthology of contemporary American women's poetry called *Early Ripening*. In 1989 she won the Sheaffer-PEN/New England Award for Literary Excellence and in 1990 she won both the Carolyn Kizer and the Golden Rose Poetry Awards.

Deirdre Raynor is a writing instructor at the University of Washington's Office of Minority Affairs' Instructional Center. She is also a doctoral student in English at the University of Washington, Seattle. Her primary academic interest is contemporary Afro-American and other ethnic minority literature.

Anna Lee Stensland was a professor of English at the University of Minnesota, Duluth, Minnesota where she taught courses in English methods, adolescent literature, images of women in literature, and teaching reading in the junior and senior high school. She is the author of *Literature by and about the American Indian: An Annotated Bibliography* (National Council of Teachers of English 1979). She has written numerous articles on Native American literature and the teaching of it. She retired from the University of Minnesota, Duluth, in 1985 and now resides in Lake Havasu, Arizona.

Diane Wakoski has published many collections of poetry, including *Emerald Ice: Selected Poems 1962–87* (Black Sparrow Press) which won the William Carlos Williams Prize from the Poetry Society of America. The first volume of her epic poem of The West, *The Archaeology of Movies and Books*, was published in 1990 under the title, *Medea the Sorceress*. She is University Distinguished Professor at Michigan State University.

Ingrid Wendt's twenty years of teaching experience includes college and university appointments, as well as Artist-in-Education poetry residences in hundreds of elementary, middle and secondary school classrooms. Her book *Starting with Little Things: A Guide to Teaching Poetry in the Classroom* has been adopted by teachers and school districts nationwide and is now in its second printing. Widely published in periodicals and anthologies, Wendt was the 1982 winner of the D. H. Lawrence Award. Her second book of poems,

Singing the Mozart Requiem, received the 1988 Oregon Book Award for Poetry from the Oregon Institute of Literary Arts. She has co-edited the anthology/textbook *In Her Own Image: Women Working in the Arts* (Feminist Press and McGraw-Hill 1980), and serves as an associate editor of *Calyx*. She is co-editing, with Primus St. John, *Oregon Poetry*: part of the six-volume Oregon Literature series, a project of the Oregon Council of Teachers of English, to be published by Oregon State University Press.

Denny Wolfe has been a high school English teacher, a state director of English and foreign language instruction in North Carolina, and a university professor and administrator at Old Dominion University, Norfolk, Virginia. He has contributed more than sixty articles to professional journals and books. He is the co-author of *Writing for Learning in the Content Areas* (J. Weston Walch 1983), *Making the Grade* (Coronado 1986), and *Teaching English Through the Arts* (National Council of Teachers of English 1990). He teaches methods courses for English teachers and serves as director of the Tidewater Writing Project, an affiliate of the National Writing Project.